Glenn Sujo

LEGACIES OF SILENCE

THE VISUAL ARTS AND HOLOCAUST MEMORY

PHILIP WILSON PUBLISHERS

IMPERIAL WAR MUSEUM

Published on the occasion of the exhibition
Legacies of Silence
at the Imperial War Museum, London
5 April – 27 August 2001

FRONTISPIECE
Felix Nussbaum
Self Portrait with Key
1941
Cat. 32

First published in 2001 by
Philip Wilson Publishers
7 Deane House
27 Greenwood Place
London
NW5 1LB

Distributed in the USA and Canada by
Antique Collectors' Club
91 Market Street Industrial Park
Wappingers' Falls
New York 12590

ISBN 0 85667 529 6 (cloth)
ISBN 0 85667 534 2 (paperback)

Designed by Andrew Shoolbred

Printed and bound in Italy by EBS, Verona

Contents

Foreword

At the heart of this exhibition lies a paradox: the overwhelming threat of the Holocaust is represented here by these silent, fragile drawings. In the artists' determined descriptions we see preserved the details of actions designed to eliminate and to change the social landscape. Their very presence challenges the intentions of the Holocaust by creating evidence of the rich culture that was being stripped away.

Who were these artists? Most of them are little known; only a few survived to have successful careers. This is not an exhibition dependent on the famous names of twentieth-century art history, but rather on the men and women driven to respond as artists in circumstances beyond belief. How did they manage to find the resources to make these drawings when the consequence of discovery was death? Where did they start, surrounded by the enormity of this evil? What visual language can possibly start to express such devastation? Yet, ironically, their responses are founded on the traditions of Western Christian art.

Making this exhibition was never going to be easy. The material is spread across a great number of institutions. Piecing together the threads required a resolute belief that the story should be told. We have been fortunate that Glenn Sujo, the curator and author of the catalogue text, had this vision and has been able to combine it with the administrative and intellectual resources that can do justice to its richness and diversity. We have also been dependent on the efforts of curators and friends and relations of the artists who have preserved these drawings and paintings. That we have been able to draw on so much material is a testament to their work and to the individuals and institutions now responsible for it.

I am especially grateful to the Posen Foundation which has generously supported the publication of this catalogue. I would also like to thank Michael Peppiatt, Karen Pitchford and Meret Graber-Meyer for their assistance in facilitating loans from particular artists. Suzanne Bardgett, James Taylor and several former members of the Holocaust Project Office have been generous with help and advice. We owe a great debt of gratitude to Glenn Sujo for his dedication to this project over the past three years and his tenacity in seeing it through, as well as to the many institutions, artists or their descendants who have lent their work.

Robert Crawford
DIRECTOR GENERAL

Introduction

In the Ashkenazi tradition the names of the deceased are passed down in an alternate line of family succession to each newborn in such a way that the memory of them and some attribute of their former selves are preserved for later generations. According to this tradition, the names of the six million Jewish men, women and children who perished in the Holocaust, severing lines of continuity and transmission, rekindle those absent voices—all that we have left of them are the names. As a visitor to the Pinkas Synagogue in Prague, like so many others, I was overcome by the unending list of names hand-painted on the walls—of Jews from Bohemia and Moravia, victims of Nazi persecution. If at the time silence seemed the only dignified response to crimes of this magnitude, silence is not of itself an empowered response. The crimes of the Shoah call on us to set apart the silence of the victims, their profound uncertainty and ignorance in the face of the unknown (echoed in the recurring phrase of bystanders, 'I did not know' or 'I didn't understand'), from the silences enforced by the terror and lies of the perpetrators. Silence effects a break in the transmission, so that knowledge, memory are severed—the silence of forgetfulness.

Only later, when roaming the streets of the old Ghetto (returning to life after years of neglect) and the Jewish cemetery (a controversial plan to build office blocks on the site has won conditional approval from the authorities) was I able to grasp more fully the weight of collective responsibility which those names and their legacies bequeath to us. As the sites of former Jewish communities, later of murder and annihilation, are turned into car parks, supermarkets or office blocks, the task of arresting the erosion of memory becomes ever more urgent.

The artists, whose works are the focus of this study, defied their Nazi captors by venturing to look beyond circumscribed patterns of behaviour, the fences and fortifications, and employed their imaginations to counter the falsehood and deception. (In selecting the drawings, I searched for intimations of this imaginative hold on life, beyond the mere record of fact.) The vast visual record amassed by the Nazis' documents in horrendous detail all aspects of their activity: party rallies, military campaigns, the sites of concentration policy, mass murder. This material—which exists in still photographs and documentary footage—was zealously guarded by the Nazi propaganda units responsible for its production. Surprisingly, though it comes from the eye of the perpetrator, it continues to dominate the visual record.

Clear away these images, for they cannot claim neutrality, tainted as they are by the perpetrators' deeds. Imagine instead a museum of the Holocaust without the now familiar photographs of atrocity, the deception, the tampered statistical record, the images of vested authority, the pressed uniforms. Imagine a museum that sees history through the eyes of its victims.

In the last months of the war the Nazis sought to destroy the evidence of their crimes and thus erase the burden of proof. The drawings produced by artists in internment counter the weight of complicitous Nazi propaganda and information, and the falsified claims, and rescue the voices of the victims, drawing us into their midst and reminding us of our responsibility to them.

This project developed out of visits to memorial sites, museums and libraries in the Czech Republic, France, Israel and Poland, during which I looked at hundreds, perhaps even a few thousand drawings. I found that, as with speech, a drawing's modes of expression can be direct and transparent or elliptical, rhetorical, their structures grammatical or colloquial. Consistently, I looked for evidence of a dialogue with *drawing as drawing*, with its tactility, rigorous analysis of line, economy of means and tonal nuances (alluding to shades of psychological depth and meaning). The resistant materiality of the paper support and the movement and pressure of the graven tool are evidence of the artist's hand and of his or her presence. In the camps, where life was contingent upon chance (a transience so daunting, so real as to defy every single moment), drawing asserted a contrary condition, of permanence. But drawings' resilience against the ravages of time proves more tentative, the precarious condition of so many of the works makes the task of recovery and preservation an urgent one.

If artists showed extraordinary courage, placing their own lives at risk, their drawings have been at the centre of a comparable struggle, marked by neglect and indifference. How is it that an art so keenly versed in the observation of life in extremity has found itself marginalized from the story of twentieth century art, a century of calamity and genocide? Perhaps one answer is found in the art itself, at the limits of representation, of the intelligible—its meanings often elude us as we countenance the breakdown of the visual language, indeed of all codified norms. The art of internment poses serious methodological questions—of authorship and attribution. Artists signed or inscribed their drawings, sensing the survival of their works, if not of themselves, adding a date, place name or other inscription (a sure mark of intentionality, vital when establishing authorship, place of internment, identity of the subject—for instance, in Helmut Bachrach-Barree's sequence of drawings made in the death marches, or in Moritz Müller's carefully annotated portraits of dying patients in the Theresienstadt infirmary). Just as often, the works remained unsigned, protecting the artists from possible reprisal, but also concealing from the world, his or her identity. These examples epitomize the struggle between assertions of individuality and the camp's relentless drive toward anonymity. Discussion is also hampered by a lack of reliable biographical information—knowledge is sketchy, at best fragmentary, and efforts to place individual works in a trajectory (adumbrating stylistic developments or thematic concerns) are often frustrated. The reader is advised to consult the biographical entries appended at the back of this book. Documentation that might assist to unravel and establish patterns of ownership, or the circumstance of a work's conduit to safety (bequeathed to friends or relations), is vital to the researcher and must be made available. The creation of a database and the sharing of information, under the aegis of an internationally recognised body (such as UNESCO, ICOM, Survivors of the Shoah Visual History Foundation), is a necessary next step in assembling this larger picture and bringing the works, now dispersed, together.

A common misunderstanding dogs our perception of them. Put simply, a question of ownership: to whom—to what constituency or community—do these works belong? Are they the preserve of any one faith (Jewish, Christian, or agnostic), aesthetic or intellectual tradition (Modern, post-Modern) or do they belong simply to the corpus of prisoners' art (along with the all too familiar chains and handcuffs whittled from broomsticks and planks of wood)? Should these works be confined to Holocaust institutions (to be regarded exclusively as part of the historical record), or ideally inserted within twentieth-century drawing traditions and discussion of the art of their own time (German Expressionism)?

On 27 January 2001, a National Holocaust Remembrance Day was launched on the anniversary of the liberation of Auschwitz. The Holocaust is today a subject in the national schools' curriculum. The permanent Holocaust wing at the Imperial War Museum in London opened its doors last year in response to this interest. In addition, new university courses and departments dedicated to the study of the Holocaust, attract increasing numbers of students and reveal an ever-growing awareness. Conferences such as the recent *Remembering for the Future 2000* provide a focus for scholarly discussion and encourage a climate of greater openness and dialogue.

Jews were not the only targets of the Nazi policy of extermination. Poles, Slavs, Romany and other racial minorities, homosexuals, socialists, Catholics and other religious groups, were victims too. The need to extend and contextualise the lessons of the Holocaust are all the more urgent in a world of escalating violence in the former Yugoslavia, East Timor, Rwanda, Sierra Leone. The process of rebuilding lives and communities, overcoming ethnic divisions, securing the return of refugees is a slow and painful one. The most meaningful legacy of Holocaust remembrance is an empowered response to racism, anti-immigrant sentiment and hate crimes. The Holocaust teaches us not to be indifferent bystanders in the great debates of our time, but impresses on us the need for repair—*Tikkun Olam*.

This book is intended as a companion to the exhibition *Legacies of Silence* and, as such, is aimed at the general reader (though it is hoped that others may find useful pointers here). I have consulted and made extensive use of published sources. Some of these are mentioned in the brief bibliography, others in the footnotes and alongside the artists' biographies on pages 104–12. The exhibition and text assert, with renewed emphasis, the centrality of witnesses' perceptions and the role of survivors as the living conduit between past and present. The text is speculative in areas, raising more questions than it can possibly answer within the length allowed. With hindsight, I might have narrowed my study to a discussion of the complexities of witnessing, an engaging subject in its own right. Inevitably, in mapping out so wide a territory, I have overlooked issues that required a more detailed response. I hope to return to these at a later date.

I owe a particular debt of gratitude to Professor Avram Kampf, Bernard Krikler, Yehuda Bacon and Avi Hurvitz who, unknowingly perhaps, pointed me in the direction of the Holocaust as the important field of cultural enquiry that it has become and specifically to the drawings produced in internment, which I responded to in my own capacity as an artist with a daily practice of drawing. Yehuda Bacon and fellow artists Isaac Celnikier and Boris Taslitzky shared with me their acute understandings of the subject, as witnesses to atrocity and opened up glimpses into the extreme conditions in which artists worked in camps and ghettos. Sadly, I did not meet Osias Hofstatter, but encounters with Theo Vardi, Yoav Dagon and Oli Alter made up for this loss and animated my conversation with his works at the Herzliya Museum of Art and the homes of his enthusiastic collectors.

In the course of my research I have benefited greatly from the practical advice of individuals, too numerous to mention here. I should however like to single out a few whose help and timely response to my enquiries proved decisive. In the Czech Republic, Arno Parik and Michaela Hajková, Jewish Museum, Prague; Dr Jan Munk, Dr Vojtěch Blodig and Ivana Melicharová, Památník Terezín. In France, Daniel Marchesseau, Conservateur en chef du Patrimoine; Laure Barbizet, Musée d'Histoire Contemporaine; Christophe Duvivier, Musée de Pontoise; Edda Maillet, Association Les Amis de Jeanne et Otto Freundlich; Elizabeth Pastwa, Musée de la Résistance et de la Déportation, Besançon; Guy Krivopissko and Jacques Swirn, Musée de la Résistance Nationale, Champigny sur Marne; Messody Zrihen, Musée Nationale d'Art Moderne; and Gérard Lefèvre, Musée d'Histoire Vivante, Montreuil. In Germany, Dorothea Nutt, Kunstmuseum Düsseldorf and Erik Riedel, Jüdisches Museum, Frankfurt responded promptly to frequent enquiries and requests, as did Yehudith Shendar and Susan Nashman Fraiman, Yad Vashem Art Museum, and Pnina Rosenberg, Beit Lohamei Haghetaot in Israel. In Poland, Irena Szymanska, Jolanta Kupiec and Jarosław Mensfelt, Auschwitz Museum; Lukasz Kossowski, Muzeum Literatury im Adama Mickiewicza; Magdalena Sieramska and the staff of the Jewish Historical Institute, Warsaw, kindly made available their archives and collections. In Britain, the advice and help of colleagues and friends, in particular, Monica Bohm-Duchen, Frances Carey, René Gimpel, Chris Green, Keith Hartley, Nini Herman, Michael Peppiatt, Deborah Schultz and Professor Edward Timms is greatly appreciated. Ezra Kahn, Marketa Luskacová, Sandra Nagel, Wojciech Nowikowski and Kate Pool likewise offered their assistance. I should also like to thank the Imperial War Museum, in particular, Robert Crawford, Director General, and Angela Weight and Roger Tolson, Department of Art, for enabling me to pursue my research and writing in an area of consuming interest, over many months. The book's fruition owes much to the generosity of Felix Posen, and to the efficiency of Philip Wilson Publishers.

I am especially grateful to my editor, Judith Ravenscroft who, with due patience, skilfully coaxed my text through successive drafts. Her professionalism, her calm under pressure and unerring judgement have been exemplary. I would like to extend my warmest appreciation to my readers Anthony Rudolf and Dr Shulamith Behr, who took time away from their own commitments to comment on the text and when necessary, to cajole. Their learned and robust views on the subject of Holocaust representation were a source of needed stimulus, especially as the writing neared an end. Notwithstanding their advice, responsibility for the text's shortcomings is entirely my own. Finally, I should like to thank my wife Carole Berman for her support and understanding, even when the goal seemed unattainable.

Glenn Sujo

Legacies

The drawings at the centre of this discussion afford a glimpse into the world of the victims of Nazi atrocity. Their clarity, singleness of purpose and immediacy confirm the centrality of witnesses' perceptions and restore a necessary link with the past. The artist, Halina Olomucki, recalled the advice of a fellow inmate: 'If you live to leave this hell, make your drawings and tell the world about us. We want to be among the living, at least on paper.'

The act of drawing elevated the artists momentarily from their position as victims, mere cogs in the relentless wheel of destruction, to that of *seers*.[1] The drawings shed light on the complexities of seeing and therefore of witnessing, and on the reconstructive task of memory conditioned by human strategies of survival. Drawing allowed an objective distancing, a temporary release from the horrors of existence in concentration and forced labour camps and ghettos. Transcending moral and physical as well as psychological thresholds, these works reach beyond the fences and camp fortifications to inform posterity. In the intimate spaces of drawing, freed by the creative imagination, we encounter the hopes and torments of a people.

Silence and Testimony

In his account of German and Soviet internment camps, Terrence Des Pres acknowledged the unresolved conflict that he felt existed between silence and the need to bear witness. While only silence seemed to offer a dignified response in allegiance to the dead, the act of witness granted the victims some continuity and established the survivor's role as a conduit between past and present, the living and the dead:

Silence, in its primal aspect, is a consequence of terror, of a dissolution of self and world that, once known, can never be fully dispelled. But in retrospect it becomes something else. Silence constitutes the realm of the dead. It is the palpable substance of the millions murdered, the world no longer present, that intimate absence of God, of man, of love…the survivor allows the dead their voice; he makes the silence heard.[2]

As Etty Hillesum awaited her deportation from the Westerbork transit camp in Holland to an uncertain destination in the East, knowing that the end was in sight for herself and for most of her fellow prisoners whose morale she had sustained for many months, she remarked: 'All that words should do is to lend the silence form and contours.'[3] So how should speech and other expressive forms contain 'the shape and vitality of silence'?

Iconography of Human Conflict
Käthe Kollwitz, Paul Klee, Jankel Adler, Isaac Celnikier

In the dense shade of Käthe Kollwitz's *Battlefield*, 1907, a grief-stricken mother bends over a sea of corpses, her dim torch held against the raised head of a youth, her dead son. In *Woman with Dead Child*, 1903 (British Museum, London), flesh is drawn across the skeletal forms as one continuous skin enveloping both mother and child, setting a precedent for representations of victims of the Holocaust.[4] These images pose the question: is there perhaps no other way to represent the body than as the container of pain—the nagging pain of being human? A consummate draughtswoman and printmaker, Käthe Kollwitz (1867–1945) employed the medium of etching, lithography and woodcut to express her abhorrence of modern warfare and her empathy with its victims. Her images shake us into the realisation of the horror of all wars.

Kollwitz established her reputation as a public sculptor in 1931, when the two figures, *Memorial for the Fallen* (that had occupied her over the previous eighteen years) were exhibited in Berlin.[5] A memorial to her son Peter, killed in Flanders' fields during the First World War, the granite monument was installed the following year near his grave in the village of Roggevelde, at Diksmuide in Belgium. As Kollwitz made her way round the site, she heard the stories of the fallen told by their mourning families, voices from the other side. Raised on plinths and imposing in their pyramidal construction and solidity, the kneeling figures of her sculpture express an unexpected reticence—that of the bereaved, disowning and recoiling from the public rhetoric that history so often demands.

2 Jankel Adler
*What a World: The
Destruction of Lodz*
1923–24
oil on board
635 x 425mm
The Israel Museum,
Jerusalem
Cat. 74

3 Kollwitz's bronze relief, *Lamentation*, 1938–40,[6] offers so clear a demonstration of the expressive mobility of the human face while its scale draws us into an intimacy with the artist's grief. Earlier, Kollwitz had explored the informing conjunction of her hands and face in *Self-portrait*, 1924 (British Museum, London). Here the shaft of an arm and a curved hand appear to support the weight of her head, while in *Nachdenke Frau* (Thinking Woman), 1920 they offer solace, protection. But *Lamentation* is a more resolute statement of the construction of identity. The artist's powerfully modelled hands are stilled, one pressed up against her mouth, as if to silence it, the other shielding her left eye. Her right eye remains closed, refusing to countenance the loss of life—though she may yet hear the victims' piercing cries, as sight gives way to the acuity of hearing. No longer able to shield herself with the visible, unwilling to magnify or betray the victims' suffering with utterances, she is drawn instead to the drone of the 'world no longer present'. *Lamentation* is both a profound statement of witness and a foreshadowing of future deaths (and Kollwitz's loss was compounded by the death in action of her grandson Peter in 1942).

Kollwitz dedicated this work to the memory of her near contemporary, the figurative sculptor Ernst Barlach (1870–1937). The artists shared a profound humanism and soon found themselves at odds with the Nazis. Barlach's *War Memorial*, 1927, for the cathedral at Güstrow was removed some weeks after its unveiling and smelted down.[7] A second commission for the cathedral at Magdeburg provoked widespread condemnation and was removed from view in 1933, the year that Käthe Kollwitz was stripped of her professor's title and forced to resign her post at the Akademie der Kunst in Berlin. Copies of Barlach's album *Zeichnungen* (containing a selection of his drawings) were seized and destroyed by the Gestapo.[8] Similar measures were aimed at writers and intellectuals of the left and right. Banished from their places of work, forced into exile or interned in concentration camps, they were ultimately silenced. In this climate of intolerance, Germany spiralled into an unprecedented barbarity.

Paul Klee (1879–1940) cultivated an image of himself as an artist 'outside history', impervious to social influences and withdrawn from world affairs, but his life was seldom unaffected by opposition of one kind or another, and he experienced political as well as artistic controversy.[9] These upheavals are reflected in the dark mood and increasing severity of his works of the last decade, in contrast with the child-like levity and charm that characterises the earlier works.[10] In a key painting of 1933, *Struck from the List*, Klee vents his anger at his increasing marginality in German society (one he had formerly embraced and which now ostracised him). His dismissal from the faculty of the Kunstakademie in Düsseldorf, and his self-defence against accusations that he was a Galician Jew, came as a humiliating blow. An 'X' is writ large across his subject's skull in a gesture of brutal annulment—struck off the register! Eyes and mouth are formed into a terse opening, a mere cipher of a face, not unlike the vacant expressions in police mug-shots. It recalls an earlier self-portrait, *Absorption (Portrait of an expressionist)*, 1919, produced at another watershed in Klee's life, his involvement in the failed Munich Revolution of 1918–19,[11] and is similarly a statement of an identity in transition.

Between February and October 1933, Klee completed a cycle of more than 200 drawings which chronicle the rise of National Socialism. With such titles as *Barbarian Mercenary, Manhunt, Demagogy* and *Fool's Celebration*, these drawings tip the balance of his production toward figuration and away from

3 **Käthe Kollwitz**
Lamentation, In Memory of Ernst Barlach
1938–39
bronze, edition of 10
265 x 260 x 60mm
Tel Aviv Museum of Art, Israel
Gift of Helen and Eric Cohn, New York, 1970
Cat. 1

4 **Paul Klee**
Forced Emigration
Erzwungener Ausweg
1934
black chalk and pencil
418 x 314mm
Private Collection,
Switzerland

4

teachings and again in his *Pedagogical Sketchbooks*,[13] Klee set out the paradigmatic elements of a non-referential, visual language detached from the realm of visual appearances. *Forced Emigration* harnesses this abstract potential. Lines and vectors are attendant on the birth of a sign, 'exactitude winged by intuition'.[14] Like a piercing arrow or a star set at speed on its ascending course—lending 'a trace of infinity to the temporal' (Novalis)—lines hurtle into space, beyond the flat, rectangular picture plane. The convergence of these dynamic elements hint at potentially explosive social forces, the very forces that Klee now fled from.[15] Exile may have freed him from the tight grip of Nazi censorship, but he was never able to throw off fully the charge of 'degenerate artist', to which the conservative art establishment in Berne also attached importance. Klee died on 29 June 1940, having had his application for citizenship turned down by the Swiss authorities.

However abstract or removed from reality Klee's works may have seemed, he was unable to exorcise the duality of realism versus abstraction: 'The more horrible this world, the more abstract the art',[16] he wrote. This view was shared by his colleague at the Düsseldorf Academy and close friend, Jankel Adler (1895–1949). Adler developed an increasingly abstract language of latent figural content in response to personal and political events, a tendency all the more apparent in his treatment of Holocaust themes. He declared that 'a revolutionary painter is one who creates a revolutionary form. The subject has absolutely no meaning.'[17] By 1931, Adler's position within German artistic circles was firmly secured. Already in 1925, he had appeared alongside other members of *Das Junge Rheinland*, Otto Dix, Gert Wollheim, Karl Schwesig and the art dealer Johanna Ey, in Arthur Kaufmann's *Group Portrait*. In January 1933, during the ill-fated elections that brought Hitler to power, Adler was a co-signatory with members of the Internationale Sozialistische Kampfbund of the *Dringende Appell* (Urgent Appeal) which denounced the Nazi Party. But it was not his political activities so much as his artistic radicalism and Jewish background that brought him the disapproval of the National Socialists and the inclusion of his work in the *Entartete Kunst* (Degenerate Art) exhibition in July 1937.[18] Ten years of wanderings in Poland, Russia, the Balkans, Spain and France followed—a period he described as 'an active struggle against the Fascist regime in Germany'. It was not until his arrival in Britain in 1941 that Adler again found a sympathetic

abstraction, as if the subject exacted from the artist a more humane response. *Emigration*, 1933, made up of cascading, elliptical lines, addresses the persecution of Jews and their mass exodus, recalling both a 'flight from Egypt' and anticipating Klee's own flight to Berne, his childhood home, on 23 December.

The diagrammatic *Erzwungener Ausweg* (Forced Emigration), 1934, marks a new phase in the artist's circumstances, expelled as he now was from his country of adoption. Some have seen in this drawing the vestigial figure of a child or woman running. Twenty years earlier, in *Das Kind und sein Stern* (Opus 1912.141), Klee had outlined the delicate contour of a small girl who gestures toward a six-pointed star as though reaching for the ineffable. A few delicate, meandering lines evoke the genius of childhood, with its inborn creative energies.[12] Throughout his

5 **Jankel Adler**
Orphans
1942
oil and gesso on paper
570 x 780mm
Private Collection
Cat. 3

audience for his work and a circle of like-minded artists and intellectuals.

5   In *Orphans*, 1942, two vulnerable figures stare out from behind the hollow and impassive masks and carapace-like bodies. The painting was a tribute from Adler to his friend and fellow painter, Josef Herman, on learning of the deaths of all the members of Herman's family in the Warsaw ghetto.[19] (Adler would lose his nine brothers and sisters.) Seated right, the more senior of the two, Adler looks up, startled as if reckoning with calamity while Herman gazes intently at the pages that convey the dire news. The close physical proximity of the two suggests a protective intimacy. Herman remarked on the bond formed by the two artists in their Glasgow exile: 'Both of us were Yiddish speaking, we were both from Poland, hence we could look into each others faces with understanding. In the company of others, we were a conspiracy of two.'[20]

The flat austerity of the forms—built up as if in shallow relief—is reinforced by a black painted border, a funereal surround. A band of colour divides the painting in two, horizontally, as if barring entry and ultimately isolating the figures (a device Adler used repeatedly in 1942, for instance in *Homage to Kurt Schwitters*).[21] This formal device underlines feelings of estrangement, as both artists struggled to establish new lives. Only the decorative flourish of tiny hands, the rounded hollow of the eye sockets and egg-shaped heads break up the echoing horizontals, a late Cubist device heralded by Picasso in *The Three Musicians*, 1920 (Philadelphia Museum of Art). The use of a black ground (a procedure also favoured by Klee) establishes the painting's sombre key and enhances the velvet iridescence of colour. The paint and gesso ground are raked across the canvas in broad bands, reinforced by closely hatched horizontal striations that simulate lines of text.

7   *The Mutilated*, 1942, portrays two veteran amputees stranded in a desolate landscape. The artist attempts to convey the experience of looking on, from the remote distance of British shores, to events in Europe—events that have proven to define his past as much as they will determine his future, but which he feels powerless to act upon. As one perceptive commentator remarked at the time:

It is very difficult in England to realise how intense is the onslaught across the Channel against the human body and the individual soul. This may be partly due to insular lack of imagination, partly to an instinct that tells us to keep our heads, that we may stamp out these atrocities the quicker…

and to an animal instinct for ignoring the suffering which does not concern us.[22]

The Mutilated draws together Adler's responses to two world wars. A summation of his artistic credo, it contains references to the German Expressionists Otto Dix and George Grosz, biomorphic Surrealism (and Picasso's Boisgeloup pictures), while anticipating the voluminous masses of Henry Moore's figure sculpture of the 1950s.[23] A matrix of tensile lines seems to entrap the figures, suggesting a game of cat's cradle, but we might also see in them intimations of Klee's linear constellations. The artificial limbs and appendages do not so much assist as hinder the bodies' mobility: beached and unable to free themselves from the web of imprisoning lines. *The Mutilated* is an apt metaphor for the artist, epitomising Adler's position as a refugee, an outsider, unable to return to his country of origin and stranded in an alien place.[24]

Silences are forms of negation and abdication of our conscience towards Hitler's crimes.[25]

The figures in Isaac Celnikier's (b.1923) paintings articulate the conflict between the reverent silence of grief and the aching need to bear witness. Following the liquidation in 1943 of the Bialystok ghetto in which he had sought refuge, Celnikier was subjected to a barbarous and prolonged internment in a series of Nazi camps at Stutthof, Birkenau, Buna (Auschwitz III), Sachsenhausen and Flossenbürg, believing all the time that he would be shot.[26] Re-establishing a life after the war in Prague, and then in Warsaw, he forged a distinctive pictorial language, steeped in the traditions of European figurative art, with which he hoped to communicate the universal experience of human suffering.

The cycle of monumental canvases painted in the 1980s, of which *Révolte*, 1983–84, is one of the   *6* most powerful, expresses his outrage and sorrow at the killing of innocent civilians by the occupying armies of the Reich. *Révolte* recalls the destruction of the Bialystok ghetto and the inhabitant's courageous uprising in August 1943. One cannot entirely free these images from the memory of other popular uprisings, in particular, the struggle played out on the streets and barricades of Paris, enduringly portrayed in Eugène Delacroix's (1798–1863) *Liberty Leading the People*, 1824 (Louvre, Paris), as well as the knowledge of more recent conflicts.[27] It was Delacroix who

6 **Isaac Celnikier**
Uprising
1981–84
oil on canvas
1970 x 2235mm
Collection the artist
Cat. 4

insisted: 'painting is above all, an art of silence'. But the shallow foreground of Celnikier's *Révolte* is anything but silent, filled with the cries and frenzied movements of the human throng. The calligraphic speed and intensity of the marks result in a rich surface complexity that cannot be taken in at a single glance but only after repeated attempts. Only then can we begin to distinguish the individuated human forms from the confusing orgy of violence. Yellow ochres and red earths are activated like coloured shards. The surface is encrusted with jewel-like daubs of paint—glistening cadmium red and alizarin. The appearance is that of wounded flesh, scars inflicted on the surface of the canvas.[28] These physical striations (made with a painter's trowel and heavily loaded brushes) are a corollary of the graven marks produced by the metal burin and the corrosive effects of acid-biting on the copper etching plate. Celnikier has successfully transposed onto the language of painting the techniques of etching developed and perfected in the making of the suite, *La Mémoire Gravée*, which he begun in 1969 and continued working on over the next twenty years.

The winged, brandishing figure at the centre of Marc Chagall's vision of *The Falling Angel*, 1923–47 (Kunstmuseum, Basle), is an instrument of history, warning of catastrophe. Celnikier too combines the record of recent historical events with Biblical exhortation. Averting catastrophe, the towering *Judith*, 1980–86 (Collection the artist), watches over the frenzied throng, a child in one arm while, with the

other, she strikes at the dark figure of Holoferness, a metaphor here for *Amalek*, a dagger held firmly in her hand. The painting intones the Jewish injunction to remember: *Remember what Amalek did to you* (Deuteronomy 25:17),[29] acknowledging the important link for the Jewish people between Biblical narrative and twentieth-century history. The composition is reversed in one of Celnikier's most memorable etchings *Gina Frydman*, 1982, which pays tribute to the courage of the artist's companion, establishing her kinship with the physical prowess of the Spanish women, wives and mothers, in Goya's etching *Y Son Fieras* (And they are like Wild Beasts) from the suite *Disasters of War*, c.1810. However, the memory of close relatives, specifically of his mother and sister, and of Gina, anchor these works in both time and place.

Resistance and Revolt

In spite of their extreme situation, tens of thousands of Jews took part in acts of resistance during the Second World War, joining Jewish fighting contingents or partisan groups in the forests, or larger fighting groups in France, Belgium, Holland, Italy and Yugoslavia, where the local populations were less hostile to them.[30] Jews also resisted the Nazis in camps and ghettos.

A defiant Aron Kobrowski, Chairman of the Jewish Council in Marcinkance, in the Bialystok region, cried out to the assembled awaiting deportation to Treblinka: 'Fellow Jews, everybody run for his life. Everything is lost!' Unarmed and unprepared for battle, men and women ran to the fences, throwing themselves on their guards with bare fists. Some 105 were shot down. Revolts like these flared up across the region, in Lomza, Zambrow, Surprasl, Drohiczyn, Ciechanowie and in a hundred other towns and villages, where armed resistance threatened to overwhelm Nazi forces. In Warsaw, in the spring of 1943, both the Polish underground outside the ghetto and members of the Jewish Fighting Organisation inside resisted the enemy, until political and ideological differences undermined their potential alliance. At Auschwitz-Birkenau, in the closing months of the war, prisoners succeeded in blowing up one of the crematoria, thus bringing the machinery of death to a partial standstill. At Sobibor, they stormed the camp gates. Most were cut down by landmines around the camp, but so much damage was inflicted that the camp ceased to function within days. At Treblinka too, a mass-rebellion and break-out seriously hampered operations.

7 **Jankel Adler**
The Mutilated
1942–43
oil on canvas
864 x 1118mm
Tate

These were not the only forms of resistance. Testimonies reveal the extent to which friendships in the camps made conditions more bearable and even saved lives. These testimonies attest to everyday acts of kindness and solidarity that militated against the camps' brutality and the inevitable pull towards self-preservation and survival. The largely clandestine works of art produced in camps and ghettos not only placed the artists' lives at grave risk but by resisting the barbarism and brutality of the perpetrator, also constituted acts of spiritual resistance.

The events of the Second World War are remembered by the different national, ethnic and religious groups in ways that heighten their ideological differences, as political boundaries are redrawn, communities rebuilt and history is rewritten. Who gets heard and what is remembered are defined by those who gain the upper hand in the struggle of political wills.[31] The genocide of an estimated one and a half million Armenians by the Turks at Deir-el-Zor and throughout Turkey during the First World War, an event still shamefully unacknowledged by its perpetrators, set a precedent that allowed Hitler, in 1939, to ask 'Who remembers today the massacre of the Armenians?',[32] as he planned the destruction of eleven million Jews in Europe.[33] In *Legacies of Silence*, I want to remember not only the lives of the six million Jews who were systematically murdered as part of a co-ordinated attempt by Hitler to destroy all traces of Jewish life, but also the six million non-Jews—civilians—who perished as a result of Nazi policy: French *déportées*, Spanish Republicans, Polish Communists and members of the underground, 'social undesirables' as well as persecuted minorities, such as Slavs, Gypsies, homosexuals, Jehovah's Witnesses, and the mentally ill, who were also targeted in the Nazi programme of genocide.[34]

The decision to focus the discussion on the works of professional artists trained in European academies and interned in camps and ghettos during the Second World War[35] is supported by the clarity with which issues of intentionality and representation are addressed there. Artists are trained to look. Their perceptual choices are of the utmost significance, even if the question of stylistic choice in a universe that allowed for no choice to speak of, remains a vexed one. All kinds of personal mementos and illustrative material, caricatures, greeting cards and so on, were produced in the camps, often at the request of fellow inmates, or by the Nazis; they constitute a kind of camp staple, produced during the few idle moments prisoners were allowed—a demarcation of privilege in the camp's hierarchy. However fascinating, these works constitute a topic of discussion in their own right. The outstanding and extraordinarily moving drawings produced by children in the Terezín ghetto, under the supervision of Friedl Dicker Brandeis, are the subject of two or more excellent studies devoted to children's art and I have refrained from commenting on them. They raise important issues which seem to me to differ fundamentally from those which I address below.

Surprisingly for an art produced in the absence of all contacts with the outside world, the works in this study reveal an informed awareness of visual precedent and iconographic sources. In Chapter 2, *Precursors*, I have reflected on some of those sources in the context of progressive cultural and intellectual developments in Germany in the years before and during the rise of National Socialism. The work of French deportees and West European immigrants caught in the widening net of Nazi influence and their internment in camps under the collaborationist Vichy administration is the subject of Chapter 3, *In Transit*. A unique instance of artistic collaboration in the 'model ghetto' of Terezín is discussed in Chapter 4. There, the Nazis contrived to conceal the destruction of Jews and their culture behind the façade of a 'Potemkin village'—a deception that the artists challenged and managed to unmask. Chapter 5, *Ghetto*, examines the responses of artists to the doomed struggle of the remnants of Europe's Jewish communities to restore a semblance of normality within sealed enclosures. Artists countered the driving anonymity and ferocious regimentation of *Auschwitz* (Chapter 6) with their drawings, restoring a glimmer of hope and dignity for themselves and for their fellow inmates. In the final months of the war, as the full realisation of the atrocities committed by the Nazis in the notorious concentration and extermination camps emerged, artists responded with works of such unmitigated force as to render them of universal significance. The easing of restrictions empowered artists to observe and draw—an act of reckoning which restored in the artists some sense of control over their surroundings. These drawings are the focus of Chapter 7, *Witness to Atrocity*. In the final chapter, *Survivors*, I look at how artists, determined to preserve the memory of events, returned to the subject of the Shoah. Their works intimate an alternative, visionary reality, opening the way to buried memories exhumed, in the case of Zoran Music and Osias Hofstatter, some twenty-five years after the events.

2　Precursors

Prophecy and Language

The Septuagint defines the Hebrew *navi*, translated from the Greek word for prophet, as one who speaks for or on behalf of others. The classical prophet's instrument was the spoken word. But words can and often do fail us. Moses protests his inadequacy for the mission which God has assigned him, to bring Israel out of bondage: *Please, O Lord, I have never been a man of words…I am slow of speech and slow of tongue.*

The notion of prophecy is radically redefined by the Holocaust. The relentless assault on human life that was the distinctive legacy of the Nazi concentration camp system was also an assault on language. Under the pressure of falsehood, brutality and deception, words lose their humane meanings. Perhaps this goes some way to explaining the survivor Elie Wiesel's paradoxical remark: *How is one to speak of it? How is one not to speak of it?*[1] The verbal transmission of testimony is a transforming act, one of empowerment, releasing the witness from the burden of unexpressed grief, of silence. Utterances like his reflect a fundamental doubt about the adequacy of words to convey our most pressing concerns and underlines a twentieth-century preoccupation with the limits of language.[2] The poet Tadeusz Różewicz, a member of the Polish underground, expressed similar sentiments:

I regard my own poems with acute mistrust. I have fashioned them out of a remnant of words, salvaged words, out of uninteresting words, words from the great rubbish dump, the great cemetery.[3]

And in his essay, *The Hollow Miracle*, George Steiner reaches a similar conclusion, 'Make of words… conveyors of terror and falsehood…Something of the lies and sadism will settle in the marrow of the language.'

The Image of the Prophet

In Emile Nolde's (1867–1956) *Prophetenkopf*, 1912,[4] the rough-hewn and primitive character of graven marks (along the woodblock, rather than across the hard end-grain) reveal the imprimatur of the artist's hand and highlight the work's emotive power. The exaggerated Semitic features suggest both an Old Testament prophet and a Jewish Christ, eliciting the memory of ancient rivalries and auguring the rupture of two traditions. Nolde restates here the principle theme of the nine-panel cycle *Life of Christ*, completed in the winter of 1911–12 when, working in the rural seclusion of Guderup, on the island of Alsen, he identified closely with the simple beliefs and way of life of its inhabitants. But he also shared the social and utopian ideals of his Expressionist peers, their desire for cultural as well as spiritual regeneration, their protest against the life style and values of an older generation, ideas echoed in the writings of Friedrich Wilhelm Nietzsche (1844–1900). A parallel notion was that of *volkstümlichkeit*, appropriated by German Nationalists (calling for the pure and inherent spirituality of the German people) and summarised by Fritz Stern as:

…a consistent aspiration toward a form of primitivism which after the destruction of existing society aimed at the release of man's elemental passions and the creation of a new Germanic society based on art, genius and power.[5]

Sentiments of this kind prompted Germany into a fierce conflict—the First World War—and changed forever the character of European society, though not perhaps in the way Nolde had anticipated.[6]

The image of the prophet as a radical iconoclast, set apart from his fellow men and consumed by doubt, is present in the works of Ludwig Meidner (1884–1966) and Jakob Steinhardt (1887–1968). In *Self-portrait with Prayer Shawl*, 1918, Meidner is the repentant seer, emerging from prayer—his head covered with the ritual *tallit* (prayer shawl) and *tefillin* (phylacteries)—in a state of rapture. Outraged at the brutality and futile destruction of the First World War (in which he served as a translator in a French prisoner-of-war camp), Meidner embraced Jewish Orthodoxy, an assertive response to the dilemmas and choices—between acculturation and

8 **Emile Nolde**
Prophet
1912
woodcut
323 x 220mm
British Museum, London
Cat. 5

9 **Ludwig Meidner**
Self-portrait as Prophet
1918
pen and ink, pencil
649 x 550mm
Marvin and Janet, Fishman
Collection, Milwaukee
Cat. 6

10 **Jacob Steinhardt**
Praying Jew
Illustration to Arno
Nadel's *In Tiefer Nacht*
c.1912
drypoint
210 x 152mm
Tel Aviv Museum of Art
Cat. 7

distinctiveness—exercising Jewish awareness in Weimar Germany,[7] at the time undergoing a cultural reawakening. And Meidner chose to affirm the culture and values of an ancestral tradition with its ordered rituals and exalted spirituality. Jakob Steinhardt's encounter with the way of life of *Ostjuden* (East European Jews) was equally defining. In etchings and line drawings he extols the virtues of a community given to prayer and devout observance, men and women bent over ancient texts—vessels of memory—or entranced by the radiant light of Sabbath candles. Steinhardt found in them an enduring connection with his own ancestral past. The rapturous expression of his *Praying Jew*, c.1912, hands raised in celebration of the holy one, recalls the luminous visions of El Greco (1541–1614).[8] Like Nolde, Meidner and Steinhardt identified with the notion (common to both Jewish and Christian traditions) that divine revelation is delivered by human intervention.

10

The Horrors of War

The initial euphoria that carried Germany into the First World War amid expectations of a swift and triumphal end was soon challenged by the stark facts: mounting casualties, a long drawn-out and seemingly pointless conflict, Germany's isolation after 1916 and its defeat in 1918. The unparalleled graphic cycles produced in Germany at the height of the war and in the second and third decades of the century expose the full horror of these events.[9] Their sequential structure, as a series of related, mutually informing images, invoke the passage of time. But the depiction of rapid, bewildering social change is wedded to the weight of tradition—a tradition of printed images, their dissemination among artists and their wider reception. The graphic works produced as a response to the First World War provided a rare impetus for artists in the camps or in hiding during the Second World War and warrants discussion here.

When Max Slevogt (1868–1932), director of a prestigious master's studio at the Berlin Academy and soon to become a full Academician, was approached with the idea of producing a suite of lithographs on the subject of war he faced a choice—to celebrate Germany's prowess in battle or to warn of its consequences. Slevogt chose the latter and the suite of twenty-one lithographs that followed, entitled *Gesichte* (Visions), constitutes a condemnation of such force that the authorities seized the prints and destroyed the lithographic stones. In the opening image, *The March into the Unknown* (Leicester City

Museums), a frail figure in a flowing tunic—an evanescent symbol of hope—descends a spiral staircase inscribed *1914, 1915, 1916* and *1917* into the unknown, a torch smouldering in one hand. She is watched by dimly lit apparitions looming out of the cavernous darkness.

11   The angry portrayal of a grief-stricken mother, her arms thrust into the air, dominates *Die Mutter*. In the background, the fallen stretch out in trenches, mass graves, as far as the eye can see. But while Käthe Kollwitz's women are a symbol of earthbound strength and resilience and woman's pain is associated with the expiatory cry and the promise of rebirth, Slevogt's *Mother* signals only atrocity and the end of generations.[10] The nihilism of Slevogt's opening sequence echoes Goya's *Desastres de la Guerra*, while his final, dramatic plate entitled *The Forgotten*, reflects the vacant determinism of Goya's *Nada!*—Nothing!

Death and the artist is the most arresting image in Lovis Corinth's (1858–1925) suite of five etchings entitled *Totentanz* (Dance of Death), produced in 1922 and intended perhaps as a distillation of the artist's life and artistic milieu.[11] Corinth gazes into the polished surface of a mirror, one eye fixed on his reflection, the other concealed beneath a shadow. A skeleton hangs ominously behind him, a statement of finality.[12]

The most encompassing and technically accomplished of the print cycles, however, is Otto Dix's (1891–1969) *Der Krieg*, published in Berlin in 1924. In 12   *Gastote, Templeux-la-Fosse, August 1916* , two ethereal Red Cross orderlies pause as if to comment on the fate of five gassed soldiers lying awkwardly against the steep walls of a trench in an advanced state of decomposition. The pristine detail of the orderlies' uniforms contrasts with the condition of the victims. Dix's memory of the war dead is distinct, prescient and loaded with significance, while the fate of Germany's petty officers is, by contrast, of little concern. While Dix worked to complete his cycle of fifty etchings and aquatints, Germany's besieged pacifists struggled to erect a credible response to the war. The Internationales Anti-Kriegsmuseum opened its doors at 29 Parochialstrasse, Berlin in 1924. Its stridently pacifist, anti-nationalist programme called on 'Human Beings in all Lands!' to wage 'War against War'. 'True heroism', it maintained, 'lies not in murder but in the refusal to commit murder'. In a section entitled 'The Visage of the War' the museum displayed a series of close-up stills of maimed victims utterly disfigured by grenade explosions, shrapnel wounds and the most rudimentary reconstruction surgery. These images were published in Ernst Friedrich's anti-war

11 **Max Slevogt**
The Mothers from the
suite, *Gesichte* (Visions)
1917
Lithograph
390 x 540mm
Leicester City Museums

12 **Otto Dix**
Gassed
from the suite, *Der Krieg (War)*
1923
etching and aquatint
194 x 287mm
British Museum, London
Cat. 9

publication, *Krieg dem Krieg* in 1924.[13] Dix had them enlarged by the photographer Hugo Erfurth and made extensive use of them, as *Sterbender Soldat* (Dying Soldier) and the figure propped against a hospital bed in *Transplantation* (Skin graft), so vividly attest.

   With titles such as *The Sacrifice*, *Volunteers*, *The Mothers* and *The Widow*, Käthe Kollwitz's suite of seven woodcuts entitled *War*, 1922–23, expresses her outrage at the victims of war.[14] Their bold simplicity and black-and-white contrasts underscore this theme. Kollwitz *War*, Slevogt's *Visions* and Dix's *Der Krieg* contain a vigorous denunciation of war, specifically the indiscriminate destruction of the First World War. Their damning assessment of mankind's inhumanity and incapacity to learn from its mistakes forcefully and prophetically foreshadows the disastrous re-enactment to come—the Second World War with its accompanying images of naked and emaciated figures, mountains of corpses, gas chambers and crematoria.

The Jewish Christ

Jews are not only the people of Christ but the Christ of the people.[15]

Taking up a theme explored some years earlier in *The Praying Jew, Rabbi of Vitebsk*, 1914 (Museo d'Arte Moderna, Venice), Marc Chagall's (1887–1985) woodcut *Praying Jew*, 1922–23,[16] may at first seem like a lamentation: an act of atonement for the rupture

inflicted on a rich ancestral tradition by war. But his reiteration of this theme also betrays his inability to embrace wholeheartedly the world of the Jew, about whom he had written:

Did you see the old man praying? That is him. It would be wonderful to be able to work in peace like that. At times, a figure stood before me, a man so old and tragic that he already looked like an angel. But I could not stand to be near him for longer than half an hour. He stank too terribly!

In turning to Christological themes in response to the events of the Holocaust, Chagall sought to locate Jewish myth in a continuous, historiographic tradition linking Old and New Testament themes with present-day events. Thus, the Crucifixion, an image long associated with the persecution and destruction of Jews, was appropriated both to indict Christians and to represent the suffering and martyrdom of Jews.[17] Chagall used this symbol repeatedly in his works of the 1930s and 1940s, notably in *White Crucifixion*, 1938 (The Art Institute of Chicago), *Yellow Crucifixion*, 1943 (Musée Nationale d'Art Moderne, Paris) and *The Crucified*, 1944. The last of these is set in a ravaged and boarded-up Jewish *shtetl* and the figure of Christ is replaced by that of a suffering East European Jew, thus completing His transformation. These works were 'the primary vehicles of Chagall's artistic response to the Holocaust'[18] and a reaction to recent historical events: *Kristallnacht*, the destruction of Jewish synagogues in November 1938; the sinking of the *Struma* in February 1942; and the crushing defeat of the Warsaw Ghetto uprising.

   Reviewing Chagall's exhibition at the Galerie Mai in Paris in January 1940 (four months after France's entry into the Second World War), the Russian painter Alexandre Benois found in his recent work an uncommon tragic power and polemical charge rooted in recognisably Jewish symbols and themes—a vision, he remarked—'prompted by events of the past few years and especially by the untranslatable horror that has engulfed Chagall's co-religionists'.[19] These themes were present two years earlier in *White Crucifixion*, a near monumental work that defines the collective memory for the Jewish people at a turning point in their history. Some five years later, Chagall was to embark on a second version, *Yellow Crucifixion* in which Old and New Testament sources, Christian and Jewish martyrology and contemporary history are tightly woven into a web of meanings that defy convention.

The figure of a Jewish Christ, placed marginally off centre, is a life-like, flesh-and-blood being (in the tradition of Zurbaran's *Crucifixions*, modelled on contemporary Sevillians). A *tallit* across his groin and phylacteries on his head and arm, he redeems humanity's sins on the Cross, the signs of Christ's stigmata just visible on his chest and foot. He seems firmly of this world, as does the figure of Mary perhaps, tenderly embracing her child whom she has suckled only moments before (her reddened nipple is a focus of the viewer's attention). The child's powerfully alert gaze pierces the inert stillness of the painting. Along the lower edge, a figure (right) throws up his arms in rapture or dread, while another beckons for help (left). In contrast with their life-like qualities, the *shofar*-sounding angel making its descent (left) looks at first glance like a scriptural embellishment or a reference to the text itself,[20] while the blue goat, a fish and the turbulent waters evoke the primal medium of dreams and allegory. The group of refugees (right) are emblematic of the experience of a people forever on the move. This encounter of different realms of reality and experience elicit contradictory readings, so that the small bearded figure at the foot of the cross is both Joseph of Arimathea (Matthew 27:37) and Chagall's familiar Vitebsk Jew: he places a ladder, a convenient pictorial devise and symbol of the bond between heaven and earth, at Christ's feet, ensuring the eternal duality of God and Man but also of Christ and Torah.[21] Furthermore, Chagall dispenses with the pictorial requirement to ground his figures, which seem rather to float in an ill-defined space suffused by yellow, sulphurous gases. The events are staged at the meeting of land and sea: on one side, the blazing *shtetl*, which Chagall has left behind, and on the other, an open expanse of sea.[22] The open scrolls of the Torah, the five books of the Mosaic Law central to the Jewish faith contain no scriptural reference, only the faintest trace of an inscription erased or embedded in the *pentimenti*.[23] Christ's eyes are averted from the suffering around him, directed instead towards an inner meditation.

A *Sketch for the Yellow Crucifixion*, 1942, differs in some important respects from the painting, revealing Chagall's attempts to weave together competing traditions into an image of universal significance. Instead of the faint inscriptions on the Torah scroll, a carving knife rips through strewn corpses, alluding specifically to news of the massacre of Jews in Europe, and more broadly to the view of history as a succession of senseless massacres.[24] The hand and knife are also oblique references to the Biblical story of the *Akedah*, the binding of Isaac, identified by later commentators with the Jewish people's historic suffering. To one side of the Torah scrolls, small hands (absent in the painting) preach or intimate divine purpose and, in a reference to the First and Second Temple animal sacrifices, an ox hangs from the vertices of the cross (signifying the duality of man and beast). These images are buried beneath subsequent layers and reworkings. Visible in both painting and sketch, however, are the upturned hull of a refugee ship engulfed in flames (a clear reference to the *Struma's* doomed passage with the loss of all but one of its 760 passengers)[25] and a naked river God (a distraught Minerva) next to a large, glistening carp jumping out of the water, in a clear reference to Chagall's *Time is a River without Banks*, 1939.

But if, by his portrayal of the Jewish Christ, this confluence of Torah and Christian messianism, of Old and New Testament sources, Chagall intended to challenge the notion of antithetical traditions, echoing the sentiments expressed by the Polish artist Maurycy Gottlieb (1856–79) in a letter from Rome: 'How much I would like…to make peace between Poles and Jews, for the history of both people is one of pain and suffering'[26] he might not have foreseen the consequence for this uneasy coexistence—at Auschwitz the notion of a Judeo-Christian tradition was shattered. The defaced scroll and the floating world of vapid gases portend a terrifying outcome: a deeper rift in the covenantal relationship of the God of Israel and his people which, like the destruction of the Temple, signalled the retreat of God from man. Chagall may be hinting at the common suffering of two traditions, thus causing the viewer to reflect on both Jewish identity and on Christian martyrdom. But the redemptive image of Christ's rebirth and resurrection is overlaid in *Yellow Crucifixion* with other shades of meaning alluding perhaps to the recurring destruction of the generation of sons by the fathers in filicidal wars.

Passover: Memory

In the collective memory of Jews, the reiterated commandment to remember, *Zakhor*, is paramount: 'Remember what Amelek did unto thee' (Deuteronomy 25:17). The events of history disclose the workings of God. The legend read during the Passover meal tells of the deliverance of Jews from bondage: 'God took us out of Egypt with a strong hand, and an outstretched arm, with awesome power, signs and wonders…' (Deuteronomy 26:8). The *Haggadah* is the book of remembrance, and the idea that the hardships and privations experienced in slavery should be relived and 'remembered' with each generation lends poignancy to the Passover meal and rekindles the values of freedom and redemption that are central to Jewish continuity. Put another way, 'Memory is no longer recollection...but reactualization.'[27] Jakob Steinhardt's illustrations to the Passover *Haggadah*[28] are more than mere decorative embellishments to the printed page. They are instructive re-enactments of the historic Exodus, not in the exotic setting of Palestine (to which the minds of the meal's participants are gently directed), but in the contemporary Germany of Kaiser Wilhelm II. Commissioned by Erich Goeritz[29] in 1924, the images are replete with contemporary references, reflecting on a society in social and political turmoil.[30] Steinhardt's frontispiece for the *Haggadah, The Ten Plagues* consists of a series of plates, arranged around a central text. Each image, incised from the densely inked surface, represents one of the ten plagues visited upon Pharaoh by the God of the Israelites—turning rivers into blood, inflicting pestilence upon the land, sending forth darkness and visiting death on the firstborn (Exodus 7:14 – 11:10). This and Steinhardt's nine woodcut illustrations for the *Book of Yehoshua Eliezer ben Sirah*, 1929 (Israel Museum, Jerusalem),[31] a ringing assault on the values and moral decay of contemporary society, published in Hebrew and German (with a foreword by Arnold Zweig), mark a high point in German Jewish book illustration and the art of lettering.[32]

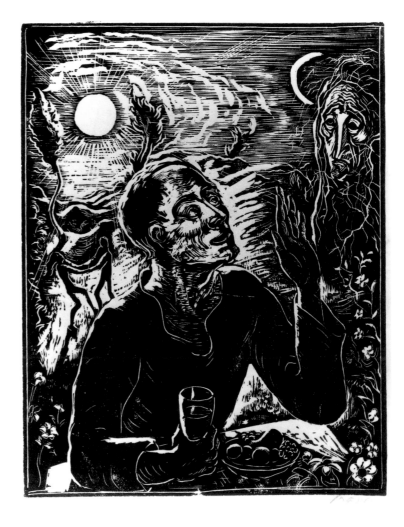

The End of Days

15 In the *Book of Yehoshua Eliezer ben Sirah*,[33] drunks and ranting figures, phantoms, sorcerers, *golem* and a triumphant death's reaper take cover under a Cosmic Night. Skeletons clamber out of the pages of the book in apocalyptic flurries, a startling vision of *Götterdämmerung* and the End of Time. Steinhardt and his contemporaries, Richard Janthur, Heinrich Richter-Berlin, Conrad Felixmüller and Carl Rabus revived the techniques of woodcut and wood-engraving synonymous with the *Die Brücke* circle of artists and German Expressionism, becoming an important example for a younger generation of artist-illustrators.[34] The brooding intensity, the quality of incised line, the density of the inked surface and the use of geometric grid to reinforce the sequential narrative of Steinhardt's *Ten Plagues*, are expressed anew in Jacob Pins' intensely nihilistic *Dance of Death*, 1945, and

in the *Apocalypse* suite, 1946 (British Museum, London), with their unmistakable references to the Holocaust.[35]

Felix Nussbaum's (1904–44) *Skeleton playing the clarinet*, 1944, is one of several studies for *Death Triumphant*, c.1944, his last great composition, produced during a sojourn in Brussels, shortly before his arrest by the Gestapo on 20 June 1944 and internment (with his companion, the artist Felda Placek) in the Malines transit camp, in Belgium. Revelling on the ruins of a bygone civilisation (or remnants of a bombed German city), Nussbaum's skeletons are informed by a wealth of art historical reference including church reliquaries and the fourteenth-century tradition of *Totentanz* (Dance of Death).[36] The unruly procession of skeletal musicians playing trumpets and kettle drums in Holbein the Younger's

15 **Jacob Steinhardt**
Illustration to *The Book of Yehoshua Eliezer ben Sirah*
1929
woodcut
280 x 195mm
The Israel Museum, Jerusalem
Cat. 14

16

16 **Felix Nussbaum**
Skeleton playing the clarinet
Study for *Death Triumphant*
c. 1944
pencil and gouache on buff
paper
306 x 223mm
Felix-Nussbaum-Haus
Osnabrück mit der Sammlung
der Niedersächsischen
Sparkassenstiftung
Cat. 16

17 **Hans Holbein the Younger**
The Bones of all Mankind
Gebeyn aller menschen
from the suite, *Totentanz*
1538
wood engraving
British Museum, London

(1497–1543) *Gebeyn aller menschen* (The Bones of all Mankind), 1538 and Alfred Rethel's (1816–59) *Der Tod als Erwürger* (Death the Destroyer), 1851[37] inspired by Heinrich Heine's account of the first appearance of cholera at a masked ball at *Mi-carême* in Paris, in 1832, have a direct kinship with Nussbaum's grimacing skeletons.

As the threat of further arrests closed in on Nussbaum, cloistered in the relative calm of his studio, it forced a new resolve and expanded powers of expression, manifest in two great paintings, *The Damned*, c.1943–44 and *Death Triumphant*. These anticipate the catastrophe descending on Europe. (Early intimations of this rapid denouement were already present in the strikingly prophetic and apocalyptic images of Ludwig Meidner and Jakob Steinhardt, produced in 1913.)[38] Nussbaum was deported to Auschwitz on the last transport from Mechelen, Belgium on 31 July 1944, only a few weeks ahead of the Allied advance on Brussels on 6 September.

The Street, the City

…Even so I will break this people and this city as one breaks a potter's vessel, that cannot be made whole again. (Jeremiah 18: 9–11)

The Impressionists conferred a fleeting theatricality on nineteenth-century cities: the crowds, the carriages and the display of banners animated by flickering gas lamps. In the twentieth century, Fernand Léger in France and the Futurists in Italy responded with vehemence to the radical transformations of this mechanistic universe, while Ludwig Meidner was first among German artists to take up the Futurists' declaration:

We shall sing the great crowds excited by revolution in modern capitals. We shall sing the nocturnal vibrating incandescence of arsenals and shipyards, ablaze with violent incandescent moons…[39]

Insisting that 'gas light is the only true light…day light is too rationalistic', Meidner preferred to work under cover of darkness, finding there the 'courage to act on one's ideas and intuitions'. But his apocalyptic visions, realised in a series of memorable canvases from 1912 onwards, are a far cry from Futurism's celebration of modernity. With their violent convergence of forces, Meidner's cityscapes are symbols of impending destruction. They effect a charged synthesis of memory and optical sensation.

Solid masses are freed from their containing borders and subsumed into infinite rhythmic correspondences. These observations are the fruit of a detached, nervous sensibility in thrall to the chaos of the modern metropolis. In *Suburban Street in Berlin*, 1913 and in related pen and ink drawings, the repeated verticals of lamp-posts, the diagonals suggested by high-rise buildings at a kilter, the curving arcs of light and swaying balconies confirm this new vision of reality—the modern city, with its unremitting speed. If Meidner's linear scaffoldings seem at first more openly derivative of Futurism, Steinhardt reclaims the human figure as the catalyst of social change. His response to the influential Futurist exhibition at Herwarth Walden's *Der Sturm* Gallery in Berlin in 1912[40] is more tentative. Meidner, Steinhardt and Richard Janthur (1883–1950) joined forces for the launch of the group *Die Pathetiker* (The Pathetic Ones) at *Der Sturm* in November,[41] and summarised their concerns as 'the big City, the Flood, the prophet, the end of the world, Apocalypse, war, plague, Jeremiah'.

In Steinhardt's *Pogrom*, 1913 a severely angular, infinitely graded line, carried with sure speed, heightens the life-threatening events depicted. Criticised by an antagonistic press, Steinhardt was aware of a wave of anti-Semitic feelings welling up inside Germany, and *Pogrom* invokes the recent memory of the Kishinev pogroms of 1905–06[42] and the renewed attacks on Jews that followed the Beilis blood libel trial[43] in the spring of 1911. The expressive angularity of Steinhardt's drypoint line, zigzagging across the etching plate, evokes the furious energies of the inebriated crowd, limbs and weapons gesturing violently, setting off the diagonals of the street and architectural backdrop. The shattered remains of windows and pavements arc scattered everywhere. Amid the whirlwind destruction, an elderly Jew (lower right) clambers desperately to regain his composure while behind him a bearded figure raises his arms in a helpless gesture of surrender. The elderly figure approaching the viewer (foreground, right) restates the central motif of Mary and Jesus from Steinhardt's etching *Pietà*, 1913. Figures, street and architecture seem to be drawn into a spiralling vortex. Rising above the street, the unmistakable dome of the great Berlin synagogue at Orianenburger Strasse 30, towers over the city's steeples. The expressive possibilities of the sharply receding, telescoped view of the street, polarising and accentuating the unbridgeable divide between the violent crowd (left)

18

18 **Jacob Steinhardt**
Pogrom
1913
drypoint
133 x 195mm
The Israel Museum,
Jerusalem
Cat. 18

19 **Max Beckmann**
Drawing for *The Street*
from the suite,
Die Hölle
1919
pencil, black chalk
673 x 535mm
British Museum, London
Cat. 19

and elderly Jews (right), may have been suggested to Steinhardt by a seventeenth-century print of *The Fettmilch Riots against the Jews of Frankfurt in 1612* which appeared in Berthold Feiwel's *Die Judenmassacres in Kischinew von Told*, 1903.[44] Steinhardt may have wanted to invoke the memory of an older conflict between the two beleaguered communities in order to draw attention to recent events.

Max Beckmann (1884–1950), a visitor to Ludwig Meidner's studio in 1912,[45] took to heart his 'exhortations to give honest expression to the unique problems of modern city life',[46] as well as the implications of Meidner's shattered pictorial space, disavowing the academic realism which had hitherto dominated his work. Instead, Beckmann embraced the city's radical transformation and its 'mathematical battles, in which the human being feels physically besieged by the riot of lines and angles'.[47] His newly

forged vocabulary is evident in the charged atmosphere of *Grenade*, 1915 (British Museum, London) depicting an exploding grenade and its ravaged victims—an event Beckmann witnessed as a medical orderly at the front.

The months leading up to the armistice on 11 November 1918 coincided with a period of marked political instability in Germany, the 'bloodless revolution'. The Berlin uprising on 5 January 1919, which received the support of the Spartacist League of Independent Socialists, was rapidly crushed and its Sparticist leaders, Karl Liebknecht, Rosa Luxemburg and Leo Jogiches, were arrested, and Liebknecht and Luxemburg murdered. Max Beckmann's narrative cycle of ten lithographs *Die Hölle* (Hell), completed in 1919, exposes this collapsing society, with its brutal ideological conflicts. The inscription on the title page (alongside Beckmann's self-portrait) announces: 'Hell. A great spectacle in ten pictures by Beckmann' and below, 'We beg our esteemed public to step forward'. This sense of heightened theatricality (strikingly apparent in Ernst Ludwig Kirchner's *Street, Berlin*, 1913, with its frenzied, gossiping crowds) is forcefully expressed in plate II, *The Street*. An unlikely mass converges on the narrow street, pressed into the fore and middle ground, a bewildering cast identifiable by the bizarre outfits and rounded, pointed and feathered headgear: war veterans and amputees, businessman and profiteers, Jewish leaders, street performers, hustlers, pimps and prostitutes, and the artist's devoutly Christian mother-in-law (centre left). The street spectacle is manifestly theatre, and its excitement is heightened by the alarming complexity of cosmopolitan culture. Weimar gave legitimacy to and paved the way for the participation of non-Germans and Jews into the culture and society of *Mitteleuropa*. If nothing else, Beckmann's *The Street* is a celebration of this diversity and difference—as his impetuous graphic marks define and shade the contours, faces and identities of figures milling in the crowd—alert to its explosive mixture. His profound feeling for the mass of his fellow humans seldom degenerates into a mocking gesture and, in contrast with George Grosz's rabid critique of society—he purportedly felt 'no kinship with this human mishmash'—Beckmann offers this compassionate assessment:

It's really pointless to love mankind, this pie of egoism to which we also belong. But I do all the same. I love them with all their pettiness and banality. With all their stupidity and cheap complacency and their oh, so rare heroism. Yet

19

nevertheless every day, each human being is a new event for me, just as they had fallen down from Orion. Where can I satisfy this feeling more than in the City?

Right now, even more than before the War, I need to remain among the people. in the city. Our place is right here. We must take part in all the misery that is to come. We must surrender our hearts and our nerves to the terrible cry of pain uttered by the poor deluded people.[48]

In *The Street*, the bearded figure with outstretched arms (in an advanced state of rigor mortis) carried by a rotund, bowler-hatted businessman is probably Kurt Eisner, a founding member of the Social Democratic Party (USPD), who for a hundred days held the post of socialist premier in the Bavarian Republic of Councils after a bloodless coup on 8 November 1918[49] and was murdered on a Munich street.

Beckmann's works reveal, in a manner that would have appealed to that inveterate observer of the street, Bruno Schulz (1892–1942), the metropolis as a hive or 'melting pot' for this vibrant melée of peoples and cultures. Not the futuristic and 'never-to-be' crystalline structures of Bruno Taut's *Cathedrals of Ice*, nor the Babel of Paul Citroen's architectural visions (1919/20), but a heaving and sighing, stick-in-the-mud humanity (drawn to the cities by the promise of employment and mass housing), getting on with life's business. And like Beckmann, Schulz observed the refractory world in his midst, for confirmation of his creative intuitions: 'It seems that the world, life, are important to me solely as raw material...To sustain curiosity, creative incentive, to fight sterilization, boredom'.[50] His works are poised uncomfortably between the provincial backwater of Drohobycz (Schulz's home town) and the city, Warsaw and he observed both from his position as an outsider. The troubled, if distant expression of Schulz's *Self-portrait* confirms the isolation of this intensely self-doubting figure and his commitment to the individual voice. He wrote: 'What do I look like? Sometimes I see myself in the mirror. A strange ridiculous and painful thing! I am ashamed to admit it: I never look at myself full face. Somewhat deeper, somewhat farther away I stand inside the mirror a little off centre, slightly in profile, thoughtful and glancing sideways. Our looks have stopped meeting.'[51] Echoes of Robert Musil's *A Man Without Qualities* surface here as do the strains of Beckmann's impassioned plea.

The *Neue Sachlichkeit* exhibition held in Mannheim, in 1925, confirmed Beckmann as Germany's

20

20 **Bruno Schulz**
Self-portrait
c.1933
pencil
115 x 98mm
Muzeum Literatury im
Adama Mickiewicza,
Warsaw
Cat. 20

foremost realist painter and granted him both public recognition and financial rewards. Schulz, on the other hand (eight years younger), while enjoying moderate recognition, continued to work in conditions of abject poverty, existing on the meagre income of a state-salaried teacher. Ostracized, misunderstood and cowed by the paralysing crisis that beset Europe in 1939, Schulz retreated into the ghetto. The bizarre *Astronomical Refractor*, part *camera concertina* and part divining instrument, is one of a series of illustrations to his collected stories *Sanatorium Under the Sign of the Hourglass*, published three years earlier. Seated at the commands, Schulz is surrounded by a group of deathly figures whose sinister expressions betray only too clearly their mistrust and foreboding. Schulz was murdered on the streets of Drohobycz by a Nazi officer during a mass action. His works and reputation were eclipsed for a number of years and reinstated only after the political and cultural 'thaw' that followed Khrushchev's rise to power and the dismantling of the Stalinist State in 1956.

Jeremiah's vision of the city as the site of devastation, shattered like the 'potter's vessel that cannot be made whole again' touched on prophetic and apocalyptic notions current in intellectual circles in Germany in the 1930s and early 1940s. Dissident artists such as Otto Pankok (1893–1966) and Carl Hofer (1878–1955) based their visions on the destruction wrought by the First World War. Stirred by his encounter with

21 **Otto Pankok**
The Synagogue
1940
charcoal and black chalk
970 x 1290mm
Otto Pankok Museum
Haus Esselt, Germany
Cat. 23

22 **Felix Nussbaum**
Bombardment I
1941
pen and ink wash
510 x 650mm
Jüdisches Museum der
Stadt Frankfurt-am-Main
Cat. 24

the way of life and identity of a gypsy community he visited at Saintes-Maries (in the south of France) in 1931 and at Heinefeld, near Düsseldorf, Pankok produced an imposing group of works, including *Großmutter spielt Geige*, 1931, and *Der Zeitungsleser*, 1933, inspired by the discovery of Van Gogh's drawings of miners in the Borinage region in Belgium. Identifying with the gypsies' predicament as outsiders in an increasingly divided society, Pankok went on to produce an extensive cycle of *Passions*, based in part on the German Renaissance tradition of the Master of Hausbuch, Albrecht Dürer and Mathis Grünewald. These images restate a theme explored by Pankok as early as 1928, in which Christ's features are recognisably those of a Jew. In *My God, My God, Why Hast Thou Forsaken Me?* (Otto Pankok Museum) executed in the momentous year 1933, Christ's head is modelled on that of his colleague Karl Schwesig, whose imprisonment and brutal torture at the hands of the Nazi SA filled Pankok's thoughts at the time. He relinquishes colour altogether, working with charcoal and black chalk to reinforce his expressive realism. Plans to exhibit the *Passion* series in his home town of Mülheim-an-der-Ruhr were opposed by the Nazis and an attempt by Kiepenheuer to publish an edition in 1939 led to its confiscation and the destruction of the printing blocks.

Armageddon

21 In Pankok's *Zerstörte Synagoge*, 1940, the ornate ruin of an archway and fragments of the synagogue's east-facing wall (whose hollow recess would at one time have housed the *Aron hakodesh* or holy ark and scrolls) are all that remain of this once proud edifice. The destruction is not confined to the ashen ruins of the synagogue, however, but to a way of life. In the distance, a burning city lights up the night sky as three figures, dressed in winter overcoats look on, dazed. The image recalls the events of *Kristallnacht*, the 'night of broken glass' on 9 and 10 November 1938, when Jewish synagogues, homes and businesses throughout the Reich were destroyed.[52] The devastation wrought by war is the subject of Carl

23 Hofer's *Man in Ruins*, 1937 which, while echoing the

robust torso of Giorgio de Chirico's *The Child's Brain*, 1914 (Moderna Museet, Stockholm), looks forward to the Allied bombing of German cities, as a naked figure emerges from the ruins of a gutted street. In Felix Nussbaum's *Fassung I* (Bombardment I), 1941, two incendiary spheres, sun and moon, light up the night sky, coverging at the centre to form an eclipse, in ominous foreboding. Two reeling figures (foreground) raise their arms as if to shield themselves from the scenes of devastation. In a vision of Armageddon, a ravaged tree descends on the crumbling buildings below, and the bodies of the dead and injured (a massacre of innocents) are strewn everywhere.[53] It would take twelve years, from the ill-fated election that brought Hitler to power in January 1933 until Germany's defeat in 1945, for society to regress to such a condition of barbarism and collapse.

23 **Carl Hofer**
Man in Ruins
1937
oil on canvas
1070 x 1035mm
Stadtische Kunstammlung,
Kassel

22

In Transit, France

3

In February 1939, Franco's Nationalist troops defeated the last bastion of Republicanism in the region of Catalonia, effectively ending three years of civil war in Spain.[1] Some 226,000 unarmed soldiers as well as members of the International Brigade and sympathisers crossed the border into France. This refugee population found shelter in makeshift camps at Argelès, Barcarès, Saint-Cyprien, Arles-sur Tech and Prats-de-Mollo in the Pyrénées-Orientales region of southern France.

The French Government responded to the crisis by constructing a more substantial camp on eighty hectares of land at Gurs, and by the onset of winter 1939, a network of camps had spread across the region. Comprising 428 makeshift wooden barracks built on a gridlock plan on either side of a central avenue, the camp at Gurs housed 19,774 inmates between August 1940 and June 1944. Most of these were foreign nationals, German refugees and recent arrivals in France, arrested by the Vichy Government at the outset of the 'phony war' in September 1939. Isolated and increasingly marginalised from the rest of society, groups like these were targeted for xenophobic attack amidst chauvinist cries of *la France aux Français*. On 25 June 1940, France became co-signatory with Germany of the armistice-convention giving the Vichy administration under Marshal Philippe Pétain new powers of arrest. France reneged on its former policy of *accueil* to asylum seekers, political refugees and victims of persecution and will-ingly participated in the arrest, sequestration and surrender to the German authorities of all aliens designated *fauteur de guerre*. These arrests entailed the collaboration of civil service functionaries at the highest level, local *préfectures* and police *gendarmes*, as well as many ordinary civilians who, acting under duress or on their own accord, turned informant on friends, former neighbours or business associates. France would be responsible for the deportation of some 76,000 French Jews who might otherwise have been saved from extermination at Auschwitz, Majdanek and Sobibor.[2]

Vichy and the Arts

Your situation is desperate, on one side the Nazis, on the other the falangists and between them the French gendarmes, but you are free to choose among these three possible ways of losing your life.[3]

The French Surrealists were among those who resisted Vichy. They disassociated themselves from the territorial concessions enshrined in the Munich Pact (signed by Chamberlain, Daladier, Hitler and Mussolini) and published a manifesto, *Ni de votre guerre, ni de votre paix!*—views espoused by other clandestine groups and journals. Salvador Dalí, Roberto Echaurren Matta, Onslow Ford and Yves Tanguy were to obtain safe passage to the United States; they were followed by the movement's leader André Breton and by André Masson, Wilfredo Lam and Claude Lévi-Strauss. Among other foreign nationals, Max Ernst and Hans Bellmer were interned at Camp Les Milles near Aix-en-Provence; Wols was arrested at La Colombe Stadium outside Paris (as was Walter Benjamin),[4] but escaped and spent the rest of the war in hiding; and Otto Freundlich was arrested by the Gestapo and eventually deported via Drancy to the Lublin-Majdanek death camp in Poland.[5] New powers of arrest in September 1940 made possible the large-scale roundup of recently naturalised French Jews, including Marc Chagall. The head of the Ameri-can Emergency Rescue Committee, Varian Fry, secured Chagall's release and then, in May 1941, after a prolonged and circuitous journey across France into Spain and Portugal, his safe departure for New York. 'Others were not so lucky', writes Fry; 'they were expelled from the district, placed in *résidence forcée* or, if they had no means, in concentration camps or sent into forced labour.'[6] Among those unfortunates who remained were artists who, finding a new role for themselves as witnesses, chronicled their lives in hiding, or inside transit camps and prisons, in drawings of unparalleled intensity.

24 **Felix Nussbaum**
Self-portrait in the Camp
1940
524 x 415mm
Neue Galerie, New York

Mapping the Confines

At St Cyprien in the Pyrénées-Orientales, a camp was established in the spring of 1939 for refugees of the Spanish Civil War, political opponents of the Vichy government, Jews and 'undesirables'. There, a close-knit group of artists, writers and intellectuals created a climate in which the arts could flourish.[7]

Two miniature pen and ink studies, *View of the Town* and *The Beach,* are among the group of landscapes produced by Osias Hofstatter (1905–95) at St Cyprien and Gurs. They offer a glimpse of the distant town and arid dunes beyond the camp's timber sheds and perimeter fences. This persistent mapping activity —examples of which are evident elsewhere[8]— suggests an overriding preoccupation with escape as well as an ingrained instinct for survival. While the man is confined to the spaces of internment, the artist's eye roams the distant terrain. The serene pen and ink drawing of a boat grounded by high tides intimates a precarious means of escape and the uncharted dangers that lay ahead. 'We began to fear the world beyond our enclosure', remarked one prisoner. The drawings anticipate Hofstatter's escape to the Swiss border, where he was arrested but eventually released to safety.

Karl Schwesig's (1898–1955) prolific output and range of subjects reflect a determination to overcome the debilitating conditions of his confinement at St Cyprien.[9] An outspoken anti-Nazi and member of the Communist Party, he fought for the Republicans in the Spanish Civil War. His regular contributions to left-wing satirical journals in Germany, and later in Belgium,[10] as well as his political activism, marked him out for detention and torture in the Reich's prisons from 1933 onward, an experience he recorded in a remarkably animated, if ferocious, suite of drawings, entitled *Schlegelkeller* (Drumstick Cellar) —the name given to the notorious torture cellars run by SA Stormtroopers or 'brownshirts'. The suite of fifty-two pen and ink drawings with such titles as *Interrogation, His hair cropped with rusty scissors so that he bled, A swastika is cut out of the hair damaged skin, Brutal man taking part in the beatings*, was completed in Antwerp in 1937, now sadly lost or destroyed.[11]

The contemplative setting of Schwesig's wash drawing *Immigrants by the Sea, Night*, executed at St Cyprien in 1940, contrasts with the raw, caustic and accusatory nature of much of his work at this time. Two figures, their backs to the viewer, gaze out to sea beneath a full moon; washes of varying intensity rendered in *grisaille* produce a mysterious light, reminiscent of the northern Romantic tradition.[12] But a devastating flood in October 1940 destroyed the camp at St Cyprien. Inmates roamed the beaches, worn out by the oppressive heat and the lack of shelter and sanitation. The scarcity of food and clean water encouraged the spread of typhus, dysentery and other illnesses. The mangled, serendipitous shapes of girders and timbers in Schwesig's *The Flood*, 1940, resemble human remains. The anatomically detailed *Naked Figure Asleep on the Beach*, 1940, and a closely related pen and ink drawing by Leo Breuer (1893–1975), *Naked Prisoner on the Sand at St Cyprien*, 1940 (Skovgaart Museet, Viborg), record these desperate conditions.

One loaf of bread a day for nine people, no soap, no clean clothing, we can't sleep because of the flees, we sleep on the earth; we have no cooking utensils (just a tin) or cutlery (just a wooden spoon). Degrading accommodation…I wish I had some watercolours to paint the impressive mountains and vineyards.[13]

Leo Breuer's topographical record of *Camp des Gurs*, 1941 (Yad Vashem, Art Museum), with its wooden barracks and surrounding landscape (a technically accomplished work which combines watercolour, pen and ink and pencil) conveys a sense of the particular, the intimate and the everyday. Even as our eye settles on the glowing snow-capped peaks of the Pyrenees beyond, a sense of the inevitable encroaches on us.[14] The remote possibility of escape, intimated in

25 **Karl Schwesig**
Immigrants by the Sea, Night
St Cyprien, 1940
pen and ink wash
210 x 261mm
Art collection
Beit Lohamei Haghetaot,
Ghetto Fighters' House,
Israel
Cat. 29

a distant view of the *Canigou Mountains under Snow VIII*, 1940[15] gives way along the bottom half of Schwesig's ethereal watercolour to suggestions of the camp's squalor. Lax security made desertion possible, even advisable, before the remaining prisoners, including Schwesig, were regrouped and transferred to the camp at Gurs, some days later.

Self-portrait as Prisoner

One of those interned at St Cyprien was the painter Felix Nussbaum, who was arrested by the Gestapo and deported on 10 May 1940.[16] His escape in mid-August,[17] and eventual return to Brussels released in him a robust response, culminating in four major works. *Self-portrait in the Camp* painted in the months of October to December 1940, marks the peak of this achievement.[18]

Karl Schwesig has explained how rigorous surveillance and the scarcity of materials made it impossible to produce works of any real substance in the early months of internment, though conditions eased after August 1940.[19] *Self-portrait in the Camp* was painted in the familiar surroundings of Nussbaum's apartment at 22 Rue Archimède in Brussels (which he shared with his companion, the painter Felka Platek), not in the camp itself. The idea grew out of earlier studies and evolved through several well-documented stages. The frail figure of a *Muselmann* in *Huddled Prisoner*, 1940 (Felix-Nussbaum-Haus, Osnabrück) bent over in exhaustion and wrapped in a threadbare blanket appears again, to the right of a group of prisoners in the imposing *Study for St Cyprien*, 1940. Seated aimlessly around a makeshift table made of wooden crates, the prisoners stare intently at the blank circumference of a globe of the world which, like their vacant expressions, reveals all too clearly the senseless nature of both their confinement and their diasporic illusions—as there was nowhere to go.[20] The hunched and now destitute figure reappears as the focal centre of *Prisoner*, 1940 (Deutsches Historisches Museum, Berlin). The barbed-wire fences (an autonomous and freely embroidered device exploited in *Self-Portrait with Key*, 1941), the glistening fragments of human bone and the distant, naked figures are positioned to the right and left of the artist in *Self-portrait in the Camp*, 1940.[21] They appear to form part of a painted backdrop, informing the sitter's space while never fully becoming part of it, and reinforcing the powerful tension between the sitter and his surroundings. Vignettes of camp life are observed and illuminated with painstaking detail. Seated to the

left of Nussbaum, his head clasped in his hands, a figure contemplates the still smouldering wick of an extinguished candle, while another, suffering from dysentery, defecates into an already filthy barrel; a third, ashen-faced and almost naked, clutches at straw.[22] Their intact humanity recalls Pieter Bruegel's (1525–69) sheet of studies of *Cripples and Beggars*, c.1600 (Graphische Sammlung Albertina, Vienna). In *The Persecuted*, 1941, and *Self-portrait with Jewish Identity Card*, 1943 (Felix-Nussbaum-Haus, Osnabrück), high walls, barred windows, and narrow corridors attest to the artist's continued sense of isolation.

If Nussbaum's investigation into the self-portrait genre was conditioned by his experience of internment, escape and clandestine existence, it was also influenced by an awareness of the traditions of portraiture. He might well have admired the rigorous objectivity of Otto Dix's *Self-Portrait at the Easel*, 1926 with its echoes of Dürer.[23] But while Dix remains comparably distant (shielded by an easel, canvas and stretcher), Nussbaum's gaze meets the viewer's head on—a conspiratorial bond is thus formed. His right eye and ear are positioned very close to the painting's centre, as if asserting the vigilance, so vital to the artist's survival. Then again, Nussbaum may have sensed an affinity with Vincent Van Gogh's (1853–90) *Self-portrait with Dark Felt Hat*, 1886 (Van Gogh Museum, Amsterdam) painted in Paris in 1886 and

26 **Karl Schwesig**
First Night: Interrogation Continues, from the suite, *Schlegelkeller* (Drumstick Cellar)
1937
pen and ink wash
Location unknown

24

revealing his sense of unease with the unfamiliar surroundings.[24] And like him, Nussbaum donned a variety of headgear and disguises (paper hats, berets and masks) as if to register different states of mind or personae. The felt skullcap pulled firmly over the back of his skull in the *Self-portrait* (a reference perhaps to the beret worn by Spanish and French prisoners in the camp) emphasises the bald curvature of the skull (where an enigmatic, inert, negative space is formed). The painting's technical range and versatility reward closer scrutiny: the flesh tints are laid on with a trowel-like instrument; dragging, glazing and the use of small brushes to clarify visual incident animate the painted surface. The sombre key sets off the brilliant lighting of the right hemisphere of the head (laid with heavy impasto or *pâte firme*) and along the horizon, where light appears to describe the day's trajectory from dusk until dawn. The focal intensity, light reflectance, clarity of illuminated detail, as well as the sense of a crepuscular orb (defined by the clouds gathering overhead) suggest the world of seventeenth-century optics, for example, Carel Fabritius' (1622–54) *View of Delft*, 1652 (National Gallery, London). Time is stilled by the intensity of the artist's gaze. Unmistakably twentieth century in its powerful assertion of the themes of witness, internment and war, and laden with a sense of doom, Nussbaum's *Self-portrait in the Camp* powerfully asserts its place within the apocalyptic tradition.

Chronicling the Quotidian

I aim to testify through drawings of everyday life.[25]

A finely graded pencil line leads the viewer along the barbed-wire fence and receding pathway to the open-air latrine at Gurs camp, in Jacob Barosin's drawing, a prescient reminder of prisoners' daily and insurmountable struggle against the camp's excremental assault,[26] the exhausting effects of dysentery and the insufficient and often complete lack of latrines, clean water or sanitary conditions. A prisoner's concern with personal hygiene was a psychological prerequisite for survival: 'It was an almost iron law—those who failed to wash every day soon died' was the remark of one survivor,[27] and Primo Levi, writing of his experiences of Auschwitz, recalled:

In this place it is practically pointless to wash every day in the turbid water of the filthy wash basins for purposes of cleanliness and health; but it is most important as a symptom of remaining vitality, and necessary as an instrument of moral choice.[28]

But the latrines elicited a markedly different response from Jorge Semprun, at Buchenwald. Advancing with measured steps through the mud, loosening 'the weight of the world that pulls on your legs, miring you in nothingness!…toward the latrine building in the Little Camp', he found a place 'of possible encounters, conversation, strangely welcoming in spite of the repulsive reek of urine and excrement, a last haven of humanity'.[29]

Following the German occupation of France's 'free zone' in December 1942, the pace of deportations intensified.[30] The individual thoughts and identities of the prisoners in Barosin's *Deportees*, 1943, elude us today. A group of ageing men, closely watched by their French guards, assemble in front of the carriages that will transport them to Auschwitz. The drawing, made with a didactically even line, is one of a group chronicling the artist's arrest in Paris, his deportation to Gurs and his escape to hiding in a Montméjèan schoolhouse.[31]

Boris Taslitzky (b.1901) endured long periods of internment in a series of prisons and camps (see biographical entry on p. 112). His drawings reflect the daily rhythms, the comings and goings, the futility of the long wait. At the Mauzac military prison he produced upward of 200 drawings, most of which were later confiscated by the prison authorities. Drawing allowed him to interpose an objective distance between himself and his fellow prisoners whose lives he observed. *Je n'ai jamais oublié que j'étais un artiste. J'ai essayé de fixer la réalité que j'ai rencontrée.*[32] A steady stream of images chronicle lives of senseless repetition, of indolence and discomfort, alleviated only by the close bonds formed with other prisoners. Figures slouch, stretch or recline, stare vacantly into space or converse before a half-opened window, awaiting orders. Deportation constantly threatened and in November 1943, Taslitzky was deported to the camp at St Sulpice-la-Pointe, thirty kilometres from Toulouse.[33] The active cultural life of the camp was the catalyst for a group of drawings of unsurpassed clarity and economy. The Comité des Loisirs commissioned him to paint large-scale, decorative murals in the prisoners' barracks. In one, two vast figures, a man and woman occupying the full length and height of the wall, raise their arms and hands in a defiant gesture, freed from the shackles that once bound them, amid libertarian scrawls of *Finissant la Marseillaise pour toute l'Humanité*. Francis Cremieux, a fellow inmate recalled:

One day in November 1943, we saw arrive at Saint Sulpice a youngster with silver-grey hair. He had come from Riom central prison…He was a painter or draughtsman, we weren't sure really. Immediately, he was commissioned to paint the theatre decors for the Leisure Committee. In a few days he completed a splendid exterior décor of a garden with foliage and birds. The eight hundred internees of the camp asked the 'Master of Saint-Sulpice' if he would give them drawing lessons and lecture them in the history of art. He gathered round him a circle of pupils…[34]

In *Durant une conférence au camp de St Sulpice* prisoners gather to listen to a lecture, one of many organised by the camp's self-styled, 'open air' university. These lectures were outspoken in their hostility towards the Vichy government and ignited passionate discussion. *27* A highly stylised pen and ink line delineates the impassive contours of the prisoners' faces. The sheer eloquence and calligraphic, near abstract simplicity of line recalls Picasso's drawing of *The Wounded Apollinaire*, 1916, and Matisse's pen and ink studies of figures in interiors. The use of an unshaded line also brings to mind Ingres' portraits of French society during the Second Empire. In the camps, stylistic and iconographic sources are invoked and reinterpreted.

The acuteness of line observed in *Three women leaning over a stove*, produced at Gurs, so unfailing in its *28* authenticity, locates this drawing within the corpus of transit camp art, even though its attribution and dating, based on the inscription found at the base of the page, *Brot Rösten, Le Pain Grillé, Rilik-Andrieux, Gurs 40* have, until recently, appeared less certain.[35] A moment of quiet intimacy—of relationships kindled in adversity—is revealed by the touching gestures of the three figures grilling thin slices of bread over a coal-fired stove, asserting the centrality of gender in the individual's experience of the camps. The women's ability to improvise a meal from miserable rations or scraps of food, bartered or stolen during the day, was vital when a nagging, incessant hunger was an overriding preoccupation.[36] Camp diaries and survivors' testimony show that the daily bread ration was the bedrock of both the prisoner's existence and of the camp's barter-and-exchange economy.

One of those interned at Gurs was Charlotte Salomon (1917–43).[37] Detained in June 1940, Charlotte and her grandfather were released soon after (on account of his old age).[38] Writing to her parents, on their return to the Villefranche (on the outskirts of Nice), Charlotte announced her intention to commence work on an extensive narrative cycle. The result was the fictionalised autobiography *Leben?*

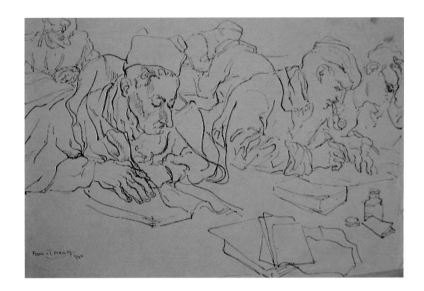

oder Theater? Ein Singespiel (Life? or Theatre? A Musical Play), a monumental task comprising some 769 images (from a storehouse of 1,325 sheets) in three movements: a prelude (which in turn is divided into scenes), a main section (into chapters) and an epilogue, completed in mid-1942.[39] It contains a wealth of visual as well as literary and musical reference, in turn revealing Charlotte's awareness of contemporary artistic trends, her place in the lively and cultivated Salomon household[40] and the influence of her stepmother, the singer Paula Lindberg (née Levi)[41] and of Paula's collaborator, the musicologist Alfred Wolfsohn, who would become Charlotte's mentor and companion.[42] With its range of stylistic experiment and breathtaking virtuosity, *Life? or Theatre?* is unique among the visual chronicles produced within the Nazi sphere. Yet, in common with other narrative cycles by Bedřicht Fritta, Leo Haas and Otto Ungar in the Terezín ghetto, *Life? or Theatre?* (with its momentous shifts in structure, ranging from the diaristic to the documentary) confirms the inextricable nature of history and biography. In asserting her own clear and inimitable voice (the voice of witness) as a continuous narrative thread, Charlotte's *Life? or Theatre?* represents a humane and courageous 'act of defiance' against Nazism. The accelerated pace and ominous content of the cycle exposes the increasing limitations placed on her movements (confined for most of this time to the safe-house in the Villefranche and the Hotel Aurore at St Jean Cap Ferrat), the death and escape of those closest to her at the time, and the dangers to her own life. Arrested by the Gestapo on 24 September,

28 Lili Rilik-Andrieux
*Three women leaning over
a stove*
Gurs, 1940
pen and ink
150 x 160mm
Art collection
Beit Lohamei Haghetaot, Israel
Ghetto Fighters' House Museum
Cat. 40

Charlotte (four months pregnant) was deported to Auschwitz where she was gassed on her arrival on 10 October.[43]

The artistic plenitude achieved by Charlotte Salomon in *Life? or Theatre?* (described by as a *dreifarben singespiel*,[44] a 'three-coloured play with music'), with its inexhaustible stream of invention, reveals both innocence and her precocious experience of life and death. In this context, we might do well to consider her mentor Alfred Wolfsohn's remark that 'to love life even more, one must have already died once'.

Drancy and Malines

Seeking to escape the grip of Nazi antisemitic policies, Central and East European Jews, like Charlotte Salomon, sought to establish new homes in France, only to find themselves victims of the Franco-German collaboration, condemned to make the tortuous return journey East in sealed cattle trucks to forced labour and extermination camps in the Reich. Aizik Feder was among these. A pupil of Henri Matisse and a close associate of the Circle of Montparnasse artists Amadeo Modigliani, Jacques Lipchitz and Otto Freundlich, Feder returned to Paris after a brief sojourn in Palestine. Following the Occupation, he joined the Resistance movement, was arrested and then deported to Drancy transit camp and from there to Auschwitz where he perished in 1943.

31   Drancy, a mass housing development still under construction on the outskirts of Paris, at La Muette, provided 70,000 detainees with temporary housing. Feder's *The Reader* (Jew with Yellow Star), 1943, one of an extended series of portraits produced at Drancy, invites the viewer to reflect on the loss experienced by a community facing the threat of deportation and death. Feder manages to restore a sense of dignity to his subject, diminished by fear and by the brutality of the treatment received at the hands of the French *gendarmes*: the forced abduction, the loss of homes, estrangement from friends and neighbours, the senseless movement in sealed cattle trucks to undisclosed destinations. Among those who passed through these concrete shells, without heating or running water, were intellectuals, such as the poet Max Jacob, the choreographer René Blum, the novelist Tristan Bernard and the playwright Itzak Katznelson.[45] Feder's *Reader* turns away momentarily from his tranquil pursuits to reveal, in an instant, the fear, the faltering hope and yearning for rescue, shared by all deportees.

29 **Charlotte Salomon**
Act Two, The Swastika, from the suite, *Leben? oder Theater? Ein Singespiel* (Life? or Theatre? A musical play) 1940–42 gouache
Jewish Historical Museum, Amsterdam

Like Feder, Leon Landau (1910–45) and his family emigrated to Palestine, returning to Belgium for a brief period, only to be caught up in a wave of arrests and deportations. Landau trained at the Academies in Antwerp and Brussels, accepting employment with the Royal Netherlands Theatre, for whom he designed sets and costumes. Interned in 1943 in the transit camp at Malines, some twenty kilometres from Antwerp, he produced a marionette theatre for a children's production of *Thyl Uylenspiegel*. Landau's nearly life-size *Portrait of a Young Man*, 1943, far surpasses his previous efforts in the severe and unadorned economy of the graphite line. The young man's shaven appearance reminds us of the degrading ordeal endured by prisoners. His dejected state suggests a period of prolonged internment. (He could well have returned from a Polish death camp, though such occurrences were rare.)[46]

30   Three drawings produced by Irene Awret (b.1921) at Malines camp in the final months before her deportation, *Open Window with Still-life, Vase and Shells (Summer)*, *Open Window (Winter)* and *Clouds* reflect the artist's shifting states of mind and increasing apprehension as she awaited the inevitable journey East. In *Open Window with Still-life, Vase and Shells (Summer)*, the camp's faint outline is just visible in the distance. The naturalistic rendering of particular

30 **Leon Landau**
Portrait of a Young Man
Malines, 1943
pencil
355 x 265mm
Art collection
Beit Lohamei Haghetaot, Israel
Ghetto Fighters' House Museum
Cat. 38

31 **Adolphe Feder**
The Reader (Jew with Yellow Star)
Drancy, 1943
charcoal and pastel
490 x 376mm
Art collection
Beit Lohamei Haghetaot, Israel
Ghetto Fighters' House Museum
Cat. 37

still-life elements gives way in the second, *Open Window (Winter)*, to broad atmospheric effects. At Malines, the buildings were arranged around four sides of a courtyard: windows opening inwards afforded a glimpse of the courtyard with its arrivals and departures, its roll-calls, and food and parcel distribution, while those facing the other way were whitewashed, depriving inmates of a view to the outside world. In the third and final drawing, a sombre, impenetrable and elemental barrier closes off the distant view in an unequivocal statement of internment.[47]

Moments of reprieve

Allow me to tell you that I am of the Jewish race…

On closer inspection, the distinction in Otto Freundlich's (1878–1943) development between the abstract works, reflecting his association with European avant-garde circles from 1911 onwards,[48] and the clandestine studies and other so-called *oeuvres retrouvé*, recording his experiences of internment and his *résidence surveillée* from 1939 onwards, appears tenuous.[49] At the assembly camp at Francillon par

32 **Otto Freundlich**
L'Indélicat
The Offending Postman
Saint-Paul-de-Fenouillet,
c.1941
pencil
283 x 231mm
Association 'Les Amis de
Jeanne et Otto
Freundlich', Pontoise
Cat. 39

Villebaron (Loire-et-Cher) Freundlich produced a series of fluid sketches of the camp's inmates. Regally dressed in a long overcoat, *Dr Mathias*[50] wears a prosecuting attorney's hat and his feet are clad in comically oversized, pointed clogs. Arms raised aloft, he holds a steaming bowl in one hand and a wooden spoon (a sceptre, perhaps) in the other. The ironic, self-deprecating stance and swift line recall Pietr Kien's caricatures of inmates in the Terezín ghetto. *Apres la réquisition des métaux précieux*[51] remarks on a visit to the dentist who, clutching a set of adequate but now fully extracted teeth, commiserates with a sorry-looking artist. His bandaged head turns him into an object of ridicule. The most poignant drawing, however, is *L'Indélicat*, c.1941–42. Inscribed with the comment, 'It seems these damned refugees don't always endure hunger. For every time that I take note of their moral conduct, I find one hundred bucks in a letter,'[52] it portrays the inquisitive postman in the small village of Saint-Paul-de-Fenouillet in the Pyrénées Orientales, who informed on the Freundlichs and regularly searched the couple's mail for small gifts of money sent by friends and collectors. The compelling power of these image lies in their oblique commentary on the uneventful dailiness of internment and *résidence surveillée*, albeit with its uncertainties and betrayal.

In Saint-Paul-de-Fenouillet, Freundlich and his companion, the artist Jeanne Kosnick-Kloss, maintained a precarious existence dependant on the help of a few close friends and collectors, among them Picasso (who paid Freundlich's studio rent), Peggy Guggenheim, who helped him to acquire artists' materials, and for a time in 1941, Varian Fry's committee. But efforts to assist his escape across the border failed. By December 1942, Germany's occupation of France was secure, enabling the authorities to close the net on 'undesirables'. Responding to a letter from the local prefecture asking him to state his religion, Freundlich declared:

Allow me to tell you that I am of the Jewish race, that my parents and grandparents were also [Jews]. I have no wealth being a painter and a sculptor, having made mosaics and stained glass, I have lived modestly and honestly from the sale of my paintings…[53]

Freundlich was employed before the First World War on the restoration of the great windows at Chartres Cathedral. This experience was to have a significant impact on his work, in which a rich orchestration of colour is reinforced by rigorous compositional

32

33 **Otto Freundlich**
Unfinished composition
Composition (inachevée)
1943
gouache on board
225 x 290mm
Donation Freundlich,
Musée de Pontoise

elements that extend the formal discoveries of Suprematism, Orphism and Neo-plasticism. By diminishing the size of the discreet taches of colour and arranging them on grids of radial and elliptical lines, Freundlich manipulated their optical activity to establish a wall of chromatic intensity, a vibrant patchwork of light, for example in the imposing oil on canvas, *La Rosace I*, 1938 (Donation Freundlich, Musée de Pontoise), and in a smaller, optically more vibrant version painted in 1942, one closely related to his experience at Chartres.

33   In what is possibly his final and bleakest statement (it remained unfinished at his death), *Composition inachevée*, 1943, breaks down the distinctions between pure abstraction and biography, symbolic and iconic languages. The prismatic elements distil reality, while also revealing the presence of a doorway or arch at the centre of the composition.[54] A discreet, shallow element within breaks up the dark rectangle and suggests a pathway or gangplank. Recalling the austerity of Malevich's *Black Square* (itself a statement of finality), *Composition inachevée* intimates a descent, entombment. An earlier instance of the artist's use of symbolic language confirms this reading. The symbolic associations of colour are frankly declared in *Mon Ciel est Rouge*, 1933. A band

of vermilion sits astride the white and blue stripes of the French *tricoleur*. This confident, even brazen evocation of the flag in this significant year was, surely, an intimation of Freundlich's allegiance to his country of adoption. In a related pencil study for the painting produced that year, the entire sheet is covered with annotations in the artist's hand. These have been ascribed variously to Freundlich's reading of Nietzsche's *Also Sprach Zarathustra* and *Der Wille zur Macht* (The Will to Power).[55] But on closer scrutiny the scribbles reveal the artist's thoughts on colour and spatial notation. Such a synthesis of the flag, a symbol of *Liberté, Egalité, Fraternité* and Nietzsche, would come as little surprise. French social aspirations and German culture both formed part of Freundlich's privileged upbringing and education and were expressed early on, in his own work. If the title of Freundlich's sculpture, *Der Neue Mensch* (New Man), 1912—reproduced on the cover of the Nazi's *Entartete Kunst* (Degenerate Art) exhibition in July 1937—contains an unequivocal reference to Nietzsche, the deft balancing of solid masses defying gravity recalls the airborne arches and butresses of Chartres.

34

Quiet before the storm

In the weeks following the German invasion of Poland and before the closure of its border with the Soviet Union on 28 September 1939, mass expulsions caused some quarter of a million Jews to journey East across the rivers Narew, Bug and San to the Soviet-administered zone. These *Aktionen*, in which thousands of Poles were murdered in cold blood, were soon followed by the mass expulsions of German, Czech and West European Jews to German occupied towns in Poland. Jews from Moravska Ostrava, in the former Czechoslovak region were deported to Lublin, where an inhospitable camp, code-named 'Central Office for Jewish Intelligence' was established.[56]

Leo Haas (1901–83) was among those ordered to leave the train at Nisko, near Lublin to help erect the wooden structures that would house fellow Jews from Ostrawa. Haas' fluid line drawing *Laundry Room*, 1939, captures the interior of the prisoner's shed which was used as laundry room, office and communal kitchen.[57] In common with the images produced at Drancy and Malines transit camps, a relative calm seems to mark the prisoners' lives. War is conspicuously absent from these drawings. A solitary figure intent on his work is seated beneath a window and surrounded by an assortment of ill-

35

34 **Otto Freundlich**
New Man
Der Neue Mensch, 1912
reproduced on the cover
of the Entartete Kunst
(Degenerate Art)
exhibition catalogue
in 1937

12.XII.39 Trockenraum
Wascherei (Brigolraum u. Kanzlei)

35 **Leo Haas**
Laundry Room
Nisko, 1939
pencil
222 x 281mm
Památník Terezín
Cat. 41

matching clothes hanging from washing lines to dry. A steam-iron, a double-handed saucepan and other domestic utensils are scattered around the room; on the work table, a set square and other drawing implements attest to the artist's task. His blunt pencil moves with speed across the sheet to record the apparent normality of this quiet domesticity and its concern with cleanliness which will, in a matter of months, be shattered by the war and the sequence of events leading to the prisoners' forced emigration. This sense of 'quiet before the storm' stands in marked contrast to the brooding intensity of the works produced by Haas, some months later, in the Terezín ghetto.

4   Theresienstadt

The German occupation of Bohemia and Moravia in March 1939 (the Protektorat) put an end to the gradual emancipation of Jews from their traditional communities and assimilation into Czech national life.[1] By October, the Nazi policy of deportation to and concentration in Polish ghettos was under way.[2] As a model for Jewish existence and sustainability, the medieval ghettos (one etymology is *borghetto*, from the Italian for small settlement), established a precedent for the notorious practices of segregation and forced internment in sealed compounds of Jews and other 'undesirables' by the Nazis. In October, a temporary enclave was established at Nisko, in Poland (the setting for Leo Haas's *Laundry Room*), housing a population of 2,900 deportees from the Protektorat and from Austria.[3] Here the Nazis appointed two communal leaders, Jakob Edelstein, former head of the Jewish Agency in Prague, and Benjamin Murmelstein, a Viennese rabbi, to administer and run the camp (thereby setting a precedent that would be repeated elsewhere in Jewish-administered settlements). In September 1941, the Nazis established a centre for the detention of prominent and elderly Jews (among them decorated First World War veterans) and their families at Terezín, situated some fifty kilometres from Prague in the Sudetenland, a conveniently marginal transit point or *Durchgangsghetto*. Theresienstadt (the Germans adapted the names of towns throughout occupied Europe) played a key role in the planned annihilation of Jews from Western Europe in concentration and extermination camps in the East under the guise of a model town for the safekeeping of Jews.[4] With the arrival of the first transport on 24 November 1941, some 342 men were assigned to the construction of lodgings inside the existing fortifications of Joseph II's garrison town, an event recorded in Bedřich Fritta's (1906–44) *Building Barracks*, c.1942 (Jewish Museum, Prague). This first group was joined on 4 December by a further 1,000 men, among them administrative officers, health service workers, the ghetto's leadership and survivors of Nisko. Edelstein was appointed to oversee the ghetto self-administration under the supervision of an *SS Lagerkommandant* and a Council of Elders (*Altestenrat*).[5] With characteristic fluency Leo Haas' *Members of the Lagerkommandantur on the Beat*, 1943–44, expresses his disdain (shared by others) for the authoritative and repressive structures that governed the lives of the ghetto's inhabitants: with heads bared and hats in hand, the Council Elders kowtow to their commanders who stride past with a self-congratulatory air. In fact, the Jewish Council was heavily circumscribed in its powers, operating in a grey area between their responsibility to the ghetto inhabitants and acquiescence to the Nazis' directives, between self-interested cooperation and collaboration. History has criticised the institution of the *Juderäte* (Jewish Councils) for subservience and unscrupulous methods in exercising its limited powers in the adjudication of privilege. For example, the Council categorised the ghetto population as *indispensable, valuable, quite useful* or *superfluous*, granting a few extra weeks of life to some, while condemning others to the transports, few of whom were seen again. But in employing upwards of 17,000 men and women, or one third of the average ghetto population, the self-administration extended at the very least a measure of protection to its members (known in Theresienstadt as *Vitamin P*, P for protection). Within this far from ideal framework a community existed. Communal values were to an extent upheld, and privation and discomfort alleviated by essential services. Education and religious observance, central to Jewish life and continuity, flourished, as did the arts.

A Human Sluice

Monde de mourants où plus rien n'a de sens.[6]

Terezín was a sorting-house for Europe's Jews. New arrivals stepped down off the trains onto the tracks at Bauschowitz and from there were escorted by foot to the *Schleuse* (the name given to barracks located outside the ghetto walls, along the banks of the Ohre river, at the point where its floodgates control the river's flow). There they were processed, their personal belongings 'sorted' or simply pillaged.

36 **Bedřich Fritta**
Fortune Teller
Kartářka
Terezin, 1943–44
pen, brush and ink wash
587 x 422mm
Thomas Fritta Haas
Cat. 57

37 **Otto Ungar**
*Street Scene with
Crowds*
Terezin, c.1943
pen, ink and gouache
440 x 600mm
The Jewish Museum,
Prague
Cat. 50

38 **Otto Ungar**
*After the arrival of the
transport*
Terezin, c.1943
gouache, pen and ink
wash
440 x 600mm
Památník Terezín
Cat. 52

Routinely, arrival and departure were accompanied by a morass of senseless bureaucracy: identity cards, ration cards, coupons, work certificates, transportation cards, exemptions from transport, permits for working indoors, permits for working outdoors—all these and more were issued to new arrivals. The Ghetto's self-administration matched their captors' zeal for meticulous record-keeping, producing large quantities of printed documents, ordinances, reports to the SS Command, records of mortalities, inoculation and medical certificates, parcel collection forms, Jews Bank savings cards, tickets for the collection of clean laundry, day permits to the ghetto kitchens or infirmary.[7] A deluge of documents is all that survives of this river of humanity, propelled through the so-called Sluice.

The intense animation of figures in Otto Ungar's *Street Scene with Crowds*, c.1943, distantly recalls Beckmann's *The Street*, from the suite *Die Hölle*, 1919, and Ungar's ability to capture the ungainly movements, the facial expressions, dress and other social demarcators strikes a parallel with the work of the exiled German artist George Grosz (1893–1959). A murky, nocturnal haze hangs over the assembled figures, a quality Ungar achieves with the overlay of washes of colour laid onto a wet *imprimatura* ground, enlivened here and there by luminous accents of cerulean, ochre and crimson. And as with other works produced in the ghetto, the buildings are less a topographical record of Terezín's incongruous eighteenth century 'baroque', than a vast theatrical backdrop, emphasising the wholly artificial nature of the setting. Fritta's pen and ink drawing *View of Theresienstadt*, 1943–44, offers a rare, aerial view of the crowded streets, rooftops, turrets, clock towers and belfries. Its tense linearity contrasts markedly with the topographical record of streets and ramparts produced by Leo Heilbrunn in the ghetto's Technical Drawing Studio.[8] Joseph Spier's album *Bilder Aus Theresienstadt*, 1944 was published to coincide with the visit by foreign dignitaries and representatives of the Red Cross Committee to Theresienstadt on 23 June 1944. Spier's *Bilder* contains eighteen delicately hand-coloured lithographs, idealised, picture-post-card views of the coffee house, a parade of modern shops, a children's marionette theatre, a bakery, neatly ordered gardens and the central square, conveying the false impression that here was a well-ordered society, a resort for Jews, sheltered from events outside.[9] Theresienstadt's isolation—an outcrop set within rolling Bohemian farmland, austere in winter, a paradise in summer—heightened

this sense of unreality for the ghetto's involuntary visitors. Maurice Rossel, a twenty-five year old Swiss worker appointed by the Committee to investigate conditions, recalled his visit in later years, 'My task was to see beyond what I was seeing…'. But beguiled by the Nazis' vile deception, he failed to grasp the misery of the ghetto's inhabitants, beyond the newly painted facades and planted walkways.[10] The different views of the ghetto by Fritta, Heilbrunn and Spier do not so much reflect individual temperaments or stylistic conventions than the artist's sense of unease and marginality amid all the artificiality of this setting.

Leo Haas' *Arrivals*, c.1943 (Yad Vashem Art Museum), records the senseless comings and goings of a transient population: a sea of migrants huddle, awaiting either deportation or initiation into the ghetto. Exhausted by their journeys, they sleep, lie awake or feverishly search their belongings in the cold discomfort and overcrowding of the Arrivals Hall. Their possessions are marked with name and destination, as if to underline their temporary status. A tiny figure, as yet unseen by the crowd, sets about dismantling the massive walls of the vaulted chamber, allowing a beam of light to filter into the windowless fortifications. Otto Ungar's *After the Arrival of a Transport* focuses on one such arrival, an ageing woman who squats, surrounded by her lumbering possessions. Trunks, bags, shoes, drapes and a copper cauldron, and her own corpulent presence, form a protective wall—a clock ticks away the long hours. Lacking more permanent materials (oil paints and canvas were not easily obtained), Ungar learnt to master the use of gouache and pen and ink to achieve a comparable density and controlled build-up of the surface.

Seated centrally in Bedřich Fritta's *Men's Dormitory, Sudetenkaserne*, 1943–44, the forlorn and emaciated figure of a *Muselmann*, his meagre rations already consumed, gazes idly in contemplation of a distant point beyond the picture's edge—a transcendent statement of internment. While other inmates do mundane chores—wash, sleep, day-dream or converse—the rotund figure (right), a recent arrival, stuffs a slice of bread into his pouting mouth, while reaching into a stash of provisions in his suitcase. Fritta sheds light on the ghetto's iniquities, in a manner that recalls Borowski's jarring observations from Auschwitz:

Several of us sit on the top bunk, our legs dangling over the edge. We slice the neat loaves of crisp, crunchy bread. It is a bit coarse to the taste…sent all the way from Warsaw—only

37

38

87

39 Karel Fleischmann
Living Quarters, Sudeten Barracks
Terezin, 1943
pen and ink wash
225 x 330mm
Yad Vashem Art Museum,
Jerusalem
Cat. 54

*a week ago my mother held this white loaf in her hands…
We unwrap the bacon, the onion, we open a can of evapo-
rated milk. Henri, the fat Frenchman, dreams aloud of the
French wine brought by the transports from Strasbourg,
Paris, Marseilles…sweat streams down his body.*[11]

39

The towering beds and telescoped perspectives in
Fritta's drawing like the spiralling bunk-beds in
Karel Fleischmann's *Living Quarters,* 1943, suggest a
despoiled, subterranean city, in a passing reference
perhaps to Piranesi's *Carceri* suite. Mořitz Nágl's silken
panel, *Ubikace ve svetnici* c.1942–43, one of several
such studies, reveals the less cramped conditions of
the dormitory at the Magdeburg Barracks reserved for
the ghetto's elite. A silken light from a nearby
window permeates the interior and inventories the
miscellany of inmates' possessions, including a suitcase inscribed with its owner's name *F. Metzl.*[12]

40

Charlotte Burešová's (1904–83) delicate ink
study, *Women's Dormitory*, intimates the futility of
waiting for Terezín's aging population. The inscription
along the base of the suitcase, *Alma Sara Schwarz
VN179*, signals the identity and transport of the figure
engrossed in her readings of psalms. Behind her, a
sleeping woman is watched by her caring companion
and beyond them, a young woman in her underwear
turns her back on us. The clarity afforded to the
sitters' faces, crumpled clothing and few personal
possessions draws the viewer into the intimacy of
the living quarters. An initial pencil outline is
subsequently strengthened with washes of ink and
watercolour and only then heightened with Chinese
white to achieve the study's inimitable quality.

Burešová attests to the solitude, privations and
uncertainties experienced by an elderly population,
notwithstanding the intense overcrowding. Likewise,
Malvina Schalková's portrayal of the women's
dormitory establishes a calm intimacy with those
fearing deportation.

Circumstances like these required absolute
resolve, as Etty Hillesum reminds us, writing on the
eve of her deportation from Westerbork to Auschwitz:
'Each moment of your life that your courage fails is a
lost moment'.[13] If Burešová and Schalková aimed to
restore a sense of dignity to their subjects, highlight-
ing ordinary virtues, it was the case that everyday acts
of kindness were central to survival. 'It seems to me',
Germaine Tillion remarked, 'that friendly support
was more consistent, more solid, and more widespread in the women's camps'.[14] A maternal instinct
for compassionate caring characterised their acts,
and also typified their role in the ghetto where
women outnumbered the men.[15] In Theresienstadt, a
workforce of 11,000 women were employed as
nurses, teachers, clerical workers, cooks, cleaners and
laundry-workers.

Like the figure of a *Muselmann* at the centre of
Men's Dormitory, Sudetenkaserne, the elderly, bespecta-
cled female inmate in Fritta's *Kartářka* (Fortune   *36*
Teller), 1943–44, is the lonely protagonist of a drama
endured in silence. Her quivering fingers move deftly
over the deck of playing cards that will disclose
her future. As she turns her gaze, and possibly her
thoughts, toward the bleak, partially bricked up
window and a life beyond confinement, the barred
gate and fortress walls come into view, as if denying
her any future at all. She is the ghetto's archetype,
aging and stranded. With its subtle gradation of tone,
fluid washes and penetrating description of line,
Fritta's *Fortune Teller,* among the truly great works
produced in Terezín, rivals the social criticism of Otto
Dix and George Grosz.

Bread and Hearses

In Fritta's *The Morgue*, 1943–44, a forbidding portrayal   *42*
of near death, three cadaverous men stretch out on
shelves in an arched recess, like figures in a catacomb.
The vertical bars lend a sinister note to the ghetto's
sleeping arrangements. One can almost hear their
low murmurs and grinding teeth; the jerking limbs
suggest the death rattle.

Inside the 'model ghetto' of Terezín, the instruments of life and death are hopelessly intertwined:
agricultural vehicles pull coffins and canopied hearses

40 **Mořitz Någl**
Small Dormitory
Terezin, c.1942
oil on linen mounted on board
295 x 398mm
The Jewish Museum, Prague
Cat. 55

distribute the day's bread ration.[16] The ghetto's health inspectorate made supreme efforts to preserve life—an ethos that was somehow also reflected in the art of the ghetto.[17] Moritz Muller's (1887–1944) *Portrait of Louis Bohm in the Infirmary*, 1944 (Jewish Museum, Prague), and similar works produced in the final months before his deportation, provide detailed insight into the quotidian lives of the sick, elderly and infirm inhabitants of the ghetto. An inscription on the reverse: *Louis Bohm, from Koca, near Breslau; in his 84th year, for 20 years he was the Head of the Jewish Community'* reveals his identity.[18] Nonetheless, between August 1942 and March 1943 the mortality rate increased fifteen-fold. Of the 139,654 Jews interned in Theresienstadt, 33,430 perished in the ghetto and another 83,934 were deported to camps in the East—only a few hundred survived.[19]

As a senior medical officer appointed by the ghetto administration (see biography, p. 106), Karel Fleischmann (1897–1944)[20] had regular access to the treatment rooms and morgue. His vivid *pochoir* studies made with a fountain pen on the lined pages of a pocket-size spiral notebook provide a detailed record of the preparation of corpses before and after autopsy: the undressing and lifting of bodies onto the articulated table, the sponging, washing and draining, cutting through the sternum, prising open the thoracic cage, to reveal the glistening organs. These studies reflect the perennial concern of artists with the analysis of human form and anatomy.[21] Their cumulative effect suggests not the inert stillness of the dead, but a sort of 'Dance of Death' animation. Indeed, Fleischmann's sketchbooks overflow with observations of the people, buildings and events—a pool of impressions from which later compositions will be nourished and their content dramatised. One of these, *Invalid veterans' prostheses*, 1943, depicts the depository of inmates' medical prostheses in the ghetto, the discarded remnants of an elderly population, veterans of the Great War who fought with the German army, receiving medals and citations for bravery. This and a closely related ink and watercolour drawing, *Furniture confiscated from Jewish Apartments*, 1943 (Jewish Museum, Prague), confirm his interest in the animation of still forms. A mêlée of ritual objects—a silver platter for the Passover *seder*, Torah scrolls and finials, a *tzedakah* box and the ark of the covenant—are unceremoniously heaped one on top of the other. Alert to the subject's expressive and technical possibilities, Fleischmann seizes on both its historic and symbolic significance as a warning of events to come. And in one of countless reworkings

43

on this theme, the evacuation of the *Sudetenkaserne Barracks*, inmates' belongings are strewn everywhere in a scene of terrible devastation, recalling the nervous fluidity of Leonardo's *Deluge* studies.

At Theresienstadt, death acquired various guises: hearses were used not only to transport the dead, but also the sick and elderly, as if to hasten their departure. They were used, too, as Leo Haas' *Funeral Hearses* shows, to carry all manner of goods. The arrival of the day's bread ration is heralded on the right, planks of timber are conveyed to the building department, while the mourning women wrapped in their hooded coats (recalling the women with mantillas in a scene from Goya's *Disparates*) make a final exit (left), with their possessions. In Fritta's *Transport of the Elderly Terezín*, 1942–44, the hearse is neither pulled nor driven, it is stationery; its passengers, perennial travellers weighed down by bundles and a dogged

41 **Charlotte Burešová**
Dormitory
Terezín, undated
pen and ink wash,
graphite
and chinese white
313 x 233mm
Yad Vashem Art
Museum, Jerusalem
Cat. 56

42 **Bedřich Fritta**
The Morgue
Terezín, 1943–44
pen and ink wash
474 x 360mm
Thomas Fritta Haas
Cat. 61

44

43 **Karel Fleischmann**
Invalid veterans' prostheses
Terezín, 1943
pen and ink wash
330 x 440mm
The Jewish Museum, Prague
Cat. 62

inertia, recall the defendants in Kafka's *The Trial*. Felix Bloch's *Rozloučeni se zemřelými* (Parting of the Deceased), 1943 depicts a burial ceremony. Presiding over the neatly laid out rows of coffins piled three high, a Rabbi and two assistants administer funerary rites to the deceased. Such occasions were conducted in rooms adjacent to the morgue and the crematorium: the coffins themselves were later reused. Bloch's drawing technique is characteristically less refined than that of Karel Fleischmann or Bedřich Fritta, manifesting a deliberate crudeness appropriate to his subjects. An incandescent ground is applied with a fine spray of ink and watercolour that sets off and dramatises the black chalk drawing.

A quarter of all Jews interned in Theresienstadt perished inside the ghetto walls. Their ashes (which until then had been stored in numbered urns in the Columbarium, awaiting dignified burial) were ejected on Nazi orders into the Ohre River,[22] ostensibly to 'remove the evidence', an execrable act which continued to prey on the minds of those charged with the deed, long after it was accomplished.

The Painters of Terezín

I feel it is my duty to accuse…the Fascist murderers named in my report—in the name of all the victims, in my own name and above all in the name of my friends who did not return, the painters of Terezín.[23]

The art produced in the Terezín ghetto ritualises the life of a community whose very existence was threatened. In this most precarious of settings, and in spite of the daily and incessant struggle to secure the basic requirements of life, artists and intellectuals countered the Nazis' repressive campaign of defamation which for a decade had marginalized them from all spheres of professional activity, while attempting to restore a tradition of political and artistic dissidence.

The embattled painters, Bloch, Fleischmann, Fritta, Haas and Ungar, made pugnacious use of a long-standing tradition of graphic images to wage a secret war against the authorities. They opposed the Nazi campaign of deception and terror, establishing tenuous contacts, through their graphic works with the world outside the ghetto, a link that would ultimately seal their fate as artists and as human beings (Bloch, Fleischmann, Fritta and Ungar lost their lives as a direct result of their clandestine activity). Like Goya, whose etchings of the Spanish Peninsular War highlight a 'loss of reason', the artists of Terezín questioned the irrationalism which had taken hold of their

44 **Leo Haas**
Funeral Hearses
Terezin, c.1943
pen and ink wash
373 x 500mm
Yad Vashen Art
Museum, Jerusalem
Cat. 69

world. The arresting anti-war protests and bitter social critique contained in the works of Kollwitz, Beckmann, Grosz and Dix[24] served as visual exemplars for those produced in Terezín. The correlation of styles and avid political commentary contained in their drawings confirm the link between artistic and political radicalism. Their presence also helped to strengthen the resolve of the ghetto inhabitants.

Leo Haas' *Kreslírna II*, 1943, presents a *tribuna*: the meeting of a group of artists, mostly associated with the Technical Drawing Studio housed in the Magdeburg Barracks. Once again, Haas' training as a graphic artist and commercial illustrator is reflected in the breathtaking fluency of this drawing. The improvisational quality of the line belies a certain command of composition. Thus, in spite of the drawing's apparent ease of execution, it required more than one sitting and was probably assembled from several preliminary studies. We know of at least one such work, the pen and ink *Technická Kancelář* (Technical Office), 1943.[25] Two inscriptions, on the recto and verso of the completed drawing help to unravel the identity of some of those portrayed.[26] Standing second from the right is Fritta, the Studio's charismatic leader and to his right, the architect Leo Heilbrunn and Felix Bloch. Petr Kien, Fritta's steadfast assistant (and author of a remarkable body of work) is seated, right foreground. Though Haas intended this primarily as the record of a typical working day in the Technical Drawing Studio and of its principal figures, we might expect to find others, not directly employed by the Studio, but who were active practitioners of the visual arts in Terezín. For example, might the penetrating

45

45 **Leo Haas**
Technical Drawing Studio
Kreslírna II
Terezín, 1943
graphite and black chalk
363 x 529mm
Památník Terezín
Cat. 63

gaze that meets the viewer's across the table be that of Charlotte Burešová? And is it Malvina Schalková who bends over her work, deep in concentration?[27] Could the small boy gazing over his father's shoulder at the far end of the table be Joseph Spier's son Peter, and the young man seated far right, Petr Ginz, author of the children's literary review *Vedem*? We might also expect to find Adolf Aussenberg, Leo Troller, Fleischmann, Ungar and Zadiková in this company. The artist's right hand and signature along the lower edge of the drawing confirm his discreet presence in the room (a device which Haas used elsewhere).[28] Recalling the work of the American painter Norman Rockwell, whose self-portrait at the easel pulls together biographical and artistic fragments, *Kreslírna* belongs to a tradition of artists' group portraits, starting with the guilds and academies painted by Zoffany, Reynolds and Fantin-Latour in the eighteenth and nineteenth centuries.

As young men, Jan Burka and his brother shared a room high up in the eaves of the *Jügendheim* (young people's home) at Theresienstadt.[29] They had brought with them a stipulated maximum fifty kilograms of personal effects, most of this consisting of paper, sketchbooks, drawing materials and art books. Intent on pursuing his artistic vocation and yet well aware of his chances of survival, Burka undertook a detailed study of the masters: reproductions of Piero and Rembrandt hung on their walls. 'We formed a small group, interested in the history of art, meeting twice a week in my studio.'[30] A *Study of Irises* and *Reclining Nude*, c.1942, executed on the two sides of a single sheet, and the sinuous line study *Nude after Rembrandt*, 1944 (Yad Vashem, Art Museum), are evidence of a wholly unexpected (in the context) affirmation of the continuity of fine art traditions. But not even the young Burka could ignore the perils faced by the community. In *Deportees* a procession of men, women and children, their backs to the viewer, descend the street and emerge through a narrow opening into infinity, the *Himmelfahrtstrasse* or 'road to Heaven'.[31] Their padded bodies (caressing marks of luminous brown chalk) wrapped in heavy overcoats stand out against the vertical accents of police bayonets and the receding diagonals of buildings on whose walls are projected dancing shadows.

46

46 Jan Burka
Deportees
Terezín (undated)
brown sanguine chalk
500 x 325mm
Yad Yashem Art
Museum, Jerusalem

Film

Fritta, Ungar, Bloch and I were so oppressed by the horrible surroundings that we devoted ourselves to our office duties by day and at night, gathered in our darkened workroom. Our sketches matured—as a cycle.[32]

Much has been written about the achievement of visual artists in Terezín, but the ground-breaking relationship of film and narrative images has gone largely unexplored. These highly charged images by Fritta, Haas, Fleischmann, Bloch and Spier, in particular, constitute a frame-by-frame cycle of life in the ghetto and, lacking the technical sophistication of film, conflate both literal and metaphorical transcriptions of reality. These artists acknowledged the power and immediacy of the time-based medium of black-and-white film, with its editing, cropping, blurring and superimposing of sound (in effect, a new language) and exploited the techniques to their own ends. For instance, Felix Bloch's *Drawing and Document Boxes*, 1943 (Yad Vashem Art Museum), constitute a panoptic, three-dimensional pop-up view of the ghetto. Each surface (front, spine and verso) is decorated with his observations: the arrival (railway tracks, boundaries and barbed fences); daily routines (barracks, ration cues, work details, uniformed members of the Judenrat); townscapes (trees, walls, gates); inmates and their possessions; the transports (coffins, luggage, hearses, agricultural machinery); the departed. This untrammelled journey through the ghetto, with its simultaneity of views, unusual perspectives and myriad details contribute to the impression of movement and recalls the rapid flickering effects and editing techniques of Pathé News.

47 Bedřich Fritta
Film and Reality
Terezín, 1943–44
pen and ink
320 x 570mm
Thomas Fritta Haas
Cat. 67

Leo Haas' essay *The Affair of the Painters of Terezín* reflects this awareness of the vast canvas on which the painters played out their own lives, as witnesses to catastrophe. Specific references to film abound in their works. Fritta's spiral bound sketchbooks (with their own sequential structure) are filled with detailed studies for larger compositions, more often than not, based on the imagination. One of these, *Film and Reality*, 1943–44, shows a young *poudreuse* (part human, part automaton), linked by an umbilical chord to the whirring sound of a film projector whose light beams on an elderly resident of the ghetto seated in front of curtain drapes. The sweeping angles afford the viewer a glimpse of a world beyond the glaring lights and sordid pretence. A skeleton agonises in a darkened alley, while in the distance, the stone walls and barbed-wire fences lay claim on reality.[33]

Fritta's *Film and Reality* preceded the making of the Nazi propaganda film entitled *Theresienstadt: Ein Dokumentarfilm aus dem jüdischen Siedlungsgebiet* (Theresienstadt: A Documentary Film from the Jewish Settlement Area) and informs our appreciation of this work.[34] Commissioned by *SS Sturmbannführer* Hans Günther and funded by the *Zentralstelle zur Regelung der Judenfrage* (Central Jewish Office) in Prague, the film relied for its production exclusively on confiscated Jewish assets. The renowned film producer and cabaret artist Kurt Gerron, interned in Theresienstadt, was a significant creative force in the early stages of the film, working under the strict supervision of the SS and the camp's commander, Karl Rahm.[35] A group of sequentially related, highly animated sketches produced by Joseph Spier during the film's shooting were intended as a visual storyboard to assist in its making. Spier may have looked through the camera's view finder before setting about the drawings, effecting a marriage of the two mediums—film and still images.[36] And unlike the frozen frames of Spier's earlier *Bilder Aus Theresienstadt*, these moved at a pace. The film itself opens with the ghetto choir led by Karel Fischer, singing Mendlessohn's *Elijah*, and is followed by footage of Martin Roman's jazz ensemble, the 'Ghetto Swingers', playing in the town's main square and public terraces; the *Kaffeehaus*, a meeting of the Council of Elders, views of the wood and metal workshops, construction and agricultural machines, a library and central laundry, precede the final tableaux, the staging of the children's opera *Brundibar* directed by Hans Krása. We can but surmise the maker's motives: to convey the impression that here was a well-ordered community, existing under the protection of the Führer

himself and safeguarded by the ghetto's walls and enclosures against the war raging beyond. But opportunities to screen the film to larger audiences in the final weeks of the war, and thus influence public opinion, as well as government and relief agencies beyond the Protektorat, in the Nazi's favour, proved of little consequence. The crew and many in the cast were deported to their deaths long before the film's completion in March 1945.[37]

Films' power to create images on an epic scale and on the big screen challenged the artists in Terezín and Fritta in particular, whose large-scale and densely executed works, such as *Deluge*, 1943–44 and *Ghetto Cinema*, 1943 (Jewish Museum, Prague) are the culmination of his experience in the ghetto. An explosive mixture of high parody and comic gesture characterises these works. In *Deluge*, the astounding contrast between the crowd of bedraggled, skeletal figures (film extras) and the hallucinatory vision of a svelte, fair-skinned doll, a poor relative of the silver-screen idols, bestows a dream-like intensity and unreality on the work. Glowing against a night sky, this cyclopean beauty raises an articulated arm in defiant celebration (a makeshift curtain and film props surround her). Beyond the elevated stage, the now familiar presence of stone walls and barbed-wire fences signal an encroaching reality.

48 **Bedřich Fritta**
Deluge
Terezín, 1943–44
black chalk, pen and ink
wash on abraded paper
420 x 583mm
Thomas Fritta Haas
Cat. 66

48

5   Ghetto

The timeless black-and-white photographs of Lithuania, Galicia and Carpathian Ruthenia, taken by Roman Vishniac in the winter of 1938, bring home the reality of the *shtetl*,[1] unsuspecting in its isolation of the profound changes which the Second World War, only a few months away, would bring. Within days of Germany's invasion of Poland on 1 September 1939, approximately three million Jews were forcibly resettled in major towns and sealed ghettos.[2] A multitude of figures encumbered with possessions edge away from the viewer or neutral bystander in Szymon Szerman's *Transfer to the Ghetto* (Beit Lohamei Haghetaot) painted in Lodz in the winter of 1939–40. The camouflage of flat, built-up areas of colour set against the snow-covered streets breaks up the containing edges of pavements, street signs, push-carts and baggage, as if to heighten the complexities of seeing in the ghetto. The overcrowding, run down housing, and lack of adequate sanitation, heating, food and medicine created living conditions unseen in Europe since the Middle Ages. In Warsaw, Lodz and Cracow, as well as Lvov, strict curfews were imposed. Those within these cities were stripped of their rights and, in a throwback to the medieval ghetto (still lodged in the European psyche), all Jews over the age of ten were obliged to wear a yellow star as an identifying symbol on the front and back of their garments. The confinement of a large section of the population in sealed ghettos signalled a transition from the Nazi policy of large-scale emigration to the systematic destruction of centuries old Jewish communities in the Final Solution.[3]

What fate awaited the occupants of the ghettos? Diaries, chronicles and artists' drawings capture the hopes and fears of their inhabitants. Yosef Zelckowicz noted in his diary: 'When a Jew rises in the morning he runs. Runs burdened with pots, bags, tickets. His eyes dart in all directions: "Where should I stand…?".'[4] Ravaged by the collapse of its markets, factories and artisan shops, the confiscation of Jewish assets and the forced closure of businesses, the ghetto economy struggled to rebuild itself from the bottom up. 'How can an entire community feed itself when it has no grip on life? For there is no trade which is not limited and circumscribed for us', wrote Chaim Kaplan in the Warsaw ghetto. This acute uncertainty is recorded in a group of pen and ink studies by Jacob Lifchitz (1903–44) produced in the weeks leading up to the liquidation of the Kovno ghetto in June 1944.[5] A winding, seemingly inexhaustible line describes the ebbing movements of the crowd, a sea of faces. Driven to starvation, ragged and barefoot, the ghetto's inhabitants showed a weary determination to preserve the institutions, the schools, soup kitchens, orphanages and libraries vital to survival and Jewish continuity: 'There was a party in the [Vilna] ghetto today, the 100,000 book was borrowed.'[6]

Seeing the Ghetto

When at the invitation of Bundist and Zionist leaders, Jan Karski, a courier of the Polish Government in exile,[7] paid a secret visit to the Warsaw ghetto, he was unprepared for the scenes he was to witness. Entering from the 'Aryan' side through one of the safe houses erected on the ghetto's boundary Karski reported seeing two children playing among the corpses,

…naked bodies on the street. Babies with crazed eyes, looking…It wasn't humanity. It was some hell…stench everywhere, suffocating. Dirty streets, nervousness, tension. Bedlam. This was Platz Muranowski. In a corner of it some children were playing something with some rags—throwing the rags to one another.

The past encroached on the present with a determined clarity, as Karski struggled to find adequate expression for the tumult of recollections—no words or figure of speech could adequately contain the burden of these memories:

I reported what I saw. It was not a world. It was not a part of humanity…nobody wrote about this kind of reality. I never saw any theatre, I never saw any movie…this was not the world. I was told these were human beings. They did not look like human beings. Then we left. [8]

49 **Jankel Adler**
*What a World: The
Destruction of Lodz*
1923–24
oil on board
635 x 425mm
The Israel Museum,
Jerusalem
Cat. 74

Simha Rottem, a survivor of the Warsaw Ghetto uprising (and one of the founders of the Lohamei Haghetaot Kibbutz), admitted to a comparable linguistic obstacle: *I don't think the human tongue can describe the horror.* Rottem recalled how he and a friend stole their way into the 'Aryan Quarter' through a tunnel under Bonifraterska Street, emerging

…in broad daylight. Imagine us on that sunny May 1, stunned to find ourselves among normal people. We'd come from another planet…exhausted, skinny, in rags…The ghetto was an isolated island amid normal life.[9]

The remarks of both Karski and Rottem, underscore the difficulty of closing the perceptual gap that existed between that which could and could not be seen, between the familiar and the unimaginable. The artists interned in camps and ghettos made a comparable perceptual leap, in defiance of their captors.

Lodz

The devastation inflicted on Lodz by an invading German army in the First World War is the subject of Jankel Adler's *Destruction of the Lodz Ghetto*, 1923–44. It foreshadows the events in the Second World War when the ghetto's 233,000 Jewish residents were the targets of repeated aggression and forced internment. Adler raises a flushed left hand as if to shield his doleful expression, only partly concealing his striking Semitic features as he points to the Hebrew word אֵין or *ein* for 'none', part of a longer inscription that reads

from (right to left), 'No God in Lodz'. Adler's eyes are mere slits and his arms are crossed in resignation at the devastation of a community (in a gesture oddly reminiscent of Käthe Kollwitz's *Lamentation*). Even as Adler turns his back on the town, he is nonetheless attuned to its cries and, anticipating Kollwitz, a lovingly fashioned ear asserts his witness. In a clear reference to the imploring Hebrew prayer, *Shema Israel*, 'Hear, Oh Israel, Hear our cry!', the Hebrew letter ש (*shin*) for *Shema*, is placed discreetly on a thin white rectangle (centre), a *mezuzah*, firmly affixed to the ghetto's boarded-up gates.[10]

In accordance with the Nazi decree of 28 November 1939, enforced throughout the General Government (territories administered by the Nazis in Central and Southern Poland), a Council of Jewish Elders or *Judenrat* was appointed to administer the Lodz ghetto. Compliance and collaboration were basic prerequisites of survival. Under its autocratic leader, *Judenälteste* Mordechai Chaim Rumkowski, the Council controlled the supply of all essentials, acceding to German demands in the hope that they would thereby save some of the ghetto's inhabitants.[11] Like Rumkowski, Ephraim Barasz, the leader of the Bialystok ghetto, believed that economic viability would secure the ghetto's survival: *We have transformed all our inhabitants into useful elements. Our security is in direct proportion to our labour productivity.*[12] Lodz became a vast factory turning out shoes, brushes, tailored garments, electrical goods and metalwork.[13] Josef Kowner's (1895–1967) presentation sheet *Untitled*, 1943, is emblazoned with bold black-and-white vignettes depicting tradesmen, tailors, a carpenter, metalworker, shoemaker and their tools: shears, a wood-plane, a jigsaw, callipers, a metal file and a cobbler's hammer; two blank tablets await inscription.[14]

In reality, labour was exploitative, wages miserable and arbitrarily set. Meagre bread rations and a watery soup hardly satisfied the workers' minimum nutritional needs. Absenteeism was met by harsh punishment and imprisonment. Death from hunger or disease significantly diminished the population of the ghetto even before the Final Solution.[15] Israel Lejzerowicz's (1905–44) *Sewage Carts, Lodz*, c.1941, depicts the punishing early morning ritual of the disposal of effluents from the ghetto's sewage system in the freezing winter of 1941–42. Three figures harnessed to the front of the cart pull as another pushes at the rear. The drawing's syntax of interrupted marks of pure colour animates the human forms and masks the surrounding poverty. In *Sewage*

50 **Josef Kowner**
Untitled sheet with decorated borders showing ghetto tradesmen: a cobbler, tailors, metal-worker and carpenter
Lodz Ghetto, 1943
pen and ink
270 x 370mm
Żydowski Instytut Historyczny w Polsce, Poland
Cat. 82

51 **Israel Lejzerowicz**
Sewage Carts
Lodz Ghetto, 1941–42
soft pastel
430 x 672mm
Yad Vashem Art
Museum, Jerusalem
Gift of Nachman
Zonabend, Sweden
Cat. 85

52 **Anon**
*Transport of the Ghetto
Effluent to the Collection
Pits*
Lodz Ghetto, c.1941
photograph
Jüdisches Musem,
Frankfurt-am-Main

53 **Esther Lurie**
Woman Prisoner,
back view
Leibitsch, 1944
pencil, pen and ink
103 x 75mm
Art collection
Beit Lohamei
Haghetaot, Israel
Ghetto Fighters'
House Museum
Cat. 79

and ink studies by Jan Burka, *Water Wagon* and *Agricultural Machine*, c.1944,[17] and the fine watercolour illustrations by Jan Munk (1898–1944)*Disinfection!* and *Bauhof* (Yad Vashem Art Museum) chronicle the transport and movement of people and supplies.

The Ghetto Feminine

The beautiful hats have disappeared. In wartime [women] put on scarves.[18]

The ghetto's population was always careful not to arouse suspicion, to be too conspicuous or to attract the attention of the ghetto's policemen and armed guards. But subtle outward changes in the appearance of women, alluded to in the line above, from Emmanuel Ringelblum's diaries, also reflect changing roles and self-perceptions. The women significantly outnumbered the men[19] and were called upon to carry out all kinds of physical work as well as feeding and caring for both the young and the old. Swathed in a large padded coat, her feet clad in wooden clogs, Esther Lurie's (1913–98) *Women Prisoner*, 1944, chronicles this change in role.[20] Tied about her waist with a length of twine are a bag and a large, twin-handled pot. Yosef Zelckowicz reminds us of the importance of this implement:

Not the bridge, nor the barbed wire, nor the gate is the symbol of the ghetto…The symbol of the ghetto is the pot… Everyone, young and old, has one. From the simplest hauler of trash to the highest, most important manager.[21]

Lurie traces the delicate outline of the thread-like figure with a pencil on the back of a used paper wrapper that once contained a cotton spool. The salient pen and ink outlines of *Women Prisoner* and *Women Prisoner, Back view*, 1944 reveal the patched-up outer layers of her clothing, a hooded garment, bandaged legs and feet bound in rags. Every scrap of cloth was salvaged and used to some end. 'Everything is useful: the wire to tie up our shoes, the rags to wrap around our feet, waste paper to (illegally) pad out our jackets against the cold.'[22] These intricately observed studies of the ghetto women confer on them a sense of the particular. Conscious as the men were of their historically appointed role as witnesses, the ghetto women were equally determined to preserve the evidence of their increasingly circumscribed existence. Works were concealed under floorboards or in cellars or smuggled to safety beyond the walls of the ghetto to the 'Aryan Quarter'. The trembling outline

Collection in Ghetto Lodz (Żydowski Instytut Historyczny w Polsce), 1943, a small, brilliantly painted and unattributed oil on panel, the proud, if frozen poses, the naturalistic setting, fine detail and intense illumination reveal the work's photographic source. The inscription in German, *Litzmannstadt Ghetto* (the name given to it by the Nazis) reveals the work's origins, painted to commission in return for meagre payment, extra rations or a favour of some kind. The same subject—so important to the inhabitants of the ghetto—is also depicted in a large, undated composition by Josef Kowner, *Carrying Faeces* (Żydowski Instytut Historyczny w Polsce), painted in umber tones on coarse flax. Hirsch Szilys' (1909–85) *Ghetto Transport*, 1942 (Yad Vashem, Art Museum)[16] combines graphite, wax and colour crayons to achieve an unusual density of surface which, in its dark allure, evokes dusk. Hand-drawn transports occur repeatedly in the drawings, reflecting the efficient system of collections run by the Lodz ghetto's *self-administration* (in marked contrast with that in the Warsaw ghetto). A similar fascination for ambulatory machines, carts and ploughs is observed in the works produced in Terezín. The exceptionally detailed pen of Halina Olomucki's (b.1921) *Girl with Arms Raised* produced on scraps of wrapping paper and brown adhesive tape, vividly recreates the atmosphere of fear, round-ups and arrests, selections, mass deportations and random executions that preyed on the ghetto's inhabitants.[23]

The Eternal Jew

The recurring themes of homelessness and wandering, pivotal to Jewish memory, are highlighted in Roman Kramstyck's (1885–1942) delicately hewn red-chalk drawing, *Jewish Family in the Warsaw Ghetto*, c.1942. Kramstyck is remembered principally for his urbane portraits of Poland's leading *culturati*, the pianist Arthur Rubinstein (Żydowski Instytut Historyczny w Polsce) and the poet Jan Lechoń (National Gallery, Warsaw). A baptised Jew interned in the Warsaw ghetto in the summer 1942, he reaffirms in his work the archetypal image of the eastern, unassimilated Jew. At the centre of *Jewish Family*, a father holds a sleeping baby in arms (swaddled in bandages); another sits on his shoulders, its legs astride, as two older children with empty pots and spoons stand by, hungry-looking and forlorn. An expression of weariness is etched into their faces and slightly stooped postures. Recalling Jean-Pierre Norblin de la Gourdine's (1745–1830) advice to his students in the Czartoryski court, to take their sketchbooks outdoors and draw the streets and market places,[24] Kramstyck's observations are based on life inside the ghetto. Like Maurycy Trębacz (1861–1941), resettled to the Lodz Ghetto in 1940, whose portraits of learned rabbis and *yeshiva* students absorbed in their readings of *Torah-Talmud* were intended primarily for the sitting-rooms and homes of Polish, middle-class collectors,[25] Kramstyck's *Jewish Family* asserts rather than questions the narrow stereotype of the Eastern Jew. The Nazis, too, understood the power of these images and exploited them to effect in racist propaganda, films and posters as well as in the antisemitic press. The ghetto is the setting for the film *The Eternal Jew*, directed by Fritz Heppler and produced by the Deutsche Filmgesellschaft. With the unknowing collaboration of its subjects, cropping and superimposing their images alongside play-acted film sequences of doubtful authenticity and unashamedly bogus statistics, the film lambasted Jewish communal life, inciting xenophobic fears and conveying the notion that Jews, like rats and vermin, reproduced in great numbers in the ghetto's streets. The myth of the corrupt Jew as a class of subhuman or *Untermenschen*

was ingrained in the German psyche by this kind of grotesque propaganda which advanced the generalised and sinister notion of contaminated Jewish 'blood' as against a racially pure Aryan nation.

By contrast, the raw expressiveness of Joseph Kowner's *Self-portrait*, 1941 (Yad Vashem Art Museum), disavows the tired stereotype and attests instead to the artist's modernity. Disenfranchised, Kowner was evacuated from Lodz in the winter of 1943–44 and his expression reflects the uncertainties of a life on the edge of society. The broad areas of umber washed across the artist's duff overcoat and soft cap lend weight and solidity to the forms while gem-like accents of iridescent colour—yellow ochres, viridian, ultramarine and alizarin—create vibrancy and luminosity.

54 **Roman Kramstyck**
Jewish Family in the Ghetto
Warsaw, c.1942
red sanguine chalk
536 x 378mm
Żydowski Instytut Historyczny w Polsce, Poland
Cat. 83

In Hiding

The observation of everyday objects and events express a reassuring ordinariness in the life of the ghetto. Arnold Daghani's (1909–85) works redeem this dailiness, the seemingly unremarkable, yet crucial incident. The works produced at Mikhailowka labour camp, east of the Bug River in western Ukraine,[26] depict the crowded dormitory building, the ritual observance of the Sabbath, the guards and fellow inmates, themes he would return to repeatedly after the war. The inscription at the base of a work made several years after the event it records, *Evensong*, 1954, reads, *Based on Evensong…first days 1942 in the extermination camp*, explaining the work's origins.[27] Characteristically, such images in Daghani work draw on a wide variety of visual, textual and documentary sources, early sketches and news clippings, diary entries and the artist's recollections. The passage of time seems to have sharpened rather than diminished the artist's powers of recall, distilling significance from the stream of images. In *Evensong*, figures are paired or arranged in small islets, ringed by a clearly defined *cloisonné* and placed against a brilliant cobalt blue ground which heightens their isolation; while along the lower half, the procession of figures, men and women in communal prayer, turn their backs on the viewer and seek each other's support. A gently inclined ladder links the two halves of the composition, an effective device found in countless depositions and in Chagall's *Yellow Crucifixion*, albeit one which here is rooted in the observation of the tiered sleeping bunks.[28] The Daghanis' perilous escape from Mikhailowka in July 1943, their concealment in the Bershad ghetto and return to Bucharest in March 1944, elicited from the artist a powerful chronicle of events, combining words and images. A first edition was published in Romania in 1946 as *The Grave is in the Cherry Orchard*. The artist recalls the atmosphere of the old stable block at Mikhailowka camp:

The bustle in the stable resembles some main street in a forlorn market-town, the shake-downs and horse-cribs tuned into infant beds…Not too far away, a young man is surrounded by men and women: he has potatoes. Another group is swaying too and fro in the rhythm of their prayer. The voices from time to time defeated by the neighing horses beyond the latticed partition…[29]

The diaries and drawings trace the couple's wanderings across western Ukraine into Poland and Romania. Daghani returned to these notes and drawings many years later, revising and reworking the material, much of which is collected in two remarkable compendium albums produced over a thirty year period: *1942–1943 And Thereafter, What a Nice World*, 1970/77 and *The Building in which we had a Narrow Escape*, 1977/78 (Arnold Daghani Collection, Centre for German-Jewish Studies, University of Sussex). The artist's clandestine world, defined by the opposing realities of indoors and outdoors, transparency and concealment, fear and elation, finds an exact correlative in the visual and textual strategies employed in the albums. These combine original pre-war material with later reworkings, collage elements, texts and personal inscriptions in challenging juxtapositions, reflecting both the artist's complex view of history and his stance as witness.[30] The albums convey the sense of a culture in transition, echoing the artist's wanderings, migrations, his close escapes and border crossings amid shifting boundaries reflecting the changing political realities of the day.

In *1942–1943 And Thereafter*, a poignant watercolour study inscribed *Nanino at the window (in Czernowitz) awaiting full of apprehension my coming home, April 1942* depicts Nonino Daghani (the artist's wife) peering beyond the half-open window, awaiting his return. There is something deeply affecting about this work, which seems to want to define the threshold between inside and out, safety and peril, her expectation at his arrival and apprehension. A closely related sheet, this time executed in the Bershad ghetto, in the district of Transnistria, between the Dnista and Bug rivers, shows a view of the encroaching roof line of a neighbouring house; its blackened windows peer at us like a pair of huge eyes. The inscription reads:

On account of the gendarmes, I was obliged to do my outdoor works clandestinely. 'Caught in the act' would have entailed my facing the court martial: 'Any person prohibited from taking photographs' —a sign with that wording was frequently fixed within the precincts of the ghetto, as if the deportees could boast of a camera.[31]

This note confirms Daghani's awareness of the risks that *seeing* posed. His determination to chronicle his escape from the camp, his clandestine existence in the ghetto and journey to safety became a powerful instrument in the artist's hand and an incentive to continue living, as one chronicler in the Warsaw Ghetto affirmed: 'I dare not hope that I shall live through this period, but I must work as though my words *will* come through. I shall act and write as though there were hope for me.'[32]

55 **Arnold Daghani**
Evensong
1954
gouache
274 x 262mm
Arnold Daghani Archive
Centre for German-Jewish
Studies, University of Sussex
Cat. 86

56 **Arnold Daghani**
The Building in which we had a
Narrow Escape
1977/78
album containing 81 sheets
mixed media
320 x 490mm (open)
Arnold Daghani Archive
Centre for German-Jewish
Studies, University of Sussex
Cat. 137

Deportation & Destruction

I have to cut off the limbs in order to save the body! [33]

This is how Chaim Rumkowski announced to an assembled crowd the deportation of 20,000 inhabitants of Lodz—children, the infirm and elderly—dispelling at once any hope of their supposed transportation to organised labour camps and instilling new fears in the population. Those who had survived the siege-like existence now faced deportation. The pattern of roundups and mass arrests quickened so that by March 1943 the liquidation of the Cracow ghetto was complete, followed in ensuing months by the destruction of the Warsaw, Lvov, Byalistok and Vilna ghettos. [34] At the Treblinka death camp, Richard Glazar was to observe the arrival of one of the trains: *'In June, the remnant of the Warsaw ghetto arrived; they were a terrible sight, more dead than alive'.* [35] Death by gas or execution awaited the ghetto's inhabitants at Belzec, Chelmno, Majdanek, Sobibor or Treblinka.

On 2 November 1942, in the Bialystok region of north-east Poland, the Nazis rounded up 100,000 Jews and held them in special camps awaiting transportation to Treblinka. A survivor of the Bialystok ghetto, Isaac Celnikier, recalled the mass arrests, deportations and massacres of innocent people. He was deported to a succession of German camps in Stutthof, Birkenau, Buna (Auschwitz III), Sachsenhausen and Flossenbürg, and was later to compile a remarkable visual narrative of his experience. One of Celnikier's earliest surviving works, *Man with a Yellow Star—And you say that God is dead!*, was painted in Prague in 1946. The implication here is of betrayal and abandonment. The dialogic relationship of mankind with an all powerful, compassionate deity is severely undermined in a world without hope. The figure seated in the foreground, his frame slouched, arms bared and head inclined, is a complex symbol, echoing both a deposition and a *Pietá*. The artist explains its origin as:

a remembrance of the man who, with thirteen other people, with my family and myself, shared a room in the ghetto. He became mad and violent, he yelled, invoked and cursed God. I started looking after him and noted his delirium. For me he symbolised the desperate cries of all the people in the ghetto. [36]

Bold contours entrap the flesh-like forms, lit as from within. A second bared figure, set back in space and recognisably a woman, hangs lifelessly. The imposing solidity and simplification of forms, their rounded cadences, the division of the surface (creating the sense of a picture within a picture), recall Georges Rouault's (1871–1958) reverential suite of etchings, *War* 1927, based on his memories of the First World War. [37] The scraping and physical burnishing of Rouault's surfaces are almost literally transcribed in *Man with a Yellow Star* in terms of the material build-up of paint applied with thickly loaded brushes and a palette knife onto the canvas. Celnikier's more recent command of a calligraphically rich surface has its origins in these early works. His own memorial to the Shoah, contained in the suite of etchings entitled *La Mémoire Gravée*, confirms his place among France's foremost living etchers. But whereas Rouault's *War* suite closes with the redemptive image of *Arise, you Dead!*, a hopeful statement of the transforming power of Christ's suffering, such a possibility is absent from Celnikier's vision of total extinction.

Auschwitz

Belying the Nazi rhetoric *Arbeit macht Frei* (Work makes Free), the underlying rationale for 'organised labour' was the exploitation of the prison population at the lowest cost to the Reich and its extermination. A total of ten million slave labourers were mobilised in defence of an ailing Nazi war economy, claiming all but 1.5 million lives. The commitment of huge material and human resources in the pursuit of a policy of total annihilation of Europe's Jews during all out war was manifestly irrational and ultimately hastened the end of Nazism. The *Konzentrationslager*—concentration camps, the system of sub-camps, munitions factories, chemical plants, quarries and a myriad of small enterprises—which was initially intended to bolster the war effort, proved its undoing. Much of this work was unproductive, punitive, serving exclusively the annihilation of the workforce.[1] Efforts by prisoners to sabotage production by using damaged components, or poor building foundations, brought conveyor-belt production to a near standstill and undermined the entire edifice of work. The complicity of the German industrial conglomerate with Nazi aims is demonstrated by the vast installation set up in the outlying camps of Dwory and Monowitz, near

Auschwitz, at the Buna-Werk factory.[2] There, the I G Farben Industries planned to manufacture a synthetic rubber (called *Buna*) and petrol products for Germany's planned post-war expansion. Auschwitz provided the pool of cheap labour which these industries required.[3] Built at a cost of 900 million German marks and more than 25,000 lives, it produced only a small amount of synthetic gasoline and virtually no rubber before it was knocked out of operation by a US air raid in the summer of 1944.

You have come to a German concentration camp, not a sanatorium and there is only one way out—through the chimney.[4]

For the entire prison population at Auschwitz, the day began at about 4.30am with cries of *Aufstehen, Zählappell. Alle aufstehen zum Zählappell!* (Get-up, roll-call!). The ritual of roll-call lasted at least two or three hours, irrespective of weather conditions. Those imposed by the punitive camp commandant, Rudolf Hoess, could drag on for up to sixteen hours. In *Roll-call*, 1942, Wincenty Gawron (b.1908), a member of the Polish underground arrested in January 1941, drew from memory the regimented rows of prisoners, the repeated counting and the endless waiting, as a thick-set SS officer (left), well shielded from the storm by his heavy overcoat and leather jackboots, relentlessly punishes the fallen victims. The detailed evidence contained in Gawron's finely honed study accords with the verbal description of a fellow witness: 'From dawn, heavy rain or sleet had been driving down and a strong northeast wind was blowing. From noon onward, frozen men began to be carried or brought in on barrows...half conscious, crawling, dying, gasping their last breath.'[5] Gawron completed the drawing some time after his escape from the Harmęże sub-camp in May 1942 and together with a diary and portraits of camp inmates, carried it to safety in a hollowed-out board.[6]

The 'friendly favour' suggested in the title of Mieczysław Kościelniak's (1912–93) *Koleżeńska przysluga* alludes to the return of the injured and the dead,

57 Wincenty Gawron
Roll-call
1942
pencil
235 x 290mm
Państwowe Muzeum,
Oświęcim

58 **Karol Konieczny**
Memorial Book
Buchenwald, 1943–44
pencil, pen and ink,
watercolour, leather
binding
235 x 340mm (open)
Państwowe Muzeum,
Oświęcim

59 **Mieczysław Kościelniak**
A Friendly Favour
Oświęcim, c.1944
black chalk
210 x 295mm
Państwowe Muzeum,
Oświęcim
Cat. 87

60 **Mieczysław Kościelniak**
Prisoners of Oświęcim
Oświęcim, 1944
pen and ink
300 x 210mm
Państwowe Muzeum,
Oświęcim
Cat. 88

hauled or carried back to camp at the end of the day's work to be propped up and counted at the next morning's roll-call. The breathtaking fluency of this sketch, the pained expressions on the prisoners' faces, the limp body of the comrade they carry in arms, leave little doubt as to his near-death state. In *Prisoners of Oświęcim*, a pen and ink line unravels at speed to fashion the shapes of two uniformed prisoners stopping to speak across a barbed wire fence that both separates them and ultimately becomes one with them. The drawing sheds light on the relationships of trust and mutual dependence struck up along the route to the camp latrines, on the *Appellplatz* and in other open spaces, relationships that proved vital to survival, as testimonies confirm.[7]

Subjected to long periods of hard labour in the gravel pits, in the paving of roads and in the infamous *Abbruch 2* (demolition section), Kościelniak succumbed to exhaustion and severe illness. He was nursed back to health by the medical corps and later was appointed as the museum's caretaker. It was here that he worked on the sketchbooks which contain a startling repertory of subjects. The repeated studies of hands in one of them may be unremarkable—their mutability has always been a source of fascination for artists—but in this instance, hands and the occasional portrait study of a fellow prisoner, the skylight window in the museum's interior, a painter's easel and palette, have a more compelling purpose: they affirm the primacy of life and meaningful patterns of existence long extinguished elsewhere in the concentration camp universe.

My commitment to drawing came out of a deep instinct of self-preservation…by taking on the role of an 'observer' I could at least for a few moments detach myself from what was going on at Auschwitz and was therefore better able to hold together the threads of sanity.[8]

One of the earliest extant drawings of Auschwitz, Włodzimierz Siwierski's (1905–84) *Soup*, 1940,[9] depicts a row of prisoners, forlorn, their heads shaven, sitting to consume the gruel on which survival depends. A feint line defines their tentative existence. The modest size and weekend fabric, the acidic condition of the paper support, are somehow inseparable from the drawing's manifest subject—a single breath might dissolve all. Siwierski's *Sculpture*, 1941, reveals a prisoner absorbed in the creative process, intent on the small clay effigy taking shape in his hands. In a world that daily conspires to eradicate all civilised values, even the value of life, the transforming power of art

61 **Włodzimierz Siwierski**
Sculptor
Oświęcim, 1941
pencil
Państwowe Muzeum,
Oświęcim

62 **Włodzimierz Siwierski**
Soup
Oświęcim, 1940
pencil
100 x 162mm
Państwowe Muzeum,
Oświęcim
Cat. 89

63 **Franciszek Jaźwiecki**
Portrait of Stefan Antoniak
Buchenwald, 1944
pencil
200 x 140mm
Państwowe Muzeum,
Oświęcim
Cat. 93

rekindles a ray of hope—at least the object (with its resistant materiality) will outlive its maker.[10] If Siwierski intended to draw attention to the need for physical as well as spiritual nourishment, both works seem ultimately weighed down by a sadness associated inevitably with transience and loss. In a letter from Auschwitz, after a long illness, the artist Xawery Dunikowski (1875–1964) reflects on the restorative powers of art: 'I feel good, for the first time in four years, I have once again begun to draw. Life acquires new meaning and purpose.' In Dunikowski's *Self-portrait*, 1943–44, the fine iridescence of tone achieved with diagonal, cross-hatching lines instils a human breath. Sleepless but exhausted and wasting, he asserts with his intent gaze the desire to remain among the living.

Self-portrait P75057 is one of more than 113 portrait drawings of fellow inmates produced by Franciszek Jaźwiecki (1900–46) in 1942 to 1945, during internment at Auschwitz, Gross-Rosen, Sachsenhausen and Buchenwald. These are faces rescued from the abyss. From Buchenwald, the sixteen-year-old Stefan Antoniak, his contoured features strongly individuated, looks intently at the viewer. The prisoner Ros Pedra wears a small red triangle embroidered with the letter F, the identifying mark at Buchenwald of a French Communist. These highly focussed, 'passport size' portraits restore the prisoners' names, 'that cardinal sign of human individuality'[11] and with them their former identities. Both the size and tonal range of the sketches recall the photographs of registered inmates taken after the selection process (which Jazwiecki may have seen), a practice that was later replaced by a tattoo marked on a prisoner's forearm. At Auschwitz, life expectancy

rarely exceeded ninety days. Was Jaźwiecki creating a counter-register of the living, in protest at the destruction of so many lives?

A key to our understanding of Józef Szajna's (b.1922) *Our biographies*, 1944-45, is suggested by the rows of faceless prisoners in striped uniforms (a comment on the camp's unremitting drive toward systematisation and anonymity). Spare in execution, they recall police mug-shots. On closer scrutiny, their heads are in fact thumbprint impressions, a mark of a person's uniqueness stamped indelibly on paper.[12] Countering Nazi efforts to falsify the historical record, Jaźwiecki and Szajna chose truth as their weapon.[13]

In Halina Olomucki's works, an almost seamless transition is evident between those produced in the Warsaw ghetto and Auschwitz-Birkenau and those completed after her emigration to Israel in 1972. How did the artist cling so tenaciously to her memories which have, as a result of this transcription, become so tangibly, so resolutely her own? Olomucki recalls her struggle to remain alive in order to convey to others the enormity of the crimes she had witnessed: 'While I was at Auschwitz-Birkenau someone told me, "If you live to leave this hell, make your drawings and tell the world about us. We want to be among the living, at least on paper" and this need to document became an extraordinary force that carried me to survival. It became the foundation of my will power'.[14] In *Women in Birkenau*, the inscription at the base of the sheet, *Halina 1945 Birkenau H O*, is a courageous assertion of authorship. A group of heads, floating effigies, surround Halina's frail figure (dressed in regulation camp uniform). Line is made with the short butt of a pencil (a rare commodity in conditions of extremity), rubbed energetically into the frayed sheet of greaseproof paper, to achieve the suggestion of a tonal veil and transparencies. These qualities transcend the prosaic and rudimentary nature of 'record keeping' and evoke other levels of artistry, indeed of consciousness, igniting the imagination's work. The precarious state of the paper support and the restrained character of the marks confirm its authenticity as a work produced at Birkenau.[15] And like the three women in Rilik-Andrieux's drawing of Gurs, intent on their mundane, life-affirming tasks, so desperately shaped by necessity, Olomucki's drawings reveal the simple virtues of caring and bonding that typified the experience for many women in camps and ghettos.[16] Such virtues are found in the drawings produced at Ravensbrück women's camp, some eighty-five kilometres north-west of Berlin, in Macklenburg.[17] These

63

64 Józef Szajna
Our Biographies
Buchenwald, 1944–45
pencil, tusche, scissors and fingerprints
340 x 298mm
Państwowe Muzeum, Oświęcim

65 Halina Olomucki
Women in Birkenau
1945
pencil on tracing paper
320 x 215mm
Art collection
Beit Lohamei Haghetaot,
Ghetto Fighters' House,
Israel
Cat. 91

66 Maurycy Bromberg
Five Jews Harnessed to a Roller
c.1945–48
wax crayon and solvent spirit
279 x 381mm
Żydowski Instytut Historyczny w Polsce
Cat. 99

chronicle the cooking, washing and repair of clothing, the removal of lice—movingly observed in Maria Hiszpańska-Neumann's (1917–78) *In the Barracks after Work*, 1945—as well as the almost constant preoccupation with personal hygiene, in spite of the scarcity of clean water, toilet paper or sanitary towels.[18] The camp at Budy, a women's outpost of Auschwitz, lay almost permanently under mud. There was no sewage system, prisoners suffered severe water shortages and disease was rampant.

Arrested for her underground activities against the Nazis, Hiszpańska-Neumann purportedly produced a large number of works at Ravensbrück (only a few of which have survived). The marvellous animation of the human figures portrayed *In the Barracks after Work*, 1945, and fluidity of line show her entirely at ease in the close intimacy of the women's living quarters. Though lacking Neumann's refinement, the works of France Audoul (1894–1977) and Violette Rougier-Lecoq describe the severity of conditions, and in a series of intimate etchings of fellow prisoners by Monique Frelaut, the spare but powerful line expresses great warmth of feeling. Rougier-Lecoq, a member of the Resistance, was imprisoned at Angoulême in 1940 and later at Ravensbrück, experiences she recorded in drawings executed from memory after the war.[19] They share with testimonies a desire to speak across the fences and fortifications to the outside world: 'We were terribly afraid that nobody in the world would notice a thing: us, the struggle, the dead…that this wall was so huge that nothing, no message about us would ever make it out.'[20]

Born in the Piotrkowie-Trybunalski district of Lodz in 1920, Maurycy Bromberg completed his training at the Akademia Sztuk Pięknych (Academy of Fine Arts, Cracow) under Professor Kazimierz Sichulski in 1939, just months before his arrest and interment in forced labour camps at Hortensia-Piotrków and Hassag-Palcery. Bromberg's *Five Jews Harnessed to a Roller, Oświęcim*, 1945–48, is one of the most discussed of all examples of 'camp art'.[21] The drawing refers to the back-breaking, mostly unproductive work carried out by the labour camp population, and specifically to the notorious steel roller used in roads building projects in the vicinity of Auschwitz, pulled by up to sixty men. The five labouring prisoners, dressed in regulation uniforms, present a generic picture, a kind of shorthand for Auschwitz, indeed for all such camps and for all enslavement. Affirming that works produced in the camps relied on visual precedent, Ziva Amishai Maisels has usefully compared

Bromberg's *Five Jews* to the work of the Russian realist painter, Ilya Effimovich Repin (1844–1930), specifically his *Volga Boatmen*, c.1872.[22] Bromberg would have known this work in reproduction (widely disseminated in its time and until recently, a top seller in the prints section of Woolworth stores in Britain), and not withstanding the obvious differences of scale, medium and portent, no less than in the cultural backgrounds of the artists, Maisels' comparison remains visually and iconographically compelling. Whether he owned a reproduction, or recalled the image while working, Bromberg manages successfully to transmute his source, while investing it with the understanding and empathy derived from his first-hand experience of the labour camps. This is apparent in the assurance and broad application of marks made with greasy or waxen crayons, thinned in solvent spirits. The prisoners' stripes merge indistinguishably and with remarkable purpose into a single, all-consuming flame, as the five gleaming heads bow in effort. The artist's use of high rhetoric to make his point is equally striking, replacing Repin's self-conscious histrionics with his own, but the assumption normally made, that Bromberg produced this work in internment, now looks more tenuous. We have no record of his imprisonment in Auschwitz and a shorthand reference to *Oświęcim* in the work's title appears to be an expedient. Its inclusion in an exhibition of recent Jewish art held in Lodz, at the Centralne Żydowskie Towarzystwo Kultury i Sztuki in January 1948,[23] suggests a completion date sometime between the end of 1945 and December 1947.[24] His own use of this widely appropriated subject has less in common perhaps with the frieze-like, narrative images of Odd Nansen at Sachsenhausen or Henri Pieck at Buchenwald, put forward by Maisels, than with the post-war renderings by Marian Kołodziej and Mieczysław Koscielniak (Państwowe Muzeum w Oświęcim Brzezinka). The sentimental, saccharine nature of the signed and dated works produced by Bromberg in the Lodz ghetto are stylistically and thematically at odds with the resolute and vigorous quality of *Five Jews*. The robust and unrestored condition of both paper and mount corroborate a later dating.

Works like these from the canon of Holocaust representation will continue to challenge. The stylistic and iconographic choices available to artists in internment, so rigorously proscribed by the severity of their existence, differed dramatically for those artists working at a safe distance, or in the war's immediate aftermath—comparison proves revealing.

To characterise this difference, the works produced in internment display a certain hesitancy, a tentativeness and lack of artifice. Their prosaic attention to the daily routines, arduous conditions and human relationships formed in adversity—underline the fact of internment. Those produced after the war tend, by contrast, to universalise extreme suffering, appropriating Holocaust images in order to comment on other events in history, thus widening its implications. They reveal an informed (if not always accurate) response to events, as well as a range of stylistic choices, materials, colour and a degree of finish rarely encountered in the 'art of internment'. Such distinctions, ultimately assist in mapping the gritty terrain of Holocaust representation and clarify questions of intentionality and process. I want now to look briefly at one or two closely related post-war examples.

For knowledge of the Lagers, the Lagers themselves were not always a good observation post. In the inhuman conditions to which they were subjected, the prisoners could barely acquire an overall vision of their universe.[25]

67 **Władysław Siwek**
Devil!
Oświęcim, c.1950
pencil, watercolour
690 x 490mm
Państwowe Muzeum,
Oświęcim
Cat. 101

The decision, in the war's immediate aftermath to extend the collections formed at Auschwitz during the war, by commissioning artists (mainly of Polish origin), former prisoners, among them Władysław Siwek and Mieczysław Kościelniak, to produce large-scale narrative cycles depicting life inside the camps, resulted in a body of exceptional, though not always historically reliable work, underlining the particular experience of this national group. These works reflect the suffering endured by Polish prisoners, next in line after Jews as victims of the Nazi programme of extermination of 'inferior races'.

The enslaving triangle of victim, persecutor and bystander is expressed in post-war representations with a degree of assurance, bordering on high rhetoric. Władysław Siwek's (1907–83) *Devil!*, c.1950, portrays an ill-tempered encounter between a guard and prisoner—Pole or Jew? From 1943 onwards, Jews made up the vast majority of the prisoner population at Auschwitz. But for Siwek's Nazi any such distinction seems an irrelevance. He stands aloof, indifferent to the abject suffering of the man beneath him, as his gleaming leather boot digs deep into the prisoner's chest. Savy, animated, punctiliously attired and armed to the hilt, this Nazi seems composed and in command. Still, all lines point to a reddened nose, tell-tale signs of drunkenness, and a bottle is surreptitiously tucked away in his trouser pocket, in a direct allusion to bar-room-brawl style caricature. Or is this

68 **Mieczysław Kościelniak**
Wheelbarrows
Warsaw, c.1947
pencil and tempera
610 x 860mm
Państwowe Muzeum,
Oświęcim
Cat. 102

the intoxication of power? Siwek remarks here on the abuses of power in the form of everyday assaults on personal, physical as well as psychological boundaries, shedding light on the 'tragic entanglement' of innocent victim and criminal aggressor, seemingly unbridgeable opposites, 'the one subservient, vulnerable, the other strong, controlling'. In fact, both are faces of the same human archetype. In the reality of the death camps, identification with the aggressor was a common and occasionally useful occurrence, assisting survival.[26] The camp's hierarchy extended privileges to a few, and the Pole, not the Jew at the bottom of the heap, was the more likely recipient.

The social demarcations between *Kapo* and prisoners are restated with biting alacrity in Kościelniak's post-war tempera *Wheelbarrow*, c.1947. A consummately gifted draughtsman, Kościelniak moves the aqueous medium deftly, orchestrating the wheelbarrows, the figures and their shadows—the position of raised arms and the angularity of prisoners' legs and bent frames are judged to remarkable effect. These contrast with the sweeping gesture of the towering *Kapo*, about to strike his victim. An air of hilarity is communicated. Such characterisation sits uncomfortably in the context of brutalisation in the camps; this post-war image normalises, even humanises the *Kapo's* behaviour, making of it an acceptable, everyday occurrence.

Bound in hand-stitched leather covers, *Pamiętnika* (Memorial Book) contains some 280 pages of illustrations and autograph materials compiled by Karol Konieczny (b.1919) including contributions from fellow prisoners in Buchenwald and Auschwitz from 1943 onwards.[27] The varied nature of this material reflects the diversity of origins and personalities of Konieczny's cellmates whose signatures and other dedications appear alongside poetry, illustrations, fully worked renditions of camp life, caricatures and song sheets. As a member and organiser of the international committee of the Polish Socialist Workers Party, Konieczny was keen to underline the camaraderie, solidarity and spirit of cooperation among the political prisoners. This sense of a collective identity, reflected in the identical blue-and-white striped prisoners' uniforms, is one of the book's evolving themes. Though Konieczny studied briefly at the School of Fine and Applied Arts in Cracow (before the outbreak of war) this is essentially the work of an autodidact and has no other pretensions, as Konieczny himself is quick to acknowledge:

I wish to emphasise that during all the time I 'created' in prisons and camps, I did not profit from any special favours or privileges. During the day, I worked with other prisoners on labour details. I drew mostly at night, when the others enjoyed their well deserved rest. My drawings ought not to be subjected to scrutiny and aesthetic artistic criticism; an aesthete will not find material in them for professional analysis. I wish them to be considered a living and shocking document of a world of horror and torment. I want the young to know how it was, so that they understand and will not allow such conditions to ever be repeated in the future.[28]

Witness to Atrocity

…you know what it is like to see 100 corpses side by side, or 500 or 1,000. To have stood fast through this—except for cases of human weakness—to have stayed decent…This is an unwritten and never to be written page of glory in our history…[1]

Some eleven million people perished in Nazi prisons and concentration, forced-labour and extermination camps. Even as reports of mass atrocity reached the West and the signs of devastation lay everywhere, Himmler could boast of this *page of glory in our history* and Hitler countermanded his officers to secrecy, banning all reference to the *Final Solution of the Jewish Question* as he pursued the total annihilation of six million Jews.[2] Against the conspirator's wall of silence, witnesses raised their protest: 'if nothing else is left, one must scream. Silence is the real crime against humanity.'[3]

Given the overwhelming scale of the killings and the weight of corroborating evidence, we should ask why, in the vast repertory of drawings produced by artists in camps and ghettos, comparatively so few grapple directly with the theme of mass atrocity. There are several explanations. First, the prisoners' movements were closely watched and heavily circumscribed. The sites of extermination—the death pits (Treblinka), mass graves (Babi Yar), gas chambers and crematoria (Auschwitz)—were out of limits to everyone except, of course, the Nazis, their victims and members of the Jewish *Sonderkommandos*.[4] The *Sonderkommando* teams that manned the gas chambers and crematoria (carefully chosen from the *Laager* and the ranks of recent arrivals) were themselves systematically put to death after no more than a few months, destroyed as they had seen others destroyed, 'hitched to the same cart, bound together by the link of imposed complicity.'[5]

But in time, artists would become remarkably adept at witnessing the atrocity and representing its salient contours, even when this meant placing their own lives at risk. Evidence of summary executions, shootings and hangings, as well as the extermination process itself is well documented in the drawings produced at Auschwitz, Buchenwald, Dora, Gusen

and Dachau. The vast majority of these, however, were produced from early 1944 onwards, and reflect an easing of restrictions and surveillance in the camps, as the Allied forces advanced steadily and the war's outcome, only months away, seemed inevitable. Depicting six million or even six thousand corpses posed significant problems, both ethical and pictorial.[6] Even a hardened Nazi like Franz Stangl could utter only a few incoherent phrases when he recalled seeing the mounds of bodies on his arrival at Belzec death camp in 1942:

The smell…Oh God, the smell. It was everywhere, the pits…the pits, full…they were full. I can't tell you, not hundreds, thousands, thousands of corpses.[7]

Jewish artists on the whole refrained from the depiction of carnage or barbarism out of respect for the dead, but others, no less respectful, like Zoran Music, Aldo Carpi and Corrado Cagli (all non-Jews), felt compelled to make use of the evidence. In Paul Goyard's *Carnage* (Musée d'Histoire Contemporaine), in the spring of 1945, the utter simplicity of the unshaded line, so lacking in pretension or pictorial embellishment, reflects the devastation wreaked in the final months of the war.[8]

But for most, the violence remained beyond the bounds of comprehension, beyond the limits of representation. And there was the problem of what artists could or could not see, what they could or could not imagine, given the camp's relentless clampdown and regimentation, and the constant grappling with everyday problems of survival, as Primo Levi explains:

prisoners felt overwhelmed by an enormous edifice of violence and menace but could not form a representation of it because [their] eyes were fastened to the ground by every single minute's needs.[9]

Arrested by the Gestapo for his wartime activity as a resistance organiser in the Franche-Comté district, Léon Delarbre was imprisoned in the Friedrich Barracks near Belfort on 3 January 1944, and

69 **Boris Taslitzky**
The Small Camp of Buchenwald
1945
oil on canvas
3000 x 5000mm
Centre George Pompidou, Paris
Musée nationale d'art moderne

70 **Jacopo Pontormo**
Dead Christ,
c. 1518
Study for a predella,
Altarpiece of San Michele
Visdomini, Florence
black and white chalk
284 x 405mm
J Paul Getty Museum,
Los Angeles

71 **Léon Delarbre**
Mort de misère,
Dora, 1945
pencil
150 x 155mm
Centre George
Pompidou, Paris
Musée national d'art
moderne
on loan to Musée de la
Résistance et de la
Déportation de
Besançon

deported in March, with fellow Resistance members to the Royallieu camp a few kilometres south of Compiègne,[10] then to Auschwitz and finally to Buchenwald. Necessarily, he set aside his earlier concern with the transcription of landscape, still-life and figure conventions in the beaux-arts manner and, in what seemed a radical and conscious shift, observed and recorded the human suffering around him.[11]

Buchenwald was situated north of Weimar, a pastoral idyll, once the home of Germany's most revered author, Johann Wolgang Goethe. The Nazis turned this once peaceable symbol of German culture into an inferno. In Delarbre's 1944 sketch, the charred limbs of *Goethe's Oak* (beneath which he composed verses) are scars left by an Allied bombing raid on the evening of 24 August.[12] It decimated parts of the camp including the Gustloff factory, where Delarbre worked in the production of small arms, regularly interrupting his duties to observe and draw his surroundings. Working with a pencil on loose scraps of paper and printed ordinances (with letterheads like *Konto Jena* or *Buchenwald*, 1944), he draws with a frenzied line which, in *Goethe's Oak*, branches out in every direction as if protesting the tree's hideous nakedness. Looking back on his experience in the camp, the Spanish Republican writer, Jorge Semprun, recalls the deathly silence of the woods: '"No birds left…They say the smoke from the crematoria drove them away…" They listen closely, straining to understand. "The smell of burnt flesh, that's what did it!" '[13] This is also the scene described in *The Crematorium, the Morning After the Bombardment*, depicting a separate bombing raid on 25 August. The crematorium's chimney, uninterrupted, defiantly spews flames out into the air as a dense cloud of smoke hangs over the camp. Other drawings by Delarbre depict the labour commandos involved in backbreaking work at the stone quarry, or fetching and carrying soup canisters, or retrieving the dead. As conditions worsened, Delarbre drew without respite and in broad daylight.

All of us walked around naked.[14]

The opening line of Tadeus Borowski's *This Way to the Gas Ladies and Gentleman* conjures a Dantesque image of the prisoners' transformation on arrival at camps. Separated from loved ones, stripped of their clothing and body hair, prisoners found difficulty in rebuilding the 'delicate web of symbolic identifications' so vital to their existence. Viktor Frankl, a survivor of Auschwitz, recalls this experience:

While we were waiting for the shower, our nakedness was brought home to us: we really had nothing now except our bare bodies—even minus hair; all we possessed literally was our naked experience.[15]

Weakened by the effects of dysentery, the small figure in Léon Delarbre's *The Little Camp, dysentery: during the drying of trousers*, 1944, supports his unsteady gait with the aid of a walking stick. Head shaven and buttocks bared, he tries to conceal his nakedness by tying a piece of sack cloth around his waist; a vestige of civilised modesty is retained which is denied to the dead and dying. The knowledge of human forms gained from anatomical dissection and the life-room underpins all Delarbre's works and indeed, four centuries of academic figure drawing. A certain gravity and corporeal presence defines the recumbent *Nue Assis*, 1933, her sinuous curves arranged in a clear 'S' shape descending vertically, the length of the picture. In the earlier *Nue de dos*, 1930 (Renee Billot Collection), our eye follows the curvature of the spine and gently contoured back. The clarity of outline and rounded morbidity of flesh recall both the unattainable ideal of Ingres' *Nue à Valpicon* and the starkly contrasting 'thirties Realism of Othon Friez (1879–1949). But the most accomplished executants of this anatomical tradition are to be found in the Italian Renaissance workshop. In Jacobo Pontormo's (1494–1557) *Dead Christ* the human and bodily attributes, so faithful to life, are transmuted into a symbol of universal suffering: an Entombment.[16] Though the analysis of anatomical form proves no less exacting for Delarbre, the bared human figure in *Mort de misère*, produced at the Dora-Mittelbau camp in February 1945 scarcely holds any promise of redemption. The pace and urgency of line link Pontormo and Delarbre across time, instilling life into their forms.

In an attempt to erase the evidence of the crimes perpetrated in the camps and fleeing the advancing Russian and Allied armies in the freezing winter of 1944–45, the Nazi SS mobilised the surviving camp population, decimated by the effects of starvation, severe illness and exhaustion, on a senseless march across the Reich's former territory. With Russian, British and American troops advancing from the east and west, Delarbre and other prisoners were transported in open trains to Bergen-Belsen on 5 April. There, during the final days of the war,[17] a virulent outbreak of typhus claimed the lives of thousands. Even after the camp's liberation, many more fell victim to exhaustion and disease (14,000 in the

period to June 1945). Faced with the transforming experience of the camp universe of Buchenwald, Dora and Belsen, Delarbre made a courageous choice. In the harrowing record of one inmate's final hour, *The Morning after Liberation: too Late!*, 1945, the ultimate futility of the subject's long wait and his resignation are expressed in a strident realism that turns the academic convention of figure drawing on its head. He observes the devastation inflicted on a man: the sickly flesh and sinew, the sagging buttocks, the rigid bone structure, and painful swelling of the knee joints and cavities. Bent at the waist and barely able to sustain his weight, he thrusts head and torso onto a supporting arm.

At Dachau concentration camp,[18] Zoran Music (b.1909) witnessed a similar tragedy: 'I started drawing one man who was so far gone that he was dead by the time I'd finished my sketch. Outside, the mountains of bodies multiplied.'[19] The subjects chosen by Music at Dachau and by Delarbre at Dora and Buchenwald reveal striking parallels. Music's *Pendu* (Figure hanging from a gallows), 1945[20] and Delarbre's *The Hanged*, 1945 inscribed, *The secretary of block 132, accused of a political plot and sabotage*[21] attest to the summary executions by which the Nazis suppressed acts of resistance or insurrection. Music believed that: 'Without Dachau I would have been a

72 **Léon Delarbre**
The morning after Liberation: too late!
Bergen-Belsen, 1945
pencil and black chalk
260 x 280mm
Centre George Pompidou, Paris
Musée nationale d'art moderne on loan to Musée de la Résistance et de la Déportation de Besançon
Cat. 106

73 **Zoran Music**
Corpses in coffins
Dachau, 1945
pen and ink
211 x 278mm
Centre George Pompidou,
Paris
Musée nationale d'art
moderne
Cat. 109

74 **United States Third
Army Photography Unit**
*Corpses lying in an open
carriage*
Buchenwald, 1945
photograph Imperial
War Museum

merely illustrative painter. After Dachau, I had to go to the heart of things.'

Music was admitted to the camp infirmary during a massive typhus epidemic (fearing for their own lives, the SS kept out of the way). For the first time he could draw without fear of reprisal: 'I could think of nothing else, *as if drawing had reawakened me to life. The reality itself was hallucinating.'* Music drew with rudimentary materials, pen and ink or brown crayon on endpapers secretly torn out of the books in the camp library (among them, a copy of *Mein Kampf*). In *Corps en Cercueils*, 1945, the line is consistently tense, paper-thin and stretched to breaking point as it cleaves through the unblemished surface of the paper, eschewing all shadows or any sense of a containing horizon. Music's desire in later years to achieve an economy of means has its origins in the austerity of these works. Arranging his figures in discreet rows, he painstakingly defines the individual features, the interstices of lips, teeth, hands and feet, and the angularity of limbs in an advanced stage of *rigor mortis*. Their identities seem highly individuated, even in a state of decomposition and when not concealed by the half-opened box coffins. The etiolated figures, unshaded contours and ivory skin recall Music's earlier, defining encounter with the works of Egon Schiele in Vienna in 1937. Some years later, he referred to the unerring beauty of the corpses at Dachau, stacked one on top of another:

like bonfires, with their arms and legs sticking out…a tragic beauty. Some of them weren't quite dead, their limbs still moved and their eyes followed you round begging for help. Then, during the night, a little snow would fall. The heap wouldn't move again.[22]

Jorge Semprun likewise recalls death's lingering presence in Buchenwald:

The fetid, faecal smell of death…I was overwhelmed by a kind of physical sadness. I sank into the sorrow of my body, a carnal distress that made me uninhabitable to myself.[23]

Visual accounts of the gas chambers and crematoria are rare, substantiated by no more than a few drawings. Although the subject would unleash a vigorous response from artists after 1945, the few contemporary examples are based on verbal, second-hand accounts. One of these, Wictor Siminski's *In the Gas Chambers*, 1944, points up the difficulties. The languid shapes and entangled outlines of the women are real

enough, but their combined effect, like the waxen figures in Ingres' *Turkish Bath* scenes, produces an erotic frisson. And while Ingres' bathers pleasure in the comfortable surroundings of the harem, Siminski's women succumb to the deadly Zyklon gas emitted by the showerheads.[24] Visible through the opening at the far end of the chamber is the skull-like head and glaring eyes of a uniformed SS officer. This overtly sexual treatment of victimisation increases the viewer's aversion, for the drawing suggests a psychotic blurring of boundaries where pain, sensual pleasure and death meet.[25] The visual description (down to the detail of the window) contained in Siminski's drawing is corroborated by the testimony of Rudolf Höss, first commandant of Auschwitz from May 1940 until November 1943, writing four years later while he awaited trial in a Polish prison:

I had to see everything…the removal [from the gas chambers] and burning of the bodies, the extraction of the teeth, the cutting of the hair, the whole grisly, interminable business. I had to stand for hours on end in the ghastly stench, while the mass graves were being opened and the bodies dragged out and burned. I had to look through the peep-hole of the gas chambers and watch the process of death itself, because the doctors wanted me to see it.[26]

Siminski has thrown open the chamber walls to the viewer's gaze, lifting the shroud of secrecy and exposing both victim and perpetrator. The humiliation, victimisation and dehumanisation of the prisoners by wanton acts of brutality, physical punishment and sexual abuse were commonplace, as Richard Glazar, a survivor of Treblinka and a key witness in post-war trials, was to testify.[27] One SS subaltern recalled: 'When Kurt Franz beat them, it was on their bare buttocks. They had to drop their trousers and count the blows of the whip. The others didn't insist on that, though.'[28] Scenes of rape and sexual assault are conspicuous in the highly rhetorical images of David Olére, produced on his return to Paris in April 1945. In *The Last Nursing* (Beit Lohamei Haghetaot), a mother breast-feeds her young child, while in the foreground a visibly distressed, naked and sibylline figure looks up to her, closing the circle. The strong 'Aryan' guard lays both hands on the mother's arm and shoulder in a gesture that seems both protective and predatory (signalling the group's imminent separation); in the background the tall chimney of the crematorium belches black smoke into the evening sky. *Killing a Women Prisoner* and *Internal Inspection* are further evidence of this collusion of unmitigated

On the banks of the Danube (Upper Austria) about twenty kilometres from Linz, near the Wiener Graben granite quarry, the Nazis established the notorious Mauthausen forced-labour camp. Valuable stone from the quarry furnished the pavements and monuments in the town of Linz, where one day Hitler hoped to retire. Revenues from the quarries, and arms and munitions factories at Mauthausen and its satellite camps at Melk and Bergkristall (Gusen II) fuelled the Nazis' planned territorial expansion. The collaboration of German companies such as Steyr-Daimler-Puch and Messerschmitt was crucial, implicating these industrial conglomerates in the crimes of the State. The relentless exploitation of the work force at Mauthausen brought about the extermination of the camp's population of 80,000 by February 1945.[30] The arrival at Mauthausen in the autumn of 1940 of the first Polish contingent (by far the largest national group) was followed some time later by Russian, Czech and Spanish prisoners (the last being Republican veterans of the Civil War) and Jews. Here, as elsewhere, Jewish prisoners were the least regarded. From this assorted population, the SS appointed the most corruptible elements, common criminals, to positions of influence in the camp's administration. This then is the rag-tag bunch of misshapen *Häftlinge* (camp prisoners) depicted in Aldo Carpi's *The Famished*, 1944. Swathed in regulation uniforms and looking stunned, the prisoners (referred to by the camp guards as *figuren*, puppets— and never addressed by their names) struggle to retain some semblance of the human.

78

The defiant group of prisoners in Boris Taslitzky's *Arrivals looking on as a corpse passes by*, 1945,[31] pressed together in triumphal unison, proclaim their hold on life as the dead (whom we cannot see) are paraded past in a cart.[32] Taslitzky's *The Small Camp of Buchenwald*, 1945 was completed in the weeks following the camp's liberation.[33] Based closely on drawings and detailed sketches produced in internment, this work is a grand summation of one man's experience of the camp. Its epic scale confirms the link between visual representations of the camp universe and the traditions of nineteenth-century history painting which, as a keen copyist trained in the beaux-arts manner, Taslitzky studied closely at the Louvre. Indeed, he felt an immediate kinship with Géricault's masterpiece *The Raft of the Medusa*, a vision of human carnage, the victims of shipwreck. Contemporary events and a sense of national humiliation are informed by Classical reference. Indeed, the corpse-laden cart tilted

75

69

75 **Boris Taslitzky**
Arrivals looking on as a corpse passes by
Buchenwald, 1945
Location unknown

brutality and voyeuristic or sexual innuendo. An implicit problem in all Olére's work is his identification with figures of authority and his crass, even sentimentalised response to the victims; the ambiguous or ill-defined relationships, the distancing devices, serve only to heighten the difficulties. The style is reminiscent of the film posters and hoardings painted by Olére (with considerable acumen) while employed as a designer for Paramount Pictures during the 1920s and 1930s.

…we do not dare lift our eyes to look at one another. There is nowhere to look in a mirror, but our appearance stands before us, reflected in a hundred livid faces, in a hundred miserable and sordid puppets…[29]

76 **Corrado Cagli**
Lying Corpses
Buchenwald, 1945
pen and ink
200 x 330mm
Archivio Cagli, Rome
Cat. 114

obliquely towards the viewer and commanding the centre of Taslitzky's monumental canvas is an effective and keenly observed device, drawn from the daily reality of the camp. Intersecting diagonals broken here and there by subsidiary groups confirm the audacity of this composition. The viewer is thrust against the teeming crowd in an already compressed foreground. An unnatural mixture of coloured gases —swirling pinks, cold grey-blues and acid yellows— rises like poisonous emissions from the crematorium into the air; sulphurous skies are cut away by the camp's outbuildings, concealing the horizon and heightening the sense of artificiality. Responding to criticism of this riotous use of colour, Taslitzky reflected that, 'Buchenwald…was in reality a carnival, horrible but striking and discordant in colour, a swarm of contradictions where barbarity clashed with the most modern techniques.'[34] The modern techniques Taslitzky had in mind were, of course, those tested by Topf of Wiesbaden for the Nazis in the crematoria ovens.

On his return to Paris in April 1945, Taslitzky found himself at the centre of another battle, that between social realists on the one hand and modernists on the other. The formal and iconographic devices employed by Taslitzky at Buchenwald contrast markedly with a contemporary work by Picasso. *Charnel House*, 1945, was displayed alongside Taslitzky's in the exhibition *Art and Resistance*, held at

the newly opened Musée Nationale d'Art Moderne in Paris, in 1946. This uneasy juxtaposition of the rasping realism of the one and the oblique distancing of Cubist-derived abstraction onthe other, provoked a fierce debate, underscoring fundamental differences between those who witnessed the events of the Holocaust at first hand and those who, like Picasso, responded from the margins.[35] The impact on the latter of the drawings by Léon Delarbre and Boris Taslitzky exhibited and published soon after the war deserves closer study.[36]

In Corrado Cagli's pen and ink drawing of a *Boy in the Camp*, 1945, an emaciated figure stares intently through dilated eyes, well aware of his own destitute state. Produced at Buchenwald (Cagli was among the front-line troops who took part in the camp's liberation), this is a grand, wrenching statement of the survivor's condition at the end of the conflict. Barbed-wire mules stretch to infinity and a thin line marks out an otherwise vacant horizon. In 1945, Cagli completed a series of drawings of the camp's victims which were published as *Scenes from Buchenwald*. Several of these are based on photographs taken by the US Signal Corps at Buchenwald, Gusen, Nordhausen and elsewhere and used in war-crime tribunals as evidence.[37] The photographs taken by Lee Miller at Buchenwald, British troops at Bergen-Belsen and the US Signal Corps made available a vast, widely disseminated visual source which would

77

77 Corrado Cagli
Boy in the Camp
Buchenwald, 1945
pen and ink
254 x 330mm
Archivio Cagli, Rome
Cat. 115

eventually find its way into the studios of artists, notably those of Leah Grundig and Gerhart Frankl in Europe and of Ben Shahn, George Segal and Robert Morris in the United States.

76 The morbidity of Cagli's *Lying Corpses*[38] belies the fidelity of line that so elegantly describes the sinuous matter, skeletal forms and strewn clothing, the repeated vertical of the receding fence and crematoria in the distance. Exerting varying pressure, this pen and ink line instils the lifeless corpse with some semblance of the human. These are drawings for the end of time, a defiant protest against the unprecedented suffering.

The collapse of language that Franz Stangl experienced amid the piles of rotting corpses at Belzec in 1942 has a curious parallel in Edward R Murrow's closing remarks in his broadcast from Buchenwald on 16 April 1945: *I pray you to believe what I have said…I reported what I saw and heard, but only part of it. For most of it I have no words…If I have offended you by this rather mild account of Buchenwald, I'm not in the least sorry.*[39] As the fires of war subsided, a human spectre emerged out of the wreckage, shocking the world into the realisation of the atrocities committed by the Nazis. For those who witnessed the spectacle it seemed as though humanity had lost its way to evil.

Remarking on the uninterrupted concern in Western Art with the ideal human form, the poet and critic Francis Ponge observed how extraneous matter had been progressively removed to reveal the figure's formal essence. Ponge had in mind the work of the Swiss-born sculptor Alberto Giacommetti, but his remarks are also coloured by his recollection of the images of the camps' victims. 'The destruction of [moral] values has speeded up', and with it the destruction of human life itself. In *Notes sur les Otages*, he remarks at length on Jean Fautrier's suite, *Hostages*, 1945 commenting that: 'He creates beauty out of the present horror of humanity'.[40] Equating the agonised, Existentialist "I" with representations of the human figure in art, Ponge concludes: 'Man not only has nothing left; there is nothing left of him but this "I".'[41] Such notions paved the way artistically and philosophically for post-war visual representations of the Holocaust.

78 **Aldo Carpi**
The Famished
Mauthausen, 1944
pen and ink wash
260 x 186mm
Art collection
Beit Lohamei Haghetaot,
Ghetto Fighters' House,
Israel
Cat. 117

So far in this essay, I have considered the unquestionable achievement of artists working in camps and ghettos in 1939–45, acknowledging the undoubted link that existed for them between seeing (and by extension, drawing) and survival, or continuity (when physical survival was no longer attainable). Their works demand to be seen alongside other twentieth-century drawing practices and traditions. Thanks to them, the names Terezín, Dachau, Auschwitz, and Buchenwald are forever endowed with the voices of those who died and those who survived. Though our impulse may be to recoil from them, tainted as they are by human suffering, we cannot shake off the memory of these drawings, which seem to want to implicate us (as intruders at the scene of a crime). They restore a link between the living and the dead and draw us into the space of the victim and the persecuted, reminding us of our responsibility to them. Through them we become conscious bearers of the truth and will in time be required to testify to humanity's crimes in our own voices.

Survivors

Survival was the supreme goal of all those interned in camps and ghettos, as H O Bluhm reminds us: 'Death in the nazi concentration camps and forced labour camps requires no explanation. It is survival that requires explanation. It is the survivors of the destruction that astonish us.'[1]

Deprived of material possessions save perhaps a treasured photograph or other memento of a vanished world, Holocaust survivors faced the monumental task of rebuilding shattered lives and identities in a post-war climate of uncertainty and indifference. 'The principle emotional reaction to liberation was emotional sadness…For us it was this: no one else had come back; we were alone and the outside world didn't care. There was a world of habits to unlearn too.'[2] The very fact of their survival presented almost insurmountable odds, as the memory of those who perished in the transports, in the forced labour, concentration and extermination camps, haunted the living fifty years on. As Jorge Semprun, interned at Buchenwald, remarked: '*you never take this voyage back in the opposite direction…you can never erase this voyage*'.[3] And in her powerful account of the Treblinka death camp, Gitta Sereny compared the resilience of the survivors' memory with the fractious, even reluctant memory of perpetrators and bystanders: 'It is quite extraordinary how the memories of the people who lived through hell remained intact, while those so infinitely less imperilled broke down.'[4]

Memory

The manner in which traumatic memories are transmuted into narrative structures and representations revealed fundamental differences in the manner in which survivors recalled the events in later years, pointing not to one but many individual stories.

What matters…is not what my past actually was, or even whether I had one; it is only the memories I have now which matter, be they false or true.[5]

The past is not intact in memory,[6] it must be articulated, represented. We live in an age of testimony, bearing witness to and forever reshaping the past. As any self-respecting artist will tell you, representational strategies abound. Memory is not pristine but flawed; it is refractory, selective and, like other cognitive processes, fluid, susceptible to change, undergoing constant editing. Shards of the personal and the public are woven inseparably and personal recollections are easily overwhelmed by the weight of historical evidence, coloured by the value and significance conferred on them by others. The recovery of memory is often painful in an uncomprehending or insensitive culture: this was the experience for many survivors in the war's immediate aftermath. The past was suppressed in order better to reproduce what was thought to be relevant to the present.

How are we to preserve Holocaust memory even as the events and their protagonists recede into the remoteness of time? In the days after the liberation of Buchenwald, one survivor offered this response: *Through the artifice of a work of art, of course*, meaning a work of fiction *narratives that will let you imagine even if they cannot let you see*.[7] Imagining a culture after the Holocaust, Yosef Hayim Yerushalmi added (in a formulation that might equally apply to artists), 'I have no doubt whatever that its image is being shaped not at the historian's anvil, but at the novelist's crucible'.[8] If the works of the survivors Robert Antelme, Primo Levi, Paul Celan or Aharon Appelfeld are the living conduit, setting down the terms for future literary representations and commentary, visual representations will in turn be shaped both, by the drawings of internment and the imaginative re-enactment of memory in the works of survivors. Thus, the centrality of witnesses' perceptions and the importance of preserving the autograph sources.

Rethinking the past: Zoran Music, Osias Hofstatter, Yehuda Bacon

The existence of a handful of carefully preserved wartime drawings as evidence of the camps rekindled memories of internment for such artists as Zoran Music, Osias Hofstatter and Yehuda Bacon, providing a vital link with the past.

79 **Osias Hofstatter**
Untitled (Heads and Hands)
undated
pen and ink wash
730 x 550mm
Collection of Herzliya Museum of Art
Cat. 132

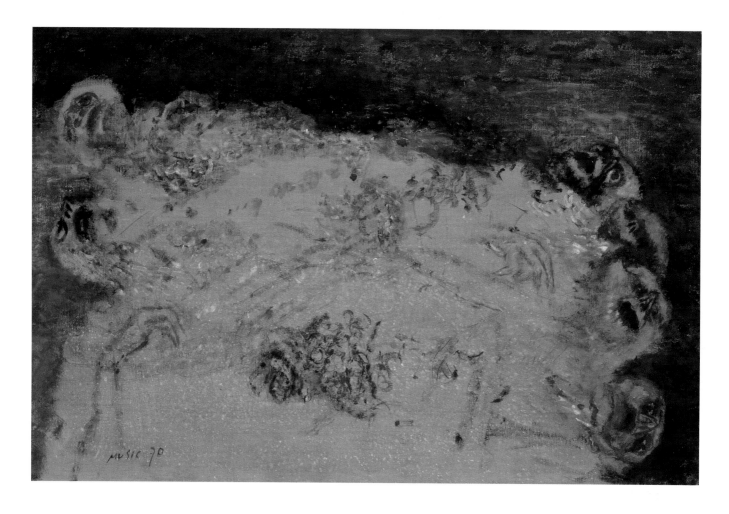

80   **Zoran Music**
We are not the last
Nous ne sommes pas les
derniers
1973
acrylic on canvas
970 x 1460mm
Collection of the artist
Cat. 121

My works are absolutely not documents…for an artist it is impossible not to work, it is like breathing. Art gave me the force to survive. (Zoran Music)

Music returned to his home in Gorizia, Slovenia, in April 1945, carrying with him a number of drawings made at Dachau.[9] Many of these recorded the corpses left to rot around the camp, as the mounting casualties overwhelmed the facilities for cremation or burial in the winter of 1944–45. Fascinated by the varied configurations which the bodies assumed, he returned to specific arrangements, clarifying and further refining the forms so that, with each study, a greater formal elegance and calligraphic fluidity were attained.[10] The tense acuity of line and the discreet placement of figures on the blank page reflect an informed and visually erudite response to his subject.[11] For all their horror, Music sensed the possibilities (already present in the Dachau drawings) which the piles of dead and rotting corpses pointed to as the lineaments of a visually abstracted, human

73

landscape. In 1970, after a lapse of twenty-five years, Music returned to the subject of Dachau in an extended series of paintings, drawings and etchings entitled *We are not the last*.[12] And he did so by invoking the landscape of his native Gorizia (which had been his subject matter in the intervening period).

Though preferring to think of himself as a person *senza fissa dimore* (of no fixed abode), Music's visual sensibility was rooted in the landscape of Dalmatia and Carsole: 'The Carso is the matrix on which all my painting is based. A desolate landscape, almost barren; petrified, one might say.'[13] Landscape was to be a route to the rediscovery of the artist's past, and of Dachau in particular. Looking out onto the hills around Siena,[14] he observed the scarred and sun-bleached soil, stripped of vegetation:

almost white, like a skin with runnel marks on them that make them look like the ribcages of human bodies…later, when I came to paint these hills, I realised that the whitish mounds reminded me of the piles of corpses that had been part of everyday life at the camp.[15]

In the series *We are not the last*, these mounds of corpses rise deflate, collapse or decompose, to become an ocean of flesh. Gossamer washes of colour absorbed into the coarse weave of the canvas and paint accretions—like protuberances of bone matter or a gleaming crown of tiny white teeth—cohere into a highly tactile, visually active surface. This vision of humanity, informed by the exhumation of earlier memories, as much as by history, literature (Dante) and Goya's black paintings, flows uninterruptedly from the artist's storehouse of recollections. And yet, even as Music embarked on the series' most intense and inventive phase of gestation in the early 1970s, he seemed unwilling or unable to relinquish the memory of the landscape with its human dimensions, a relationship explored in a group of paintings entitled *Racine*, 1972 (Collection the artist) or *Motif végétal*, 1972, a metaphor for the earth's latent energies. The gnarled and truncated roots and tubers are brutally uprooted and exposed to the elements, their fine tendril shapes almost interchangeable and contiguous with the lifeless, bare and pale corpses of Dachau. A similar metamorphosis is apparent in Music's small self-portrait, *We are not the last*, 1975. The etiolated beauty of hands and hopelessly entangled fingers—their veined patterns and almost transparent skin recalling El Greco—become indistinguishable from the now familiar heap of corpses. Above them, the artist's bloodshot and agitated face looks on in horror.

Music's large tableau *We are not the last*, 1973 (Private Collection), evokes stillness, not the stillness of death, but an indefinable state somewhere between life and death. The entire canvas is alive with the sense of touch and a raw beauty:

…I became fascinated by the heaps of bodies…because they had a kind of beauty, a tragic beauty. Some of them weren't quite dead, their limbs still moved and their eyes followed you round, begging for help. Then, during the night, a little snow would fall. The heap wouldn't move again.[16]

The vast expanse of flesh is punctuated here and there with the gaping eyes, genitals and orifices of the corpses, endowing them with a semblance of individuality. Their nakedness and progressive decay once again recall the hapless victims in Géricault's *Raft of the Medusa*. But Music has deliberately avoided the excessive trappings and anecdotal content of the large *pompiers* painted in the previous century. His works

are informed by an extreme economy of means—the spare language of drawing. A group of charcoal and red chalk drawings of the 1970s depict the small, naked figures with charred heads, vaporised against the bleached whiteness of the paper—their evanescence confirmed by the fugitive nature of marks:[17] 'My experience of death had transformed my experience of life. I was only interested in images that were stripped down to their essence'.[18] In Music's etchings, the figures seem poised between being and non-being—fine incisions of line and the acid's corrosive properties, threaten to remove all vestiges of the human image. In the reactive and generative processes by which memories become form, his figures emerge out of the nebulous washes or abstracted fields like a slow afterimage. *I never try to*

81 **Zoran Music**
We are not the last
Nous ne sommes pas les
derniers
1978
brown chalk
500 x 350mm
Collection of the artist
Cat. 122

will it into existence. The only worthwhile images are those that come about of their own accord. With his suggestion of an unwilled image and thus, a renunciation of the self, Music's concerns echo those of two other artists-survivors, Osias Hofstatter and Yehuda Bacon.

Israel: Post-War

By virtue not only of their Jewish origins but of their stateless condition, Hofstatter and Bacon felt they had compelling reasons to look to Israel, in the years following the war. It was there that the two men, so different in inclination and temperament, found the conditions, as artists, to revisit their experiences of internment from a safe distance. If not its central myth, the *Shoah* is one of the defining themes and narratives of the country's history. And yet, as the world examined its own responsibility in the events of the Holocaust soon after the war, Israel seemed to want to bury this past. Reflecting a newfound confidence as an emerging regional power in the wake of the Six Day War, it struggled with the painful legacy connecting its origin as a State with the death of the six million, as refugees and survivors sought to build new lives in Israel.[19] Similarly, a tendency within progressive artistic circles in the 1940s and '50s to embrace abstraction over narrative, and language over empirical reality, further marginalized the *Shoah* as a viable subject for artists.[20]

A tradition of draughtsmanship with its origins in schools and workshops in Central Europe flourished in Israel, away from the cosmopolitan centres of art and culture, and thus, from the dominance of conforming modernist orthodoxies. This was due, in part, to the presence of a group of artists who immigrated in the early years of the century, principle among them, Leopold Krakauer (1890–1954), Yosef Zaritzky (1891–85) and Anna Ticho (1894–1980).[21] Their influence in turn fired a younger generation of artists and informed a tradition of excellence evident today, in a strong and viable graphic sensibility. The works of Osias Hofstatter and Yehuda Bacon are nourished by and in turn enrich this tradition.[22]

Osias Hofstatter's floating world

Strange and monstrous beings stir out of the dark and iridescent pools of ink in Hofstatter's drawings, exhuming inchoate memories. These are the anomalous beings that inhabit an uncertain universe after the wholesale destruction of Auschwitz, a world 'inverted by the passions of man's lower nature', as

82 **Osias Hofstatter**
Untitled (Man-Beast-Child)
undated
gouache, ink, graphite
615 x 405mm
Collection of Herzliya
Museum of Art
Cat. 131

83 **Anon**
Sciapod
from Hartmann Schedel's
Liber Cronicarium,
1493
wood engraving
Courtesy of the Warburg
Institute, London

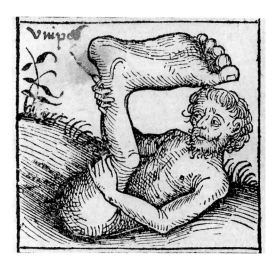

Goya readily acknowledges in the suite of etchings, *Los Caprichos*: 'The sleep of reason produces monsters'.[23] Goya's *Sueño* reminds us that dark and predatory forces intrude uncomfortably on our waking thoughts. In Hofstatter's works, disembodied heads ascend into the ether (in a reference to Odilon Redon's *Les noires*), demons embrace winged angels and monstrous figures elope with women with sylph-like waists, while a solitary creature stares into the night.[24] The human figure is subjected to remorseless, physical attack. Only the waif-like silhouette of an earlier, more corpulent figure survives the artist's repeated assault in *Diagonal*, 1968 (Herzliya Museum of Art), echoing Francis Ponge's remark, 'Man not only has nothing left; there is nothing left of him but this "I".' Defined by the void, she floats serenely. A more benign light suffuses *Three profiles*, 1968. Its constellation of heads cohere in the sitter's multiple identity. Pure, undiluted washes of Indian ink or *tusche* are built up into rich, carbonised surfaces, producing deep, lustrous areas of black. Layers of tissue or newsprint are adhered to the paper support and worked repeatedly, to endow the images with a memorable intensity.

Like a traveller on a post-exilic journey, the victim of a Chernobyl-like meltdown, *Untitled (Man-Beast-Child)* recalls the monstrous hominids, the sciapods and antipodes found in early *mappa mundi* such as the great Hereford map. (As the surface tension of ink attracts and repels the viscosity of gouache and bodycolour, the materials coalesce and, losing their pristine identities, gain in strength and plasticity.) Summoning all their human and animal powers, they remain at a fixed point, while the earth spins beneath their tangled feet. Believed to inhabit the extremities of our planet, these beings were integral to the superstitious lore of late medieval and early Renaissance societies until the explorations of the New World and the discovery that the world was not flat, but round. The Shoah demands of us a comparable reassessment.

A thinning down of the ink medium and loosening of gesture are discernable in a later composition *Untitled (Hand and Heads)*, undated.[25] At the point where Hofstatter's image seeks to dissolve into the flux of matter, he reclaims the figural theme with bold outlines, arresting its disintegration and holding the surface. This unfettered freedom of invention confirms the fluency of his graphic processes. An outsized hand shields the troubled eyes of a stunned witness. In Hebrew, the word for hand and memorial are the same, יד *yad*. We are reminded here of the mute gestures of Käthe Kollwitz's hands shielding the artist in *Lamentation*; the pointing hand of a tearful Jankel Adler after the destruction of the Lodz ghetto in 1927; and the wringing hands of Music's *Self-portrait*, transmuted into a pile of corpses. Twenty years later, in *Luminous Figure on Dark Ground*, 1999, Music's hands are transformed into instruments of light.

The female nude— as personifier of *Eros* or *muse* is a recurring symbol in Hofstatter's late and most inventive group of works. Dye-like magentas, indigo and saffron are freely applied over dark, iridescent grounds, their luminosity a response to the violent passions the nude figure arouses. The fluidity of the eroticised drawing restores a life-like quality to her contours: braced hips, swollen breasts rising to meringue-like peaks, miniature feet and hands elegantly curled into tiny flames. This carry-over of tradition (the nude) is no harbinger of the New World. And yet, she persists, albeit transformed as Queen of the Night, a lantern adumbrating the path of art.[26]

Yehuda Bacon's Workbooks

Unusually, for an artist working at the end of the twentieth and beginning of the twenty-first century, Yehuda Bacon has consigned a significant part of his creative output to his workbooks and diaries,[27] as if to establish an intimate dialogue between the reader and the text or image. The workbooks are the products of an inspired and prodigious memory, granting him uninterrupted access to the past.

When in 1961, at the Eichmann trials in Jerusalem, Jewish survivors were called up to give evidence, their voices broke through the silence that once threatened to engulf the memories into a prevailing forgetfulness. One of those called to testify, Yehuda Bacon,[28] remembered with surprising acuity his experiences of internment in Theresienstadt, Auschwitz, Mauthausen and Günskirchen. A pair of cathartic images, *Memorial Candle I & II*, 1950, recall the loss of his father in the crematoria at Auschwitz: 'We were separated from our parents; we knew the precise moment when they were sent to the gas chambers. I believe we could have seen them walking there. However, none of us could cry. Something inside us had broken; we were transformed.' Bacon's memories of the camp, the fences and fortifications (he was thirteen at the time of his deportation to Theresienstadt and internment in Auschwitz) are recorded in *Night in Auschwitz*, 1946. Night is a cover

82

for disorientation and fear, a symbol of that 'sleep of reason' which the Nazi concentration camps epitomized.

Entering Yehuda Bacon's studio in Jerusalem, we are soon surrounded by workbooks, sketchbooks, diaries and literally hundreds of loose drawings; his work table is piled high with unsorted papers, letters, photographs of mentors and close friends, journals, ink bottles, pots containing pens, brushes, a letter opener. Bacon begun the suite of workbooks in the autumn of 1973, on his return from a sabbatical year in the United States (one month before the Yom Kippur War), a task he persists in, almost without interruption, to this day.[29] Each book contains upward of seventy drawings, disposed vertically, to the right of a blank page. Notwithstanding the economy of his medium which has remained largely unchanged—a metal stylus, reed pens, brushes and black ink of varying shades and intensity —the workbooks disclose a startling range of iconographic, stylistic and technical experiment. His workbooks are not intended as a 'practice run' or a subsidiary statement in thrall to painting (unlike a traditional sketchbook) but as the depository of thoughts and pure visualisation in an inexhaustible stream of predominantly abstracted images. They unlock the imagination's reserves, inviting us to explore the porous layers of memory and retrieval, a cathartic process for Bacon, prising open the pathways to as yet unearthed memories.

84

Bacon prefers to work with Indian ink or *tusche*, strengthening or diluting the medium as required. Subtle variations occur in the chemical composition and pigmentation of the inks, which range from warm ivory black or bone black to cooler shades of blue grey, violet or jet black. A variety of tools—a metal stylus, reed pens, brushes of varying sizes unleash a powerful array of marks—delicate, whimsical, determined, staccato-like or impetuous. Line unfurls from the point of a stylus pen, arcs, pivots and spirals before coming to a stop at the foot of the page. These marks have a musical, improvisational elegance and confirm Bacon's mastery of the medium of pen and ink wash.[30] Corrections are rare. Accidents are integral to the process and encouraged. A seemingly inconsequential mark can ignite a presence on the page; repeated reworkings endow this incipient shape with individuated form and accentuate its three-dimensionality. The dazzling spectre of a women—a powerful female archetype—appears in manifold guises.[31] She gazes admiringly at us through vaporous washes of ink. Rembrandt's *Saskia* and the Old

Testament matriarchs, Sarah, Rebecca and Rachel, as well as the artist's companion Leah are invoked.

So how do Bacon's workbooks enshrine the memory of the Shoah and what is their significance? Parallels with the well-stocked shelves of the *Beit ha Midrash* (house of study) or *Beit Knesset* (the synagogue) are inescapable, although valuable and sacred texts were also found in the *genizah* (a book repository usually in the upper storey or attic of a synagogue where threadbare tomes are deposited).[32] For the 'people of the book', the study of *Torah* is the most sacred of *Mitzvot* (commandments).[33] But perhaps the key to Bacon's workbooks lies in the *Memorbücher* (memorial books), preserved in the community's archives, which record the names of the deceased, to whom communal prayers are addressed.[34] In one sense then, the workbooks are a link to lost relatives and friends, to a whole community.

Bacon was immersed in books from an early age, absorbing the culture of Max Brod and Franz Kafka as a young man.[35] Soon after his arrival in Israel in 1947, the eminent historian Hans Günther Adler, author of the seminal post-war study *Theresienstadt 1941–45*,[36] introduced him to the circle of writers and intellectuals associated with the Hebrew University, among them Gershom Scholem (1897–1982) and Martin Buber (1878–1965). Scholem opened up for Bacon a Jewish mystical tradition unfettered by orthodoxy, while Buber lent authority to Bacon's personal understanding of the dialogic relationship ('I and Thou') between man and God. The universalist implications of Bacon's more recent spiritual pursuits and his readiness likewise to embrace and reach across to other faith traditions including Christianity, invites the reading of particular works as a 'Christian fulfilment of Jewish foreshadowing'.

Bacon's exploration of visual signs has its counterpart in Klee's private notebooks which contain the seeds of his teaching at the Bauhaus. Access to Klee's teachings was granted through the intermediary of Mordechai Ardon (1896–1992), Bacon's tutor at the Bezalel Academy of Arts and a pupil of Johannes Itten at Weimar and of Klee at Dessau. The levity and luminosity which are the hallmarks of Bacon's pantheism, recall the earlier, more ethereal Klee than the post-exilic works with their gravitas and contemplation of death and foreboding.[37] One in particular, Klee's *Angelus Novus*, 1920, is apposite to this discussion.[38] It was acquired by the German Jewish philosopher Walter Benjamin (1892–1940) in 1921. He attached great importance to *Angelus Novus* and based two

86

84 **Yehuda Bacon**
Forty workbooks
1973–2001
pencil, black chalk, pen
and ink wash, water-
colour and mixed media
bound in black covers
285 x 435mm (open)
Collection the artist
Cat. 133

85 **Yehuda Bacon**
Forty workbooks
1973–2001
pencil, black chalk, pen
and ink wash, water-
colour and mixed media
bound in black covers
285 x 435mm (open)
Collection the artist
Cat. 133

autobiographical essays on Klee's enigmatic work *86* which became something of a talisman for him, symbolising the angel of history. (Significantly, at his death, Benjamin bequeathed the work to his life-long friend and correspondent, Gershom Scholem and today it forms part of the Israel Museum Collection.) The taut, spare precision of Klee's diagrammatic lines, off-set by luminous washes of colour, wrap themselves around a pin figure, whose gaping teeth, Olympian curls and wide open eyes are not devoid of humour.

85 Leafing through the pages of Yehuda Bacon's workbooks, we are made aware of the repetition of certain themes, unfolding effortlessly, without a willed outcome. A man balances precariously with outstretched arms on the high wire. A plume of smoke rises into the air from a vast chimney. Constellations of straight and curved lines converge to form a loose counterpoint structure. Such simply formulated themes (echoing the bird or crane motif used by Georges Braque in the latter years of the artist's working life, a symbol of spirituality; or Picasso's bull, a metaphor for virility, sanguinity and the artist's unbridled powers), structure and contain our reading of his works. Bacon has long felt an affinity with the work of these artists, and with Jankel Adler, whose exhibitions in London and Jerusalem in the 1950s moved him deeply. Indeed, Bacon's linear constellations and pictorial invention share with Adler's Cubism's analysis of penetrable objects and the suggestion of a space-time continuum.

Ultimately, Bacon shies away from too literal an interpretation of his works, preferring instead to emphasise their pure, abstracted and lyrical qualities. And, as we turn the pages of his workbooks, not a word, date or numbering sequence intrudes upon our contemplation of the page and pure visualisation (echoing Paul Klee's aphorism that 'Art does not render the visible but makes visible'). Renouncing the written word, these are actions of the spirit rooted in the silence of remembrance.

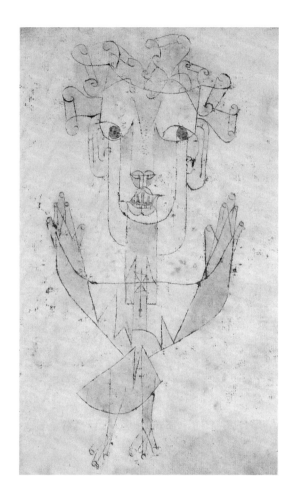

86 **Paul Klee**
Angelus Novus
1920
Indian ink, colour chalks
and brown wash
322 x 242mm
Department of Prints and
Drawings
The Israel Museum,
Jerusalem
Gift of Fania and
Gershom Scholem,
Jerusalem, John Herring,
Marlene and Paul
Herring, Jo-Carole and
Ronald Lauder, New York

Art of the Holocaust, a Reader

The Holocaust has engendered a vast amount of historical research and published material. This brief note on the sources is intended as a guide for the student and general reader. Any discussion of the art produced in internment in camps and ghettos must, of necessity, take place within an overall understanding of the dominant social and political forces inside occupied Europe, from the ill-fated election of 1933 and the rise of National Socialism as an institutional party to Germany's defeat and liberation in 1945. For an analysis of the events and their causes, the condensed version of Raul Hilberg's seminal *The Destruction of the European Jews* (New York, 1985) is a most useful source. Martin Gilbert's vivid chronicle *The Holocaust, The Jewish Tragedy* (Glasgow, 1986) is based on first-hand witness accounts. Yitzhak Arad, Israel Gutman, Abraham Margaliot, eds., *Documents on the Holocaust, selected Sources on the Destruction of the Jews in Germany and Austria, Poland and the Soviet Union* (Yad Vashem, Jerusalem 1981; eighth edition, 1999) presents key documentary sources in a single volume.

Though separated by nearly twenty years, both Terrence Des Pres' *The Survivor, An Anatomy of Life in the Death Camps* (New York, 1976) and Tzvetan Todorov's *Facing the Extreme, Moral Life in the Concentration Camps* (Paris, 1991/ New York, 1997) emphasise the centrality of witnesses' testimony when grappling with human strategies of survival in extremity. Gitta Sereny's harrowing account of the Treblinka death camp *Into that Darkness* (London, 1974), through interviews with its commander Franz Stangl and survivors offers the reader a window onto this extremity. A more recent and useful addition, from the field of gender studies is Dalia Ofer, Lenore J. Weitzman, eds., *Women in the Holocaust* (New Haven, 1998).

The following accounts of life in internment are essential reading: Primo Levi's *If this is a Man* (originally published as *Se questo é un uomo*, 1958/ London, 1987) and *The Drowned and the Saved* (*I Sommersi e i salvati*, 1986/ London, 1988); Robert Antelme, *The Human Race* (*L'Espéce Humaine*, 1957/ Vermont, 1992); Tadeusz Borowski, *This Way to the Gas Ladies and Gentleman* (translated by Barbara Vedder,

London, 1976); Jorge Semprun's *Literature or Life* (*L'ecriture ou la Vie*, 1991/ New York, 1997) and *The Long Voyage* (London, 1997); Aaron Appelfeld, *For Every Sin* (London, 1995). After the war, the survivors constructed identities from the fragments of the past. An important addition in the rescue of individual voices has been the publication in Britain of a number of survivors' testimonies by *The Library of Holocaust Testimonies* (Vallentine Mitchell) and *Witness Collection* (Beit Shalom), among them Trude Levi, *A Cat Called Adolf* (1995) and Kitty Hart-Moxon, *Return to Auschwitz* (1997). Of an entirely different order is the remarkable, albeit controversial fictionalised account of a childhood in a Polish concentration camp by Benjamin Wilkomirski, *Fragments* (London, 1997), which raises many issues regarding the appropriation of memory and fictional autobiography. George Steiner's landmark essay on the decline of language after Auschwitz, 'The Hollow Miracle' is contained in *Language and Silence* (London, 1967). For a discussion of the Holocaust and literary theory see Lawrence Langer's *The Holocaust and the Literary Imagination*, 1975 and *Holocaust Testimonies* (New Haven, 1991).

For the relationship of Biblical narratives to Jewish historiography and contemporary history Yosef Hayim Yerushalmi's *Zohar: Jewish History and Jewish Memory*, University of Washington Press, 1982, is stimulating and highly readable. The legal and political emancipation of Jews in Germany in the late eighteenth and early nineteenth centuries augured a renaissance of Jewish culture and an opening out to secular culture, known as the Haskalah or Enlightenment, and led to the rapid assimilation of Jewish writers, artists and thinkers into mainstream culture. These trends are discussed in Michael Brenner's *The Renaissance of Jewish Culture in Weimer Germany* (New Haven, 1996) and R. I. Cohen, *Jewish Icons: Art and Society in Modern Europe* (Berkeley, 1998).

An account of Nazi policies toward the visual arts and culture is contained in Stephanie Barron's *Degenerate Art, The Fate of the Avant-Garde in Nazi Germany* (Los Angeles County Museum of Art, 1991). Looking beyond, James E. Young's *The Texture of Memory* (New Haven, 1993) is the most useful consideration of Holocaust memorials, monuments and counter-monuments, containing useful methodological pointers for students of the Holocaust.

Work in this field has been significantly enhanced by the appearance of Ziva Amishai Maisels, *Depiction & Interpretation, The Influence of the Holocaust on the Visual Arts* (Oxford, 1993) by far the most comprehensive account to date. Maisels' contribution in so many areas, and in particular, her discussion of visual precedents has established a new ceiling for researchers. This work was preceded by Janet Blatter, Sybil Milton, *Art of the Holocaust* (New York, 1981) and Miriam Novitch, Lucy Dawidowicz, Tom L. Freudenheim *Spiritual Resistance, Art from Concentration Camps, 1940–45* (Kibbutz Lohamei Haghetaot, 1981) which, if more condensed, have proven nonetheless invaluable in the twenty years since they were published. Two studies on the arts in Terezín have been particularly useful: *Seeing Through Paradise, Artists and the Terezín Concentration Camp*, Massachusetts College of Art, Boston, 6 March–4 May, 1991 (with contributions by Arnošt Lustig, Arno Parik) and Sabine Zeitoun, Dominique Foucher *La Masque de la Barbarie: Le ghetto Theresienstadt 1941–1945*, Centre d'Histoire de la Résistance et de la Déportation, Lyon, 1998. Our understanding of the role of artists in French transit camps has been significantly enhanced by the appearance of Véronique Alemany-Dessaint, Danièle Baron, *Créer pour Survivre*, Fédération Nationale des Déportes et Internés Résistants et Patriotes, Musée des Beaux Arts de Reims, 1995 and Pnina Rosenberg, *Salon des Refusés, L'Art dans les Camps d'Internement Français 1939–45*, Beit Lohamei Haghetaot, spring, 2000.

A number of exhibitions in Britain over the past decade have surveyed the response of artists. Avram Kampf's *Chagall to Kitaj, Jewish Experience in Twentieth Century Art*, Barbican Art Gallery, London, 1990, discusses the Holocaust as part of the diverse story of Jewish Art and life in the twentieth century. The response of post-war artists, survivors and their descendants, are usefully examined in Monica Bohm Duchen, ed., *After Auschwitz, Responses to the Holocaust in Contemporary Art*, South Bank and Northern Centre for Contemporary Art, London, 1995; and Elizabeth Maxwell, Roman Halter, *Remembering for the Future, Original Drawings and Reproductions by Victims of the Holocaust 1940–1945*, Oxford, 1988 and Glenn Sujo, *Artists Witness the Shoah, Camp Drawings from the Collections of Beit Lohamei Haghetaot and Yad Vashem*, Sheffield, 1995, have focussed specifically on the works produced by artists in camps and ghettos.

Artists' Biographies

The following entries refer to those artists interned in camps and ghettos from 1939 to 1945 whose works appear in the exhibition.

Irene AWRET (Berlin 1921–lives in Virginia)

Née Irene Spicker, Awret fled Germany to Belgium in 1939 where she continued her studies at the Académie des Beaux Arts, Brussels. Arrested by the SS in 1943, she was interned in the Malines transit camp in Belgium. There she met her future husband, the sculptor-ceramist Ariel Awret. Together, they succeeded in concealing and preserving the works of fellow inmates, Claus Grünewald, Leon Landau and Jacques Ochs. Awret and her husband emigrated to Safed, Israel in 1947.

Sybil Milton, Janet Blatter, *Art of the Holocaust*, Rutledge, New York, 1981, p.241. Miriam Novitch, Lucy Dawidowicz, Tom Freudenheim, *Spiritual Resistance, Art from Concentration Camps, 1940–45*, Kibbutz Lohamei Haghetaot, Israel, 1981, pp. 44–47.

Yehuda BACON (Ostrava, Czechoslovakia, 1929–lives in Jerusalem)

Born into a traditional Jewish family, Bacon was interned in the Theresienstadt ghetto at the age of thirteen. The presence there of Leo Haas, Bedrich Fritta and Otto Ungar encouraged Bacon to develop his abilities as a draughtsman, working mainly from the imagination, a practice he continues to this day. In the winter of 1943 he was deported to Auschwitz and in January 1945 to Mauthausen. His parents and a sister perished at Auschwitz and Stutthof. Bacon has recorded these experiences in a group of drawings and workbooks. Following his liberation from Günskirchen on 5 May, Bacon spent a period of convalescence in Prague, under the care of Přemysl Pitter. The historian H. G. Adler introduced him to the German artist Willi Novák, a committed anti-Fascist who had befriended Kafka and Max Brod and took Bacon on as a pupil (he paid for these classes with his own ration of bread and eggs secured from the children's hostel). Bacon emigrated to Israel in 1946, studying at the Bezalel Academy of Arts under Mordechai Ardon and Jakob Steinhardt, becoming a long serving member of the faculty (1959–93).

Anton Gill, *The Journey Back From Hell, Conversations with Concentration Camp Survivors*, Grafton Books, London, 1988, pp. 442–459. Gerhard Durlacher, *The Search, The Birkenau Boys*, Meulenhoff, Netherlands, 1991. Glenn Sujo, *Artists Witness the Shoah, Camp Drawings from the Collections of Beit Lohamei Haghetaot and Yad Vashem*, Graves Art Gallery, Sheffield, 1995.

Jacob BAROSIN (Latvia 1907/8–)

Born of Russian Jewish parents, Barosin spent his childhood in Berlin, attended the Kunst Academie and was awarded a PhD in the history of art from the University of Freiburg. In 1933, he and his wife Sonia emigrated to France. During the German occupation, Barosin was interned at Gurs and Gignac labour camp, before his escape and hiding in a Montméjèan schoolhouse on the outskirts of Paris. A suite of drawings and texts by Barosin chronicle his arrest and deportation. In 1947, the Barosins emigrated to the United States. He illustrated a Jewish Family Bible and worked for NBC Television in New York. Eighteen portraits of Old Testament prophets, conceived while in hiding, toured the United States.

Jacob Barosin, *A Remnant*, The Holocaust Library, New York (undated publication). Irit Salmon, ed., *Testimony, Art of the Holocaust*, Yad Vashem, The Holocaust Martyrs and Heroes Remembrance Authority, Art Museum, Jerusalem, 1986, p.25. Jacob Barosin, *The World was Silent*, The Rockland Centre for Holocaust Studies, New York, 8 January–29 June, 1989 (exhibition handlist).

Felix BLOCH (Vienna 1898–1944 Terezín)

Details of Felix Bloch's life are scarce. Bloch trained and worked in Vienna as a graphic designer and illustrator, escaping to Prague during the Nazi *Anschluss* in the spring of 1938. He was employed by the *Altestenrat der Judein* (Jewish Community in Prague) until his arrest by the Gestapo and deportation to Terezín (Transport AAv) on 30 July 1942. In Terezín, he became a prominent figure in the *Technische Abteilung* (Technical Drawing Office) where he produced a group of clandestine drawings, from memory. He was arrested with fellow artists Bedrich Fritta, Leo Haas and Otto Ungar for allegedly distributing 'horror propaganda' on 17 July 1944, following a visit by the International Red Cross to Terezín. Bloch was murdered during interrogation by SS Nazi officials in the Small Fortress prison in Terezín.

Arnošt Lustig, Arno Parik, Leo Haas, *Seeing Through Paradise, Artists and the Terezín Concentration Camp*, Massachusetts College of Art, Boston, 6 March–4 May 1991, p.83. Sabine Zeitoun, Dominique Foucher, *La Masque de la Barbarie: Le ghetto Theresienstadt 1941–1945*, Centre d'Histoire de la Résistance et de la Déportation, Lyon, 1998, p.102.

Maurycy BROMBERG (Piotrkowie-Trybunalski, nr. Lodz 1920–)

Bromberg studied at Szkoła Sztuk Zdobniczych w Sosnowiec (School of Decorative Arts) in 1935 and completed his training at the Akademia Sztuk Pięknych (Academy of Fine Arts, Cracow) under Professor Kazimierz Sichulska in 1939. At the onset of war, Bromberg found shelter in the Piotrków ghetto near the Pilnika River, southeast of Lodz. Interned in the labour camp in Hortensia-Piotrkow, he worked in the glass factory. He was later transferred to the Hassag-Palcery labour camp. Liberated in 1945, there are two conflicting versions of his life after the war. One of these, Jozef Sandel's *Lexicon of Jewish Art*, 1946 (unpublished typescript), remarks that the artist travelled to Zamarkand (in the former USSR). Bromberg emigrated to Israel in 1950 where he continued to paint and draw. A retrospective exhibition was held at the Ramat Gan Museum of Art in 1972 and in Toronto the following year.

Jozef Sandel, *Lexicon of Jewish Art*, 1946 (unpublished type-script) Archives of Żydowski Instytut Historyczny w Polsce, Warsaw. Efraim Kaganowski, *Wystawa Zbiorowa* Centralne Żydowski Towarzystwo Kultury I Sztuki, Lodz, 1948 (exhibition handlist). Milton, Blatter, *Art of the Holocaust*, 1981, illus. p. 195. Ziva Amishai Maisels, 'The Complexities of Witnessing', *Holocaust and Genocide Studies*, vol .2, no. 1, 1987, pp.123–47; reprinted in Monica Bohm-Duchen, ed., *After Auschwitz, Responses to the Holocaust in Contemporary Art*, Northern Centre for Contemporary Art, Sunderland and Lund Humphries, London, 1995, pp.25–48.

Charlotta BUREŠOVÁ (Prague 1904–83 Prague)
After completing her studies at the School for Applied Arts and the *Akademie Výtvarných Umění* (Academy of Art) in Prague, Burešová was interned in the Theresienstadt ghetto in July 1942. She worked in the official *Lautscher* workshop, producing copies from the old Masters. She was drawn to the performing arts, producing animated posters as well as portraits of the noted theatrical impresario Kurt Gerron and the composer Gideon Klein. She remained in the ghetto until liberation, after which she once again settled in Prague.

Lustig, Parik, *Seeing Through Paradise*, 1991, p.83. Zeitoun, *La Masque de la Barbarie*, 1998, p.102.

Jan BURKA (Prague 1924–lives in Vaucluse)
A pupil of Peter Kien in Prague (1939), Burka was exposed to both the Old Master tradition and to contemporary theories of expression. Burka's father (a non-Jew), was sent to a labour camp near Pilsen; his (Jewish) mother survived the war in the family's apartment in Prague. With his brother Raymond, Burka was deported to Theresienstadt on 8 August 1942 (Transport BA-115). In the empty space below the mansard roof in the children's quarters, the Burka's opened a studio, furnished with illustrated art books and reproductions. A small circle of friends met twice a week to discuss art theory. Notable among the works produced are a group of studies after Lippi, Dürer and Rembrandt, life drawings and detailed drawings of agricultural machines (ploughs, wagons and wheels). Jan's ambition had long been to enrol in the Royal Academy of Fine Arts in Amsterdam, and this he succeeded in doing at the end of the war. In 1951, he left Europe for Canada, making regular visits to France, where he settled at L'Isle-sur-la-Sorgue in 1979.

Jan Burka, *Terezín after fifty-five years, Awoken Memories* (unpublished manuscript),Yad Vashem Art Museum.

Corrado CAGLI (Ancona 1910–1976 Rome)
A co-founder of the Second Rome Art Group, Cagli was admired for public commissions, such as the Fontana de Terni (1931–35). His works were widely exhibited, notably at the Milan Triennale (1933, 1936), Venice Biennale (1936, 1948, 1952, 1957), in San Francisco and New York. An opponent of Fascism, he emigrated to Paris in 1938, and from there to New York in 1940, where he designed sets and costumes for the City Ballet. Cagli served with the US Army during the Normandy landings and took part in the liberation of Buchenwald and Nordhausen (Third Army Division). In 1945, he completed a series of pencil drawings of emaciated victims, some of these based on photographs, entitled *Scenes from Buchenwald*. After the war, he travelled through Belgium, Germany and Switzerland, returning to Rome in 1947.

Corrado Cagli, *Trenta Disegni, 1944–1945*, Edizione d'Arte Amilcare Pizzi, Milan, 1947. Corrado Cagli, *Corrado Cagli, From Cherbourg to Leipzig* (introduction by Leon Kochnitzky), Hugo Gallery, New York, 22 January–February, 1946 Enrico Crispolti, Giuseppe Marchiori, *Corrado Cagli,* Fratelli Pozzo, Turin, 1964. Ziva Amishai-Maisels, *Depiction & Interpretation, The Influence of the Holocaust on the Visual Arts*, Pergamon Press, Oxford, 1993.

Aldo CARPI (Milan 1886–1973 Milan)
Born Aldo Carpi de Resmini, he studied at the *Accademia di Brera*, Milan and held a teaching post. Arrested in 1944 for his series of paintings *Arriva l'Uragano* (The Hurricane Comes) and suspected collaboration with the Resistance, he was deported to Mauthausen and Gusen camps. Liberated in 1945, Carpi published a harrowing account of these experiences in *Diario di Gusen*, an illustrated diary containing 150 drawings.

Aldo Carpi, *Diario di Gusen*, Garzanti, Milan, 1971. Novitch, *Spiritual Resistance*, 1981, pp.64–73.

Isaac CELNIKIER (Warsaw 1923–lives in Paris)
Between 1934 and 1938, Celnikier was placed in the care of the notable educator and paediatrician Janusz Korczak, who encouraged Celnikier's precocious talent. Escaping Warsaw with his mother and sister in November 1939, Celnikier found refuge in Bialystok. The town fell to the German Army on 28 June 1941 and thereafter its Jewish population was confined to the ghetto, and Celnikier remained there until its violent liquidation in August 1943. He was arrested in Lomza and deported to camps in Stutthof, Birkenau, Sachsenhausen, and Flossenbürg. After the camp's liberation in April 1945, he was briefly interned in a Soviet refugee camp at Šumperk, Moravia from where he fled, settling in Prague. From 1946–52, Celnikier studied painting under the Czech modernist Emile Filla. Returning to Warsaw in 1952, he organised (with Andrzej Wróblewski) the controversial 'Arsenal' exhibition. In 1957, Celnikier settled in France, whose culture and language he felt a deep affinity with. He was awarded the distinction of *Chevalier des Arts et Lettres* (1967). In 1969, he began the suite of etchings *La Mémoire Gravée*, completed some twenty years later. The Israel Museum, Jerusalem (1967), Tel Aviv Museum of Art (1976), Musée des Augustins, Toulouse, National Gallery, Warsaw and Musée Fabre, Montpellier (1993), have held major exhibitions.

Isaac Celnikier, Musée des Augustins, March–April, 1991. *Isaac Celnikier, Mémoire, Révolte, Vie*, Pavillon du Musée Fabre, Montpellier, 16 April–10 May, 1993. *Isaac Celnikier*, Arsenal de Pratifori, Sion 8 November–20 December 1994. Véronique Alemany-Dessaint, Danièle Baron, ed., *Créer pour Survivre*, Fédération Nationale des Déportes et Internés Résistants et Patriotes, Musée des Beaux Arts de Reims 1995, pp.62–63.

Arnold DAGHANI (Bukowina 1909–1985 Hove)
Living in Czernowitz at the time of the German invasion, Daghani (a Romanian citizen) and his wife Nonino were deported across the Bug river to the Mikhailowka labour camp in western Ukraine, where they were forcefully employed in the construction of a strategic military road (DGIV) by the Dohrmann company. Daghani and his wife witnessed the arbitrary execution of many of their fellow prisoners by the German *SS Einsatzgruppen D* and Lithuanian armed guards. Self-taught, Daghani completed a series of

portraits of camp prisoners, the living quarters, camp routines and duty guards, chronicling the precarious survival of a community. His works aroused considerable interest and Daghani was commissioned to design a mosaic emblem for the Dohrmann company's headquarters in the neighbouring town of Gaissin. In July 1943, Daghani and his wife escaped to the Bershad ghetto (aided by a Jewish shoemaker, a member of the resistance). In January 1944, while preparing to return to Bucharest, they learnt that the remaining prisoners of the Mikhailowka camp, transferred to Tarassiwka, had been murdered. On reaching Bucharest, Daghani began compiling a diary of events and continued to expand on it over the next forty years. A later, German edition of the diary, *Lasst mich leben*, was published in Tel Aviv in 1960. The detailed information contained there precipitated a judicial enquiry into the crimes committed in slave labour camps in south-western Ukraine. In 1958, the Daghanis emigrated to Israel, though they did not remain; after several years in France and Switzerland, they settled in Hove, England in 1977. His diaries and albums are held in the Arnold Daghani Archive at the Centre for German Jewish Studies, University of Sussex.

Arnold Daghani, *The Grave is in the Cherry Orchard*, Adam International Review, ed., Miron Grindea, XXIX, 1961. Monica Bohm-Duchen, *Arnold Daghani*, Diptych, London, 1987. Edward Timms, *Memories of Mikhailowka Labour Camp Testimonies in the Arnold Daghani Archive*, Centre for German Jewish Studies, University of Sussex, Research Paper no. 4, June 2000.

Léon DELARBRE (Masseveaux, Upper Rhine 1889–1974 Belfort)

A painter and curator of the Museum of Fine Arts at Belfort in the Franche-Comté district, Delarbre was a member of the Resistance branch, 'Libération-Nord'. Arrested after a tip-off from a Gestapo informer and imprisoned in January 1944 at the Friedrich Barracks near Belfort, he and fellow resistance workers were deported in March to Royallieu camp, south of Compiègne, and in April to Auschwitz and Buchenwald. Allied bombing on 24 August decimated the Gustloff factory at the entrance to Buchenwald, where Delarbre worked. In January 1945, he was deported to Dora-Mittelbau and in April to Bergen-Belsen, where he was liberated. He returned to Paris on 29 April, carrying the drawings to safety. They were acquired almost immediately by the State for the newly formed Musée Nationale d'Art Moderne and published by Editions Michel de Romilly. They were exhibited soon after at the Salon de la Libération, Salon d'Automne and in Berlin and Vienna.

Léon Delarbre, *Croquis Clandestins Auschwitz, Buchenwald, Dora, Bergen-Belsen*, Musée de la Résistance et de la Déportation de Besançon, 1995 (first published 1945). Renée Billot, *Léon Delarbre, Le peintre déporté*, Editions de l'Est, Belfort, 1989. Anne Drizard, *Léon Delarbre 1889–1974, Les Effets de la Guerre dans l'Oeuvre de Peintre Déporté*, Université Franche-Comté, 1997 (unpublished dissertation).

Adolphe FÉDER (Odessa 1887–1943 Auschwitz)

As a member of the Jewish *Bund*, 'Aizik' Feder took part in the 1905 Revolution. He fled the Ukraine at the age of nineteen for Berlin and Geneva, where he enrolled at the *Ecole Supérieure d'Art Visuel* (School of Visual Arts). As a pupil at the Académie Julian in Paris and at the Matisse Academy, he formed friendships with artists of the Montparnasse circle, among them, Otto Freundlich, Jacques Lipchitz Mané-Katz and Amadeo Modigliani, and exhibited at the *Salon d'Automne* in 1912. In 1926, Feder travelled to Palestine, where he painted and drew the locality. Returning to

Paris, he obtained French citizenship and widened his circle of artistic and intellectual contacts. After the occupation, he joined the Resistance. Arrested by Pétain's militia in June 1942, he and his wife Sima were interned at the Cherchemidi prison and in September, transferred to the Drancy transit camp. The large group of portraits of fellow inmates predates his deportation to Auschwitz in December 1943.

Novitch, *Spiritual Resistance*, 1981, pp.76–79. Kenneth Silver, Romy Golan, *The Circle of Montparnasse, Jewish Artists in Paris 1905–1945*, The Jewish Museum, New York, 1985, p.99. Pnina Rosenberg, *Salon des Refusés, L'Art dans les Camps d'Internement Français 1939–45*, Beit Lohamei Haghetaot, Spring 2000, p.49.

Karel FLEISCHMANN (Klatovy 1897–1944 Auschwitz)

On completing his studies in the Southern Bohemian town of České Budějovice, Fleischmann was admitted to the Faculty of Medicine in Prague. During a visit to Germany in 1928, Fleischmann saw and was deeply impressed by an exhibition of the works of Albrecht Durer marking the 400th anniversary of his death. Fleischmann's father (a professional graphic artist and calligrapher) encouraged his son's gifts. From then on, Fleischmann combined his vocation as an artist, an accomplished draughtsman, poet and novelist, with his medical career. He was a founder of the avant-garde group *Linie* (Line) and member of its editorial board. From 1928–38 he published several collections of short stories, poems and a novel, *Návrat* (Return), inspired by his experiences as a student in Prague. *Prázdninová cesta* (Holiday Trip), 1928, an account of a holiday in Europe, contains wood engravings and linocuts by Fleischmann; a collection of poems, *Pěsti do oblak* (Hitting the Clouds), was his last before internment (1938). In April 1942 (having rejected an invitation to emigrate to Palestine), he was deported to the Theresienstadt ghetto. He held an important post in the ghetto's health administration. The decorative flourishes that characterize his earlier works are superseded in Terezín by an altogether freer handling of line, culminating in a prolific and remarkably vivid chronicle of the ghetto, a large part of which is held at the Jewish Museum in Prague.

Karel Fleischmann, *Návrat*, České Budějovice, 1933. Markéta Petrášová, Jarmila Škochová, *Karel Fleischmann*, The Klausen Synagogue, State Jewish Museum in Prague, March–November, 1987. Lustig, Parik, *Seeing Through Paradise*, 1991, p.83. Zeitoun, Foucher, *La Masque de la Barbarie*, 1998, p.102.

Otto FREUNDLICH (Stolp, Pomerania 1878–1943 Lublin-Majdanek)

Freundlich grew up in a largely assimilated, middle-class Jewish household. He studied art history, music theory and philosophy in Berlin and Munich (1903–04) for part of this time under Heinrich Wölfflin. He broke away to spend time painting and sculpting, first in Florence and then in Paris, where he met with leading avant-garde figures. These early contacts led to his participation in the *Neue Sezession* in Berlin in 1910, the *Sonderbund* exhibition in Cologne in 1912 and the *Erster Deutscher Herbstsalon* in Berlin in 1913. Conscripted as a medical officer in the German Army in the First World War, he spent much of this time in Cologne, Bonn and Berlin until 1924. A brief association with the *Novembergruppe* and the Dadaist circle followed. Freundlich exhibited regularly at the *Salon des Indépendants* (from 1924), *Cercle Carré* (1930) and *Abstraction Création* (1934). The sculpture *Der Neue Mensch* (The New Man), 1912, was reproduced on the cover of the *Entartete Kunst* (Degenerate Art) exhibition in 1937. This same year, he participated in the international

Konstruktivisten exhibition in Basel, and with Kandinsky and others at the Salon des Réalités Nouvelles in 1938. With France's entry into the war, Freundlich was arrested as a German national and held at the *Camp de rassemblement* at Francillon par Villebaron (Loir-et-Cher), Cépoy (Loiret) and Bassens (Gironde). Freed from the camp, he found temporary refuge in Saint-Paul-de-Fenouillet in the Pyrénées orientales, where he was joined by his companion, the artist Jeanne Kosnick-Kloss. An incriminating letter to the local *préfecture* led to his arrest and transfer, on 23 February 1943, to the Degostinet assembly centre outside Paris. Freundlich was deported to the Lublin-Majdanek camp where he died on 9 March, shortly after his arrival.

Günter Aust, *Otto Freundlich, 1878–1943*, Verlag DuMont Schauberg, Cologne, 1960. Joachim Heusinger von Waldegg, *Otto Freundlich 1878–1943 Monographie mit Dokumentation und Werkverzeichnis*, Rheinland-Verlag, Cologne, 1978. Association Les Amis de Jeanne et Otto Freundlich, *Otto Freundlich* (with essays by Alain Bonfand, Christophe Duvivier, Edda Maillet, Jerome Serri, Guy Tosatto), Musée Départemental de Rochechouart, 9 June–31 August, 1988. Christophe Duvivier, Edda Maillet, Jerome Serri, eds., *Otto Freundlich et ses amis*, Musée de Pontoise, 1993.

Bedřich FRITTA (Višňová u Frýdlantu, Bohemia 1906–1944 Auschwitz)

Known in Prague for his work as a caricaturist, polemicist and graphic designer, Fritta was among the first group of inmates interned in Theresienstadt in 1941. Active in the *Aufbaukommando* (construction department), he became director and an influential member of the *Technische Abteilung* (Technical Drafting Studio), a centre of artistic life in the ghetto. Arrested with his wife and three-year-old son Tomáš for allegedly distributing 'horror propaganda' (with Felix Bloch, Leo Haas and Otto Ungar), he was tortured during interrogation in the Small Fortress and deported to Auschwitz on 26 October 1944, where he perished. His images are a scathing critique of life in detention.

Lustig, Parik, *Seeing Through Paradise*, 1991. Maisels, *Depiction & Interpretation*, 1993. Zeitoun, Foucher, *La Masque de la Barbarie*, 1998, p.102.

Wincenty GAWRON (Stara Wieś, Limanowa 1908–1991 Poland)

Studied at the National School of Decorative Art, Lvov and from 1935 at the Akademia Sztuk Pięknych w Warszawa (Academy of Fine Arts, Warsaw). Arrested in January 1941 and imprisoned in Nowy Sącz and Tarnów, he was later deported to Auschwitz. There he worked in the *Abbruch commando* (building works) and in the carpentry workshops. While planning his escape, Gawron sought refuge in the camp's hospital, volunteering to work in the sub-camp Harmęże from where, in May 1942, he was able to escape, taking with him his diary and portraits of camp inmates. He fought in the Warsaw uprising in 1944. After the war Gawron emigrated to the United States. Employed by the firm Marshall Field & Co to design and produce stained glass windows and lettering, he was subsequently appointed as Curator of the Pilsudski Museum, Chicago. His post-war works derive their subjects from his camp experiences.

Milton, Blatter, *Art of the Holocaust*, 1981, p.248. Jerzy Dałek, Teresa Świebocka, *Cierpienie I Nadzieja*, Państwowe Muzeum w Oświęcim, Katowice, 1989.

Paul GOYARD (active in Paris–)

Painter, poet and member of the Popular Front, Goyard ran a clandestine press in his Paris studio. Before the war, he worked for a time with Boris Taslitzky, designing and building theatrical backdrops. Deported to Buchenwald in 1944, he produced a group of line drawings which show scenes of carnage. Several of his drawings are in the Musée d'Histoire Contemporaine, Paris. Goyard returned to the subject of the camps after the war.

Alemany-Dessaint, Baron, *Créer pour Survivre*, 1995, pp.76–77.

Leo HAAS (Opava, Moravia 1901–1983 Berlin)

Haas studied at Karlsruhe and Berlin, forming links with the revolutionary *Spartacus* movement and establishing a reputation as a painter and illustrator. Influenced by the works of George Grosz, Otto Dix and other Expressionists, he worked for the working-class press in Vienna. Arrested by the Gestapo, he was interned in Nisko camp near Lublin, in German-occupied Poland. Deported to Theresienstadt in December 1942, he was active in the *Technische Abteilung* (Technical Drafting Studio) with Felix Bloch, Bedrich Fritta and Otto Ungar. Arrested and imprisoned in the Small Fortress for allegedly distributing *Greuelpropaganda* or 'horror propaganda', he was interned at Auschwitz, Sachsenhausen and Mauthausen concentration camps. Liberated at Ebensee, he returned to Prague, working as a caricaturist on the Czech Party daily *Rudé Právo*. In 1947, Haas produced a suite of 12 lithographs based on his camp experiences. A committed socialist, he moved to East Berlin in 1955 and was appointed Professor of the *Akademie der Künste* and editor of the Journal *Eulenspiegel*. Haas was instrumental in securing the works of other artists in Terezín. His essay, *The Affair of the Painters of Terezín* (published in 1965), documents the experience of besieged artists in the ghetto.

Leo Hass, 'The Affair of the Painters of Terezín', reprinted in Lustig, Parik, *Seeing Through Paradise*, pp.63–68. Lawrence Langer, ed. 'Painters of Terezín' in *Art from the Ashes, A Holocaust Anthology*, Oxford University Press, New York 1995, pp.663–81. Zeitoun, Foucher, *La Masque de la Barbarie*, 1998, p.103.

Osias HOFSTATTER (Bochnia, Galicia 1905–1995 Ramat Gan)

Osias Hofstatter grew up in an observant Jewish household. When the Russian army invaded Galicia in 1914, the family moved to Vienna and soon after to Schevenin-gen, Holland. In 1919–20 they settled in Germany where Hofstatter attended the Jüdische Realschule, Frankfurt-am-Mein and took a precocious interest in the German language, philosophy and culture. There followed a 'quiet period' in Vienna (1921–38). With the *Anschluss*, all the members of Hofstatter's family were arrested and his parents deported to death camps. In 1937, Hofstatter met his future wife, Anna-Maria Schebestova. The couple sheltered in the Marneffe refugee camp (60km outside Brussels). But on his return to Brussels, Hofstatter was arrested and interned at St Cyprien (May 1940) and Gurs camps in the Pyrénées orientales. In October 1941, he obtained leave from the camp on medical grounds. With the help of Anna Manuguettes, he escaped to the Swiss border where he was detained at the Igel, Wald and Birmensdorf camps. In 1943 he was released and moved to Zurich, where he studied at the *Kunstgewerbeschule* under Johaness Itten and Walter Rosshardt and after May 1945, at the *Akademie für Angewandte Kunst* (Academy for

Applied Art) in Vienna. Reunited after the war, the Hofstatters returned to Poland where he worked for the Warsaw communist press. In 1957, they emigrated to Israel, where he returned to themes of the Holocaust.

Benjamin Tamuz, Dorit Levité, eds., *Hofstatter*, Hakkibutz Hameuchad, Israel, 1980. Yoav Dagon, Benjamin Tamuz, eds., *Hofstatter, Paintings*, Massada, Tel Aviv, 1989. Yoav Dagon, Osias Hofstatter, Masterpieces from the Artist's Collection, Herzliya Museum of Art, November 1990–January 1991. Rachel Sukman, *Osias Hofstatter, The Early Years*, Yad Vashem Museum of Art, Jerusalem, 1992.

Franciszek JAŹWIECKI (Cracow 1900–1946 Świdnica)

He completed his studies at the Akademia Sztuk Pięknych (Academy of Fine Arts, Cracow) in 1933. While working as a civilian in the transit camp in Waska Street, Cracow, he helped prisoners escape by forging false identity papers. Arrested at Montelupich prison in Cracow, on 1 December, he was deported to Auschwitz. He worked in the camp's 'painting room' producing signs, posters and other artefacts. In March 1943 he was transferred to the Gross-Rosen camp, and from there to Sachsenhausen and Helberstadt (a satellite of Buchenwald). He was liberated near Zwönitz. He is perhaps best remembered for the series of more than 113 portraits of fellow prisoners produced in Auschwitz and other camps.

Milton, Blatter, *Art of the Holocaust*, 1981. Dałek, Świebocka, *Cierpienie I Nadzieja*, 1989, p.141.

Karol KONIECZNY (Cieszyn 1919–   )

Active in various Communist youth organizations before 1937, he enrolled at the Cracow School of Fine and Industrial Arts. His studies were interrupted by the war. He was captured by the German army while working on defensive fortifications around the town of Cierlic on 18 September 1939, and deported to Buchenwald, escaping from the train at Katowice. There followed a series of arrests and escapes culminating in his trial before a *Volksgericht* (People's Court) in Berlin. Konieczny was interned at Buchenwald where, after hard labour in the camp's stone quarry, he was placed by Communist comrades in Block 36, Class A. As head of the Socialist Worker's Party (RPPS) he organised various cultural activities in the main camp. He then survived a series of pseudo-medical experiments. Evacuated on 10 April, he was liberated by the US Third Army on 3 May 1945. After his liberation, Konieczny resumed his studies at the Warsaw Academy of Art.

Milton, Blatter, *Art of the Holocaust*, 1981, pp.253–54.

Mieczysław KOŚCIELNIAK (Kalisz 1912–1993 Słupsk)

Painter and graphic artist, he studied at the Akademia Sztuk Pięknych (Academy of Fine Arts, Cracow) under Professor J Mehoffer before moving to Warsaw where, in 1935, he published a suite of ten illustrations to Homer's *Iliad*. In 1939, he was called up to military service with the Polish army, fought against the Germans at Kutno and was wounded in the defence of Warsaw. In Kalisz, he joined the *Związek Walki Zbrojnej* (Association of Armed Struggle). Arrested and imprisoned in 1941, the Nazis insisted that his painting, *Aznyka Aznyk*, 1928 (which commemorated the shooting of Poles under Kaiser Wilhelm,) was evidence of his nationalist sympathies for which, in the spring of 1941, he was deported to Auschwitz and his papers stamped *Rückkehr Unerwünscht* (return unwanted). Employed in the gravel pits and road-paving division, the infamous *Abbruch 2*

(demolition squad), he became critically ill and was helped by the camp's Polish medical corps. With Wincenty Gawron, Kościelniak was transferred to the SS-owned *Deutsche Ausrüstungswerke* enterprise and later appointed *Unterkunftskammer* (sorting personal effects from recent arrivals). His duties included the custody of the museum's collection. He was also commissioned to paint frescoes in *Der Haus den Waffen (*the SS officer's club in Oświęcim). A store containing artist's materials and a small printing press provided valuable materials. Kościelniak's clandestine works and correspondence were smuggled out of the camp by Josef Szpyra. In January 1945, he took part in 'death marches' to Mauthausen, Melke and Ebensee (liberated 6 May 1945). After the war, Kościelniak produced a series of larger drawings and fully worked watercolours recording the lives of prisoners (Auschwitz Museum).

Milton, Blatter, *Art of the Holocaust*, 1981, p.248. M. Koscielniak, *Bilder von Auschwitz*, Dominikanerkloster, Frankfurt, 6–24 November, 1982. Dałek, Świebocka, *Cierpienie I Nadzieja*, 1989, p.143.

Josef KOWNER (Kiev 1895–1967 Colmar)

Kowner's father was a respected professor of Latin and Mathematics and established a Gymnasium in Lodz. Josef went on to study at the Academy of Art in Saint Petersburg and Düsseldorf, Kassel and Paris. He held exhibitions in Cracow, Warsaw, Lvov and Lodz. He joined the avant-garde circle of artists *Forma*, and became a member of its editorial board, together with the constructivist artist Władysław Strzemiński (1893–1952). At the outbreak of the war he entered the Lodz ghetto, working in the rug factory and producing cartoons and designs for handmade rugs based on his drawings. He is one of only two artists to have received official sanction from the ghettos *Judenälteste* Mordechai Rumkowski (the second, was Vincent Brauner), enabling them to work and exhibit their works freely. During the liquidation of the ghetto, Kowner was able to conceal his drawings and later recovered them. In August 1944 he was deported to Birkenau and from January was forced to take part in the 'death march' ,which ended for him in Döblin, Germany. In July 1945, ill and wounded, he applied for and obtained asylum from the Swedish authorities, settling in Colmar, where Kowner continued to paint and exhibit his work.

Susan Nashman Fraiman, Yad Vashem Art Museum.

Roman KRAMSTYCK (Warsaw 1885–1942 Warsaw)

Kramstyck first exhibited with the *Zachęta* group in Warsaw (National Institute for the Visual Arts). In 1912, he took part in exhibitions in Paris, Barcelona, the Berlin *Sezession* (and after 1914, the *Neue Sezession*). Following the First World War, he also participated in the Venice Biennale as well as exhibitions in London, Moscow and New York. A gifted portraitist, his works included a *Portrait of the pianist Arthur Rubinstein*, 1914 (Jewish Historical Institute, Warsaw) and *The poet Jan Lechoń*, 1919 (National Museum, Warsaw). During the German occupation of Poland, Kramstyck (a baptized Jew) was interned in the Warsaw ghetto where, in the summer 1942, he was killed in a Nazi *aktion*.

Magdalena Sieramska, Żydowski Instytut Historyczny, Warsaw.

Leon LANDAU (Antwerp 1910–1945 Bergen-Belsen)

Landau's family emigrated to Palestine in the 1920s and returned to Belgium, where Landau studied theatre design at the *Koninklijke Academie voor Schone Kunsten* (Academy of

Fine Arts), Antwerp and *Ecole National Supérieure des Arts Visuels de la Cambre*, Brussels. He was employed as a stage and costume designer by the *Koninklijke Nederlandse Schouwburg* (Royal Netherlands Theatre). After the German invasion of Belgium, Landau was interned in Malines transit camp where he designed a marionette theatre for a children's production of *Thyl Uylenspiegel*. Deported to Auschwitz, then to Bergen-Belsen, Landau perished shortly after liberation on 15 April 1945, while nursing a friend during the camp's typhus epidemic.

Novitch, *Spiritual Resistance*, 1981, pp.112–15.

Israel LEJZEROWICZ (1905–1944)
Details pertaining to Israel Lejzerowicz's life and work are scarce. A painter and graphic artist, he was active in the Lodz ghetto c.1941–4. Two colour drawings (Yad Vashem, Art Museum) describe the disposal of effluents from the ghetto during the harsh winter 1941–42. The treatment of similar subjects by Josef Kowner and Hirsch Szylis suggests a possible association with these artists. According to Nachman Sonnabend, an exhibition of the work of ghetto artists was held in Lodz. This included works by Victor Brauner, Sara Gilksman-Fajtlowitz, Josef Kowner, Amos Szwarc, Szymon Szerman, Hirsch Szylis and Maurycy Trębacz, as well as Israel Lejzerowicz.

Jacob LIFCHITZ (Kovno 1903–1944 Dachau)
Lifchitz spent his entire professional career in Kovno. He studied at the Institute of Art, eventually joining the faculty, teaching etching and engraving techniques. He was highly regarded for his illustrations, a number of which were published in books and teaching manuals. Lifchitz contributed with Esther Lurie and Josef Schlesinger to the ghetto's clandestine archive, commissioned by the *Altestenrat* Elkhanan Elkes. The similarities in their choice of subjects and medium (pen and ink on paper) are revealing.

Dennis B. Klein, ed., *Hidden History of the Kovno Ghetto*, United States Holocaust Memorial Museum, Washington, 1997, pp.168–170.

Esther LURIE (Liepaja, Latvia 1913–1998 Tel Aviv)
Lurie studied at the *Ecole National Supérieure des Arts Visuels de la Cambre*, Brussels and the *Koninklijke Academie voor Schone Kunsten* (Academy of Fine Arts) in Antwerp under René Leclerq. There she came into contact with the work of the Expressionists James Ensor and Constant Permeke. In 1934, she joined her family in Palestine and worked at the Hebrew Theatre. Awarded the prestigious Dizengoff prize for art in 1938, Lurie returned to Antwerp and resumed her studies under Isidor Oppenheimer. A visit to Kovno at the outbreak of war, prohibited her departure and she remained in the Kovno Ghetto until its liquidation in July, 1944. She was deported to Stutthof and Leibitsch camps until liberation in 1945. Lurie was able to reconstruct the subjects of the drawings and watercolours produced in the ghetto, later lost, from photographs of the originals taken by Avraham Tory. Lurie emigrated to Israel, returning to camp themes in late works; her book *A Living Witness*, tells of her wartime experiences.

Esther Lurie, *Edut Haya*, Dvir, Tel Aviv, 1958. Novitch, *Spiritual Resistance*, 1981, p.118. Milton, Blatter, *Art of the Holocaust*, 1981, pp.256–67. Klein, *Hidden History of the Kovno Ghetto*, 1997, pp.168–170.

Ludwig MEIDNER (Silesia 1884–1966 Darmstadt)
Meidner studied at the Königliche Kunstschule (Royal Art School), Breslau (1903–5) and the Académie Julian, Paris. The most gifted member of the short-lived *Pathetiker* group, he exhibited with Jakob Steinhardt and Richard Janthur at Herwarth Walden's Galerie Der Sturm in November 1912. His works were reviewed in the journal *Die Aktion*. In 1916–18, he served in the German infantry as a French translator in a prisoner-of-war camp. His first solo exhibition at the Galerie Paul Cassirer in Berlin (1918) coincided with the publication of his book *Im Nacken das Sternenmeer*. He was a founding member of the socialist Arbeitsrat für Kunst (Workers' Council for Art) and the Novembergruppe. But in the 1920s, Meidner disavowed his expressionist works. In 1929, in the *Deutsche Allgemeine Zeitung*, he published an article proclaiming his Jewishness. Escalating anti-Semitism forced him to leave Berlin in 1933. Eighty-four works were seized from public institutions. *Selbstporträt*, 1912, was displayed in the Nazi's *Entartete Kunst* exhibition under the heading 'Revelations of the Jewish Soul'. Following the events of *Kristallnacht* on 9 November 1938, Meidner and his family prepared to leave Germany. With the help of Augustus John, they found refuge in England. On arrival, Meidner was interned as an 'enemy alien' in Liverpool and the Isle of Man (finding there a community of German-speaking Jewish and non-Jewish exiles). Aware of the tragedy that had befallen his fellow Jews, he produced a cycle of images he referred to as *Massacres in Poland*, 1943–48 (Jüdisches Museum, Frankfurt am Main). He returned to Germany in 1953 and was awarded the Order of Merit from the Federal Republic and the Villa Romana Prize. He was elected to the Berlin Akademie der bildenden Künste in 1964.

Stephanie Barron, ed., *Degenerate Art, The Fate of the Avant-Garde in Nazi Germany*, Los Angeles County Museum of Art, 1991. Gerda Breuer, Ines Wagemann, *Ludwig Meidner, Zeichner, Maler, Literat 1884–1966*, Mathildenhöhe, Darmstadt, 1991. Palais des Beaux Arts, Brussels *Art et Résistance, Les Peintres Allemands de l'Entre Deux Guerres, La Collection Marvin et Janet Fishman* Snoeck-Ducaju & Zoon, Gent, 1995. Shulamith Behr, *Expressionism, Movement in Modern Art*, Tate Gallery, London, 1999.

Zoran MUSIC (Gorizia 1909–lives in Paris)
Music studied at the Académie des Beaux Arts in Zagreb under the Croatian painter Babic (a pupil of Franz von Struck). Babic awakened in him an admiration for Spanish painting and for Goya and El Greco in particular. He spent a year copying the masters in the Prado, the Escorial Palace and Toledo (1935–36). The civil war ended his sojourn in Spain and Music returned to the Carsole. In 1943, he made the first of several visits to Venice. Italy invaded Slovenia. Music was detained by the Gestapo and accused of collaborating with anti-Nazi groups. He was imprisoned in Trieste and deported to the Dachau concentration camp. Music succeeded in drawing the mounds of corpses and the crematorium. Liberated in April 1945, he returned to Gorizia, and to Venice (two works were exhibited in the 1948 Venice Biennale). Music's first Paris exhibition at the Galerie de France, in 1952, proved a turning point for his career. He established friendships with Alberto Giacometti and Francis Bacon (two artists he admired greatly). In 1970, he began work on the series *We are not the last*, which recaptured his experiences in Dachau. A retrospective exhibition was held at the Grand Palais, Paris in 1995.

Jean Clair, *Zoran Music*, Réunion des Musées Nationaux, Grand Palais, Paris, April–July 1995 (with essays by Michael Peppiatt, Michael Gibson). Jean Leymarie, *Zoran Music, Nous ne sommes pas les derniers, Peintures, Dessins, Gravures*, Musée des Beaux-Arts de Caen, 18 May–16 August 1995 (essays by Michael Gibson, Patti Cadby Birch). Michael Peppiatt, *Zoran Music*, Sainsbury Centre for Visual Arts, University of East Anglia, Norwich, February–April 2000 and Estorick Collection of Modern Italian Art, London, June–September 2000.

František Mořitz NÁGL (Telč 1900–1944 Auschwitz)
After studying at the School for Applied Arts and
Akademie Výtvarných Umění (Academy of Art) in Prague
under Professor Schweiger, he was deported from Třebíč
to Terezín on 22 May 1942 (Transport Aw169). He
produced a large body of watercolours and gouaches
which observe in detail the dormitories, courtyards and
fortifications (these were discovered in the attic to the
Magdeburg Barracks in 1950). He was deported on the last
transport to Auschwitz (Ev 1351) on 28 October 1944.

Lustig, Parik, *Seeing Through Paradise*, 1991, p.85. Zeitoun,
Foucher, *La Masque de la Barbarie*, 1998, p.104.

**Felix NUSSBAUM (Osnabrück 1904–1944
Auschwitz)**
Nussbaum studied in Hamburg and *Akademie der Künste*,
Berlin (1924–29). In 1932, he exhibited at the Berlin
Sezession and was awarded a Rome Prize. Much of his early
work was destroyed in a studio fire. The rise of anti-Semi-
tism forced him to flee Rome in 1933 and, unable to
return to Germany, he travelled through France and
Belgium, settling in Brussels with his wife, the artist Felka
Platek (1899–1944). Following Germany's occupation of
Belgium, Nussbaum was arrested and deported to St
Cyprien in the Pyrénées orientales. He escaped and spent
the next four years in hiding. The works of this period are
among his most powerful. In 1944, he and Felka were
recaptured and deported to Auschwitz in the last wave of
Jewish deportations. Major retrospective exhibition were
held at Osnabrück Kulturgeschichtliches Museum,
Wilhelm Lehmbruck Museum, Duisburg (1988) and the
Israel Museum, Jerusalem 1998.

Avram Kampf, *Chagall to Kitaj, Jewish Experience in Twentieth
Century Art*, Lund Humphries, Barbican Art Gallery, London,
1990. Palais des Beaux Arts, Brussels, *Art et Résistance, Les Pein-
tres Allemands de l'Entre Deux Guerres, La Collection Marvin et
Janet Fishman* Snoeck-Ducaju & Zoon, Gent 1995. Karl George
Kaster, *Felix Nussbaum: Art Defamed, Art in Exile, Art in Resis-
tance, A Biography* (translated by Eileen Martin), The Overlook
Press, Woodstock, New York, 1997.

David OLÈRE (Warsaw 1902–85 Paris)
On completing his studies at the Academy of Fine Art in
Warsaw (at the age of sixteen), Olère moved to Danzig
and Berlin. In 1921, he was hired by Ernst Lubitsch at
Europäische Film Allianz to build sets for the film *Les Amours
de Pharaon*. In 1923, he moved to Paris, settling in Montparnasse. There he designed costumes and publicity
posters for Paramount Pictures. In 1930, he married Juli-
ette Ventura and became a French citizen. Arrested by the
French police and interned at Drancy, he was deported to
Auschwitz on 2 March 1943. Olère was one of only six
survivors of the 49th convoy, attached to the *Sonderkommando* in Crematorium III. In January 1945, he took part
in the 'death march' to Mathausen and Melk, and was
liberated by the American Army at Ebensee on 6 May.
Olère returned to Paris. He recalled his experience of the
camps in a series of over seventy drawings produced after
the war.

David Olère, *The Eyes of a Witness, A painter in the Sonderkom-
mando at Auschwitz*, The Beate Klarsfeld Foundation, New
York, 1989. Serge Klarsfeld, *Memorial to the Jews Deported from
France 1942–44*, The Beate Klarsfeld Foundation, New York,
1983. Serge Klarsfeld, ed., *Out of the Depths, David Olère, An
Artist in Auschwitz*, Yad Vashem, The Holocaust Martyrs &
Heroes Remembrance Authority. Pnina Rosenberg, *David
Olère, Witness, Images of Auschwitz*, Beit Lohamei Haghetaot,
Israel, 1998.

Halina OLOMUCKI (Warsaw 1921–lives in Ashkelon)
Olomucki was interned in the Warsaw Ghetto. Self-taught,
her harrowing portrayal of ghetto life includes the faces of
vanished friends, the deportation and transport of prisoners
from the *Umschlagplatz* (railway station), the ghetto uprising
of March–May 1943 and the liquidation of Dr Korczak's
orphanage. With the help of friends, she was able to
smuggle her works to the Aryan Quarter of the city.
Deported to Majdaneck and Auschwitz-Birkenau (employed
by the *Stubendienst* to make signs and decorations), she
survived to see the liberation. She returned to Warsaw,
pursuing formal studies at Lodz Academy of Art under
Stefan Wegner, emigrating to Paris in 1957 and Israel in
1972.

Milton, Blatter, *Art of the Holocaust*, 1981, p.260. Novitch,
Spiritual Resistance, 1981, pp.154–59.

Otto PANKOK (Mulheim 1893–1966 Hünxe-Drevenack)
Pankok studied at the Kunstakademie, Düsseldorf and
Weimar. Van Gogh's drawings of miners in the Borinage
and the tragic perception of life encountered in the works of
Käthe Kollwitz and Ernst Barlach made a deep impression.
Pankok was severely wounded in active duty during the
First World War. In 1920, he became a member of *Das Junge
Rheinland* with Jankel Adler, Otto Dix, Karl Schwesig and
Gert Wollheim. From 1924 he increasingly gave up colour,
producing bold black-and-white drawings executed in
charcoal, which best suited his expressive realism. His
encounter with the gypsy communities at Saintes-Maries
and at Heinefeld, near Düsseldorf (1931) gave rise to a group
of drawings on this subject. His plans to exhibit a cycle of
drawings on the *Passion* was opposed by the Nazis and printing blocks for an edition were destroyed. Examples of his
work were included in the Nazi's *Entartete Kunst* exhibition
in 1937. After the war, Pankok was reinstated to his post as
professor at the Kunstakademie, Düsseldorf. In 1950, he
was commissioned to paint the *Gelsenkirchen* memorial to
Jews and Gypsies who perished in the camps.

Bernhard Mensch, Karin Stempel, ed., *Otto Pankok 1893–1966,
Retrospektive zum 100 Geburtstag*, Plitt Verlag, Oberhausen, 1993.

Lili RILIK-ANDRIEUX (Berlin 1914–)
Growing up in a largely assimilated, middle-class Jewish
family, Rilik-Andrieux (née Abraham) attended the
Hochschule für Kunsterzeichnung in Berlin (1933–37) and
the Académie Ranson in Paris (1938). In May 1940 she was
interned, via Alençon, at Gurs camp (the subject of a small
number of recently identified works) until November 1941.
Housed briefly at the Terminus Hotel in Marseilles (a shelter
for women and children), she was transferred to camp Les
Milles. She contracted typhus and was hospitalised in Aix,
where she remained until 1946, working as a translator for
the American Army and emigrating to the United States
later that year.

Novitch, *Spiritual Resistance*, 1981, pp.160–61. Rosenberg, *Salon
des Refusés*, 2000, p.46

Bruno SCHULZ (Drohobycz 1892–1942 Drohobycz)
The youngest son a Jewish rag merchant, Schulz grew up
outside the dominant German-speaking culture of Galicia,
adopting Polish rather than Yiddish as his language. He
enrolled briefly in Lvov Polytechnic, studying architecture
and joining the *Kelleia* circle of artists which included the
writer Emanuel Pilpel and the collector Stanisław

Wiengarten. The group of etchings, *A Book of Idolatry*, was published in 1922 and Schulz moved to Warsaw in the following year. An exhibition of his drawings in Truskawiec attracted adverse attention but was vehemently defended by supporters. His first book, *Cinnamon Shop* (1933), was enthusiastically received. While working on the Polish translation of Kafka's *The Trial*, in 1937, Schulz formally rescinded his former ties with the Jewish Community to remove legal barriers preventing his marriage to Józefina Szelińska, a Roman Catholic (their engagement was broken off). Schulz's *Sanatorium under the Sign of the Hourglass* was published in 1937. His stories, articles and drawings appeared regularly in leading journals. Schulz was awarded the 'Golden Laurel' by the Polish Academy in 1938. In July 1941, German troops seized Drohobycz. Jews were confined to the ghetto or deported to the Belzec death camp. Schulz was offered a post as librarian of a valuable collection of Judaica, entrusting his own manuscripts, drawings and papers to friends outside. On 'Black Thursday' 230 people were killed in the streets. Schulz was shot twice in the head by *SS Scharführer* Karl Günter. After the war, his works were banned as ideologically unacceptable and reinstated only after a loosening of Stalinist controls during Khrushchev's premiership.

Bruno Schulz, The Book of Idolatry (introduction by Jerzy Ficowski, translated by Bogna Piotrowska), Interpress, Warsaw, 1988. Wojciech Chmurzynski, ed., *Bruno Schulz (1892–1942), Ad Memoriam. Drawings and Documents from the Collection of the Muzeum Literatury im Adama Mickiewicza w Warszawie*, Adam Mickiewicz Literature Museum, Warsaw, 1995. Jerzy Ficowski, ed., *The collected works of Bruno Schulz*, Picador, London, 1998.

Karl SCHWESIG (Gelsenkirchen, 1898–1995 Düsseldorf)

Schwesig studied at the *Kunstakademie*, Düsseldorf. A member of the Weimar *Novembrists* and *Das Junge Rheinland*, he exhibited with Jankel Adler, Otto Dix, Otto Pankok and Gert Wollheim. A member of the Communist Party and outspoken anti-Nazi, he was arrested in 1933 and brutally tortured, an experience recorded in the cycle *Schlegelkeller*. After his release, Schwesig obtained political asylum in Belgium. He was active for the Republican cause in the Spanish Civil War. During a visit to Moscow in 1937, his German citizenship was revoked. In 1940, Schwesig was arrested and interned in Antwerp, and deported to St Cyprien, Gurs and Noe camps in the French Pyrénées orientales. On 1 June, 1943, he was imprisoned at the Fort Romainville in Paris, from where he was transferred to the Ulmer Hoch prison in Düsseldorf in 1945. His suite of etchings *Les Inutiles*, published in 1949, contains a searing account of the camp system and its hapless victims.

Karl Schwesig, Paintings, Watercolours, Graphics, Documents, Galerie Remmert und Barth, Düsseldorf, 9 September–7 November 1981. Ulrich Krempel, *Am Anfang, Das Junge Rheinland, Zur Kunst und Zeitgeschichte einer Region, 1918–45*, Städtische Kunsthalle, Düsseldorf, 9 February–8 April 1985. F. Schaaf, *Radierfolge Les Inutiles (Die Nutzlosen) von Karl Schwesig (1898–1955)*, Justizvollzugsschule, Rheinland-Pfalz, Wittlich, July 1997.

Władysław SIWEK (Niepołomice 1905–1983 Warsaw)

Siwek studied at the Akademia Sztuk Pięknych (Academy of Fine Arts, Cracow). Arrested in January 1940 for his collaboration with the Resistance, he was imprisoned at Montelupich and Tarnów from where, on 8 October, he was deported to Auschwitz. Assigned to hard labour, he was later appointed to the camp's 'painting workshop', which produced a variety of signs and posters, construction drawings and models, as well as works of a decorative kind. In the *Baubüro*, Siwek and fellow inmates built a maquette of

Auschwitz camp. In October 1944, he was transferred to the Heinkel aircraft factory at Sachsenhausen and was liberated near Schwerin on 3 May 1945, returning to Poland two years later. A gifted draughtsman and caricaturist, he produced a series of portraits of SS officers facing trial for atrocities committed in Auschwitz. In 1948–53, Siwek, Kościelniak and others were commissioned by Państwowe Muzeum w Oświęcim Brzezinka (Auschwitz Museum) to make drawings and other works depicting the lives of prisoners in the camp.

Milton, Blatter, *Art of the Holocaust*, 1981, p.264. Dałek, Świebocka, *Cierpienie i Nadzieja*, 1989, p.24.

Włodzimierz SIWIERSKI (Chelmno 1905–84 Warsaw)

Painter and conservator, Siwierski studied at the Chudozestwienno-Promyszlennom Institute in Omsk (1918–20), the Chudozestwiennych Mastierskich in Moscow (1921–23) and the Sorbonne in Paris (1929–33). During the German occupation he lived in Warsaw, painting portraits, landscapes and still lives. Arrested in September 1940 he was placed in the Pawiak prison, from where he was transferred to Auschwitz. Employed in the carpentry workshop, he made children's toys and decorative ornaments on commission. Released in March 1942, he succeeded in smuggling his drawings of fellow prisoners and work details out of the camp. These are preserved in precarious condition at Państwowe Muzeum w Oświęcim Brzezinka (Auschwitz Museum). After the war Siwierski resumed a successful career as an exhibiting artist and founder in 1945 of the Association of Polish Artists (ZPAP).

Milton, Blatter, *Art of the Holocaust*, 1981, p.264. Elizabeth Maxwell, Roman Halter, *Remembering for the Future, Original Drawings and Reproductions by Victims of the Holocaust 1940–1945*, Oxford, 1988. Dałek, Świebocka, *Cierpienie i Nadzieja*, 1989, p.25.

Joseph E A SPIER (Zutphen 1900–1978 USA)

Spier is known principally for his album of lithographs *Bilder Aus Theresienstadt* containing eighteen views of the ghetto produced for a visit by Red Cross officials on 23 June 1944. With titles like *Am Marktplatz, Im Stadtzentrum, Kasperltheater im Kinderheim*, the hand-coloured booklet portrayed Theresienstadt as a sanitized community where life continued normally in spite of the war, reinforced the Nazi view. He was a member of both the *Lautscher* workshop and the *Technische Abteilung* (Technical Drafting Studio) under Bedřich Fritta, remaining in the ghetto until May 1945, when Spier returned to his home in Holland and emigrated to the United States.

Lustig, Parik, *Seeing Through Paradise*, 1991, p.85. Zeitoun, Foucher, *La Masque de la Barbarie*, 1998, p.104.

Jakob STEINHARDT (Poznan 1887–1968 Nahariya)

An accomplished painter and printmaker, Steinhardt trained at the school of the Berlin Museum of Arts and Crafts. He was co-founder with Ludwig Meidner and Richard Janthur, of the short-lived *Die Pathetiker* group, exhibiting his work at Herwarth Walden's Galerie Der Sturm, in November 1912. As a conscript in the German Army in the First World War, Steinhardt visited Jewish communities in Eastern Europe, awakening in him an interest in Jewish popular culture or *Yiddishkeit*. As a member of the Berlin *Sezession*, he attended its social and artistic gatherings, meeting Lovis Corinth, Conrad Felixmüller, Arno Nadel and Arnold Zweig, among others. Shortly after Hitler's accession to power in 1933, Steinhardt emigrated to Palestine, settling in Jerusalem and joining the Bezalel Academy. He became its director in 1953.

Jakob Steinhardt, *Hagaddah shel Pesach*, Berlin, 1924 (facsimile edition by Franzisca Baruch, DVIR, Tel Aviv, 1979). Ziva Amishai Maisels, *Jakob Steinhardt, Etchings and Lithographs* DVIR Jerusalem, 1981. Inka Bertz, *The Prophet's Pathos and the Communality of the Ghetto: Jakob Steinhardt's Work Before and After WWI*; reproduced in *Jacob and Israel, Homeland and Identity in the work of Jakob Steinhardt*, The Open Museum Industrial Park, Tefen, January, 1998.

Józef SZAJNA (Rzeszów 1922–lives in Warsaw)

A member of the Polish underground, Szajna was arrested while crossing the border into Hungary in January 1941. He was detained in prisons at Spisz, Murszyna, Nowy Sącz and Tarnów and deported to Auschwitz on 25 July. He was placed on two occasions in the infamous punishment cell, Block 11. On 21 January 1945 he was transferred to Buchenwald and to the Schönebeck sub-camp near Magdeburg. In a deliberately abstract and highly conceptual group of drawings, he portrayed the terrible conditions and degrading anonymity of the camps. Assertions of this kind represented an act of resistance. In 1948–53, he trained at the Akademia Sztuk Pięknych (Academy of Fine Arts) in Cracow, joined the MARG group of artists and was co-founder and director of the *Teatr Ludowy* (Peoples Theatre) in Nowa Huta. Szajna's installation *Reminiscencje* (Reminiscences), 1969, combines painting, with theatrical props and life-size photographs of the artist in the striped uniform of a prisoner, to evoke memories of internment.

Elżbieta Morawiec, Jerzy Madayeski, *Józef Szajna*, Wydawnictwo Literackie, Cracow 1974. Aleksander Wojciechowski, *Młode malarstwo polskie 1944–1974*, Ossolineum, Warsaw, 1983. Venice, Biennale, *Józef Szajna*, 1990. Maisels, *Depiction & Interpretation*, 1993, pp.248–50, 285–86.

Boris TASLITZKY (Paris 1901–lives in Paris)

The son of Jewish refugees from Russia, Taslitzky studied painting, sculpture and tapestry design under Jacques Lipschitz and Jean Lurçat at the Ecole des Beaux Arts. From 1935, he was Secretary of the Union of Painters & Sculptors, Maison de la Culture and founded the *Journal des peintres et sculpteurs de la Maison de la Culture*. An activist in the Communist Party, he designed and built floats for the *Front Populaire* in 1936. Taslitzky served briefly in the French Army and was arrested at Melun prison in July 1940. In October, Lurçat gave him refuge at the Aubusson tapestry workshops. Restless and isolated, he returned to Paris and was active for the *Front National pour la Libération de la France*. Arrested in November 1941, he was interned at Guéret, Clermont-Ferrand and Riom prisons where, obtaining paper and ink, he drew incessantly. Two hundred drawings were confiscated at the Mauzac military prison. In November 1943, Taslitzky was interned in St Sulpice-le-Point and in August 1944, he was deported to Buchenwald. He made several hundred drawings of the camp. One of these was published by André Fougeron in the Resistance journal *Vaincre* in 1944. He continued to work illegally, 'for myself, for my comrades and for the future'. Liberated in 1945, he returned to Paris. He was decorated with the Légion d'Honneur, *Médaille Militaire, Croix de Guerre* and remained an ardent Realist, committed to the struggle of oppressed people.

Henri Mougin, 'Boris Taslitzky ou Les Jeudis des Enfants d'Ivry', *Arts de France*, no. 4, March 1946, p.38. Jacques Gaucheron, 'Entretien avec Boris Taslitzky', *Arts de France*, nos. 29–30, 1950, pp.36–37. *Boris Taslitzky, Cent onze dessins faits à Buchenwald*, Association Française Buchenwald-Dora, Editions Hautefeuille, Paris, 1978. Günter Rieger, *Zeichnungen Boris Taslitzky, Paris*, Zentrum für Kunstausstellungen der DDR, Berlin, 1987.

Otto UNGAR (Brno 1901–1945 Blankenheim)

Ungar studied at the *Akademie Výtvarných Umĕní* (Academy of Art), Prague and taught drawing at a Jewish Gymnasium in Brno. Interned in Theresienstadt in January 1942, he was active in the *Technische Abteilung* (Technical Drafting Studio) with Felix Bloch, Bedrich Fritta and Leo Haas. Imprisoned in the Small Fortress for allegedly distributing 'horror propaganda', he was deported to Auschwitz in October 1944. In January 1945, he took part in the 'death marches' from Auschwitz to Buchenwald and survived to see the camp's liberation in April, but perished soon after from typhus in a sanatorium in Blankenheim.

Lustig, Parik, *Seeing Through Paradise*, 1991. Zeitoun, Foucher, *La Masque de la Barbarie*, 1998, pp.91–141.

Notes

Chapter 1

1   The prophetic role of the artist as *seer* or witness, transcending his or her predicament and conscious of the historical process, is discussed at length in another context. See, Peter Parshall, 'The Vision of the Apocalypse in the Sixteenth and Seventeenth Centuries', in Frances Carey, ed., *The Apocalypse and the Shape of Things to Come*, The British Museum, London, 1999, pp.99–124.

2   Terrence Des Pres, *The Survivor, An Anatomy of Life in the Death Camps*, Oxford University Press, New York, 1976 (1980 edition), p.36.

3   Etty Hillesum, *An Interrupted Life: The Diaries and Letters of Etty Hillesum, 1941–43* (translated from the Dutch by Arnold J Pomerans, with a preface by Eva Hoffman and introduction by Jan G. Gaarlandt), Persephone Books, London, 1999, pp.167–68.

4   For instance, in the graphic works of Lea Grundig, *Treblianca* or *Terror (from the series Niemals Wieder)* and Vera Nilsson's, *The Mothers*. Kollwitz worked from a mirror reflection of herself holding her son Peter (b.1896). A full-scale preliminary drawing (private collection) was followed by eight successive reworkings of the soft ground etching.

5   Our understanding of Kollwitz development as a sculptor during the 1930s and '40s is fragmentary at best. Her house in the Weissenburger Strasse and its contents, including a number of her works and printing plates, were destroyed during an allied bombing of Berlin in 1943.

6   The bronze cast made from clay and plaster originals are now in the Leopold Hoesch Museum, Düren. A cast is reproduced in *Ernest Barlach, Käthe Kollwitz*, Marlborough Gerson Gallery Inc., New York, September–October 1968, where it is dated 1940.

7   This event is discussed in some detail in Richard Cork, *A Bitter Truth, Avant-Garde Art and the Great War*, Yale University Press, New Haven & London, 1994, p.293.

8   Barlach's sculpture *Das Wiedersehen* was included in the *Entartete Kunst* (Degenerate Art) exhibition in 1937.

9   In fact, Klee had personally witnessed the social divisions and chaos of the First World War and the November Revolution; his disappointment with the outcome of the Revolution may partly explain his position.

10 Klee's late work has been the focus of extensive critical attention which has acknowledged the effect of National Socialism and other social forces on the artist. See Richard Verdi, 'The Late Klee' in Joachimides, Rosenthal, Schmied, eds., *German Art in the 20th Century, Painting and Sculpture 1905–1985*, Royal Academy of Arts, London 1985, pp.457–459; Stephanie Barron, ed., *Degenerate Art, The Fate of the Avant-Garde in Nazi Germany*, Los Angeles County Museum of Art, 1991; Stephanie Barron, ed., *Exiles + Émigrés, The Flight of European Artists from Hitler*, Los Angeles County Museum of Art, 1997. See, for instance, the distinct unease, the monstrous, grimacing heads and masks which appear in Klee's work at this time, for instance: *Prophet* 1930 (private collection) and *Tête de Martyr* 1933 (private collection).

11 Klee is reported to have felt 'torn between the ideology of progressive culture and the revolutionary politics of mass movements'. See O. K. Werckmeister 'From Revolution to Exile', Carolyn Lanchner, ed., *Paul Klee*, Museum of Modern Art, New York, 1987.

12 Josef Helfenstein, 'The Issue of Childhood in Klee's Late Work', Jonathan Fineberg, ed., *Discovering Child Art, Essays on Childhood, Primitivism and Modernism*, Princeton, New Jersey, 1998, pp.122–56.

13 Paul Klee, *Pedagogical Sketchbooks*, Faber & Faber, London, 1953 (first published as *Pädagogisches Skizzenbuch*, Walter Gropius, ed., Bauhaus Books, Dessau, 1925).

14 Klee continued to grapple with these ideas in, for instance, *Stricken City*, 1936 (Berggruen Collection, Metropolitan Museum, New York).

15 Paul Klee, *On Modern Art* (introduction by Herbert Read), Faber & Faber, London, 1948.

16 Paul Klee, *Tagenbücher*, Cologne, 1957, p.323; quoted in Harten, J Pollakowna, N Guralnik, *Jankel Adler 1895–1949*, Städtische Kunsthalle, Düsseldorf, Tel Aviv Museum of Art, 1985, pp.249–50.

17 'A revolutionary painter is one who comes with a revolutionary form. The subject matter doesn't matter at all.' S K Schaidermann, 'Jankel Adler' in *Literarische Bleter* 38, 1933, p.614. Reprinted in Harten, ed., *Jankel Adler 1895–1949*, 1985, p.29. This translation from Ziva Amishai-Maisels, *Depiction & Interpretation, The Influence of the Holocaust on the Visual Arts*, Pergamon Press, Oxford 1993. See also Ziva Amishai-Maisels, 'The Iconographic Use of Abstraction in Jankel Adler's Late Works' *Artibus e Historiae*, no.17, 1988, pp.55–70.

18 Adler's works were also included later in the year in the Nazi *The Eternal Jew* exhibition, under the heading 'Revelation of the Jewish Racial Soul'. One of these is reproduced in the catalogue of the exhibition alongside the declaration: 'The eternal Jews are those people with a destructive effect upon politics and culture'. *Beamten Zeitung* 24, 21 November 1937, p.615; quoted in Harten 1985, p.33.

19 'In 1942, the Red Cross transmitted to me a message that my whole family in Poland had perished. I was terribly distressed. One day, Jankel Adler appeared at my studio and brought me this picture he had painted as a gift. There are two orphans in the picture; after a while I understood that one was me and the other, he himself.' Avram Kampf, *Chagall to Kitaj, Jewish Experience in Twentieth Century Art*, Lund Humphries, Barbican Art Gallery, London, 1990, p.87.

20 Josef Herman *'Memory of Memories' The Glasgow Drawings 1940–43*, Ben Uri Gallery, London and Third Eye Centre, Glasgow, 1985, p.7.

21 In this work Adler uses lengths of dyed, coloured strings adhered to the painting's surface. See Harten, *Jankel Adler*, 1985, cat. 91. See also *Jankel Adler* (introduction Stanley William Hayter) Nicholson & Watson, London, 1948, no.16.

22 Cyril Connolly, 'Comment', *Horizon, A Review of Literature and Art*, London, October 1943, Vol. VIII, no.46, pp.221–22.

23 Moore reportedly saw his reclining figure sculptures laid out on the grounds of his studio at Much Hadam, as fallen warriors on a battlefield.

24 The above, detailed discussion of Adler's working methods demonstrates how precise was the requirement of visual language in addressing political adversity.

25 Letter from the artist to the author, 14 April 1999.

26 These were the notorious 'death marches' during Germany's retreat from the approaching allied armies in the winter 1944–45, during the final weeks and months of the war.

27 For Celnikier, who has resided in Paris since 1957, the students' uprising in the summer of 1968, and the emergence of a people's uprising in Poland under 'Solidarity', may have symbolised the continuity of a libertarian struggle. These experiences were still fresh in his mind when working on *Révolte* in the mid-'80s.

28 Celnikier began work on the painting at the end of 1981; it was exhibited in 1982 and reworked in 1983–84. The combination of colour harmonies offset by their complementaries reveals similarities in treatment to the methods of Delacroix, whom Celnikier admired.

29 Amalek has come to symbolise the archetypal enemy of Israel. The Amalekites, descendants from Esau (Gen. 36:12), attacked their kinsmen, the Israelites, during the Exodus to the Holy Land (Deut. 25:18) by ambushing and then killing the children and the elderly who formed the rear guard.

30 These small, poorly armed Jewish fighting groups sabotaged railway lines, raided German utility stores, and killed a number of German soldiers, policemen and functionaries.

31 Remarks to this effect were made during the

'Memory, Representation and Education' plenary at *Remembering for the Future 2000*, Academic Conference, Oxford, 19 July 2000. Author's conference notes.

32   Words attributed to Hitler in a speech to his army chiefs, shortly before the Nazi occupation of Poland on 1 September 1939. See Ronnie Landau, *The Nazi Holocaust*, I B Taurus, London, 1992, p.267, fn.10.

33   Hermann Gö, Memorandum to SS *Gruppenführer* Reinhard Heydrich addressing 'The Final Solution of the Jewish Problem', 31 July 1941. Reprinted in Yitzhak Arad, Israel Gutman, Abraham Margaliot, ed., *Documents on the Holocaust*, Yad Vashem, Jerusalem, 1981 (8th edition, 1999), p.233.

34   For civilian casualties see Martin Gilbert, *Atlas of the Holocaust*, Pergamon Press, London, 1989 (third edition). I am indebted to Anthony Rudolf's remarks in *At an Uncertain Hour: Primo Levi's War Against Oblivion*, Menard Press, London 1990, pp.50–51, fn. 4.

35   The reader should refer to the biographical entries provided on pp.104–12.

Chapter 2

1   Elie Wiesel, *One Generation After* Weidenfeld & Nicolson, London 1971. Quoted in Monica Bohm-Duchen, Ed., *After Auschwitz, Responses to the Holocaust in Contemporary Art*, Northern Centre for Contemporary Art, Sunderland and Lund Humphries, London, 1995, p.103.

2   Nowhere more acutely expressed than in the philosophical writings of Ludwig Wittgenstein, Theodor Adorno and Emmanuel Levinas.

3   Tadeusz Różewicz, quoted in Daniel Weissbort, ed., *The Poetry of Survival, Post War Poets of Central and Eastern Europe*, Penguin Books, London, 1993.

4   A copy (Kupferstichkabinett, Berlin) was included in the Nazi *Entartete Kunst* (Degenerate Art) exhibition and later destroyed. Other copies, Israel Museum, Jerusalem and Tel Aviv Museum of Art; see G Schiefler, *Emile Nolde, Das Graphische Werk* 1927, no. 110; F Carey & A Griffiths *The Print in Germany 1880–1933, The Age of Expressionism*, The British Museum, London 1984, cat. 111.

5   Stern is addressing the issues raised in Julius Lengbehn's highly influential book, *Rembrandt as Educator*. Fritz Stern, *The Politics of Cultural Despair*, Berkeley, Los Angeles, 1961, p.118. I am indebted to the discussion in Irit Rogoff's 'Representations of Politics' published in *German Art in the 20th Century, Painting and Sculpture 1905–1985*, Royal Academy of Arts, London 1985, p.127.

6   Nolde was directly affected by the political climate of his day. Abiding notions about the revival of German culture, 'purity' and the superiority of 'northern people', prompted him to side with National Socialism and become a member of the Nazi Party. But his works were attacked and later removed from public exhibition. Forty-eight of his paintings were shown in the *Entartete Kunst* exhibition and Nolde was banned from painting. During this period he produced a series of clandestine works entitled *Ungemalte Bilder* (Unpainted Pictures).

7   See 'Between Acculturation and Distinctiveness, Nineteenth Century Roots' in Michael Brenner, *The Renaissance of Jewish Culture in Weimer Germany*, Yale University Press, New Haven & London, 1996, pp.13–19.

8   Steinhardt's *Prophet*, a vision of a levitating figure underscores the effect made on him by the Spanish sixteenth century artist. Eight works by El Greco from the private collection of Marczell von Nemes were shown at the Alten Pinakothek, Munich in 1911. I am indebted to Dr Shulamit Behr for pointing this out to me. Steinhardt exhibited two major paintings, *Der Prophet* (no.337) and *Jeremiah* (no.338) at the *Erster Deutscher Herbstsalon* held at Der Sturm Gallery between 20 September and 1 December, 1913 that confirm this trend.

9   Britain too experienced a parallel resurgence of interest in printmaking and print publishing. Christopher Nevinson (1889–1946) produced his first dry-point, *A Dawn, 1914*, 1916 and the lithograph *The Road to Arras to Bapaume*, 1918. In that year Edward Wadsworth (1889–1949) also completed a group of striking woodcuts of the camouflaged ships in the Liverpool drydocks, and Paul Nash (1889–1946) his scenes of devastation in the battlefields of Flanders. In 1919, Percy Smith (1882–1948) published a suite of seven etchings, *The Dance of Death*, comparable to Adolf Uzarski's suite of lithographs with the same title, published in 1917. In a particularly savage image by Percy Smith, *Death Awed*, a skeleton stands in a decimated landscape of creeks and hollows; a soldier's boots are rooted firmly to the ground as his severed body lies rotting in a ditch nearby.

10   Both artists resided in Berlin and were elected to the Berlin Akademie der Kunst within a year of each other. Slevogt's contacts in Impressionist circles included Lovis Corinth and Max Liebermann (1847–1935), though he was certainly familiar with Kollwitz's images.

11   Frances Carey, Anthony Griffiths, *The Print in Germany 1880–1933, The Age of Expressionism*, The British Museum, London, 1984, pp.91–95.

12   Two other plates show the painter and etcher Hermann Strück (1867–1944), author of *Die Kunst des Radierens* (The Art of Etching), 1907 with his wife Mally, communing with the same human skeleton (part of Corinth's studio furniture). Strück was also a conduit for new ideas in the burgeoning artistic environment of *Eretz Israel*, touring pre-state Israel in 1903 and returning there in 1923, at a time when university and museum institutions were rapidly establishing a presence. He exerted a significant influence on the Bezalel Circle of artists, eventually settling in Haifa.

13   Ernst Friedrich, *Krieg dem Krieg*, Malik Verlag, Berlin, 1924.

14   Letter to Romain Rolland, 23 October 1922; quoted in Hans Kollwitz, ed., *Käthe Kollwitz, Brief der Freundschaft und Begegnungen*, Munich, 1966, p.56.

15   Israel Zangwill (1864–1926), British novelist and dramatist, author of *Children of the Ghetto*.

16   Eberhard W Kornfeld, *Verzeichnis der Kupferstiche Radierungen und Holzschnitte von Marc Chagall, 1922–66*, vol. I, Verlag Kornfeld und Klipstein, Bern, 1970, cat. 31, pp.70–71.

17   Christian symbolism had dominated western painting and a tradition of Christian iconology ran uninterruptedly through Jewish art. From the Enlightenment onwards, a strain in Jewish thought saw Jesus as a law-abiding Jew, a Jewish prophet 'in a direct line from Moses and David'. For a detailed discussion of this theme, see Ziva Amishai-Maisels, 'The Jewish Jesus' *Journal of Jewish Art*, vol. 9, 1982, pp.83–104.

18   Matthew Affron, quoted in *Exiles and Emigrés, The Flight of European Artists from Hitler* (ed., Stephanie Barron), Los Angeles County Museum of Art, Los Angeles, 23 February–11 May, 1997, p.115.

19   Alexandre Benois, 'Chagall, oeuvres récentes', *Cahiers d'Art*, vol.15, nos. 1–2, 1940, p.33.

20   The particular correlation of the child and angel recalls the story told in the Talmud (*Tractate Niddah*), and echoed in other oral traditions: a foetus in the mother's womb knows the Torah by heart and has seen the world from end to end. At the moment of its birth, however, an angel sweeps by and brushes the baby on the lips, at which point he forgets everything and must begin anew the process of learning. The Shofar or ram's horn in the angel's hand (traditionally sounded at the Jewish New Year) is perhaps a reference to the Jewish injunction to remember.

21   Franz Meyer, *Marc Chagall*, Thames & Hudson, London, 1964, p.446.

22   This lack of rootedness may well be attributable to Chagall's own lack of a base at this time, his crossing by sea to America on 23 June 1941 and his status there as an exile.

23   In a related sketch the words 'Chagall' and 'Vitebsk' appear at the foot of the Torah scrolls, suggesting a close indentification with his subject.

24   The mound of corpses is too generalised as to warrant the possibility that Chagall knew or had seen early published photographs of the mass graves; though news of the events (by now fairly widespread), could well have elicited these images. Photographs of the Armenian genocide of 1915 were, of course, known.

25   The decision to refuse the ship permission to dock safely in Turkey or Palestine led to its sinking with the loss of all but one of the 760 people on board. Though it may have prompted waves of protest, it did little to alter the immigration policies of the major Allied countries involved.

26   Maurycy Gottlieb *Letters and Diaries*, Mossad Bialik, Jerusalem, 1957, pp.24–25; quoted in Amishai-Maisels, 1982, pp.98.

27   Yosef Hayim Yerushalmi, *Zohar, Jewish History and Jewish Memory*, University of Washington Press, Seattle and London, 1982, p.44, fn.28.

28   The *Haggadah* presented artists of the stature of El Lissitzky (1890–1941) and Chagall with an unparalleled opportunity for pictorial invention and an imaginative response to the text.

29 Goeritz was a Jewish textile manufacturer and one of the key art collectors in Weimar Germany. He supported Steinhardt by purchasing a copy of every print the artist produced.

30 The most discussed is the image of the four sons, central to the Passover legend. Here, the wicked son is dressed in the stiff uniform and onion-shaped helmet of a Prussian soldier.

31 Jakob Steinhardt, *Book of Yehoshua Eliezer ben Sirah* (foreword by Arnold Zweig), Soncino Society, Berlin, 1929.

32 Publications like these are best understood in the context of a renascent interest in Jewish book illustration in Weimar and the formation of bibliophile societies to which well-educated middle-class Jews subscribed. The Soncino Society of the Friends of the Jewish Book was the first of these. See 'Aesthetics and the Jewish Book' in M. Brenner, op. cit., 1996, pp.165–77.

33 *Ben Sirah* is Hebrew for Ecclisiasticus, the Greek text of the Apocrypha, based on the Hebrew source (discovered only three decades before) and regarded as part of the scriptural canon by some Christian denominations. The book emphasises the greatness of Israel, as well as the enjoyment of worldly pleasures. The relationship of the images to the typographic design by Abraham Horodisch, are a tour de force.

34 After his arrival in Palestine in 1933, Steinhardt ran the Printmaking Department at the Bezalel Academy, a forerunner of the national museum and art school, becoming its director in 1953.

35 Pins emigrated to Palestine in 1936, studying under Steinhardt at the Bezalel Academy (1941–45) and concentrating thereafter almost exclusively on the woodcut medium. See Frances Carey, ed., *The Apocalypse and the Shape of Things to Come*, The British Museum, London, 1999, pp.316–17.

36 Nussbaum may have known Adolf Uzarski's, *Totentanz*, 1916/17 (Stadtmuseum, Düsseldorf).

37 This forms part of the cycle of wood engravings *Auch ein Todtentanz aus dem Jahre 1848* (Dance of Death for the Year 1848), published in Leipzig in 1894.

38 Years later, conscious of the tragedy that had befallen his fellow Jews, Meidner produced a cycle of works entitled *Massacres in Poland*, 1943–48. Jakob Steinhardt emigrated to Palestine shortly after Hitler's accession to power in 1933 and, settling in Jerusalem, turned his attention to Biblical themes and the region's landscapes.

39 From Filippo Tommaso Marinetti (1876–1944), 'The Founding Manifesto of Futurism', originally published in *Le Figaro*, 20 February, 1909. Quoted in Norbert Lynton, 'Futurism' in Nikos Stangos, ed., *Concepts of Modern Art*, Thames and Hudson, London, pp.97–98.

40 This took place between 12 April and early May 1912.

41 The exhibition of *Die Pathetiker* took place between 2 and 15 November 1912.

42 During the Kishinev pogroms, 60,000 Jews were killed by Ukranian Nationalists and 'white Russians' in attacks across Russia.

43 The death of a young boy Andrei Yustshinski, on the outskirts of Kiev, elicited accusations of 'Jewish ritual murder'. Mendel Beilis, the manager of a brick factory, was arbitrarily accused. The prosecutions case was shown to be fraudulent and overturned, but only after repeated incidents of mob violence against Jews and mass demonstrations met with Czarist support. Beilis was released two years after his arrest and eventually reinstated by the courts.

44 Berthold Feiwel, *Die Judenmassacres in Kischinew von Told*, Judischer Verlag, Berlin 1903. This appeared alongside I M Lilien's (1874–1925) illustration, *Dedicated to the Martyrs of Kishinev*, 1903.

45 See Thomas Grochowiak, *Ludwig Meidner*, Recklinghausen, 1966, p.38.

46 Sarah O'Brien-Twohig, 'Beckmann and the City' in *Max Beckmann Retrospective*, Los Angeles County Museum, Los Angeles, 9 December–3 February 1985, p.97.

47 Sarah O'Brien-Twohig, ibid., pp.91–109.

48 Max Beckmann 'Schöpferische Konfession' in *Tribune der Kunst und Zeit*; quoted in 'Confession 1918', in *Der Zeichner und Graphiker Max Beckmann*, Hamburg Kunstverein, 8 September–4 November 1979, p.11–12.

49 While the head is unquestionably that of Eisner, the figure is identified elsewhere as that of Gustav Landauer, an acquaintance of Beckmann's and briefly Minister of Education for the Bavarian Republic, the moving spirit behind Berlin's first cooperative society and a co-founder of the Berlin People's Theatre. A friend of Martin Buber, he was perhaps the only leading figure in the revolutionary movement who maintained close ties with Jewish life. Eisner did not. Landauer was murdered by the Freikorps volunteers on 2 May 1919, shortly before Beckmann began work on the series, thus perhaps encouraging speculation that the figure in question is Landauer.

50 Letter to Romana Halpern, 30 August, 1937; quoted in Wojciech Chmurzynski, *Bruno Schulz 1892–1942: Drawings and Documents from the Collection of the Muzeum Literatury im Adama Mickiewicza w Warszawie*, Adam Mickiewicz Literature Museum Warsaw 1995, vol. II, p.21.

51 Bruno Schulz, excerpt from *Loneliness, About Myself*; quoted in Chmurzynski, ibid., 1995, p.11.

52 *Kristallnacht* was a night long campaign of violence aimed at the physical destruction of Jewish lives, property, homes and synagogues. 91 Jews were killed, 7,000 Jewish-owned shops destroyed and approximately 300 synagogues razed to the ground. In one of the first mass arrests, 25,000 Jews were sent to concentration camps at Dachau and elsewhere. The Jewish community was held responsible and were demanded to pay 1,000 million marks by the Nazis in 'reparations'.

53 The mounds of rubble visible here appear again in the pencil study for *The Damned*, 1944, and the disgorged tree and archway (right) appear in *Death Triumphant*, 1944 (Felix-Nussbaum-Haus, Osnabrück), suggesting perhaps that Nussbaum intended to produce a painting on this theme.

Chapter 3

1 The capitulation of Madrid in March 1939 finally brought the Spanish Civil War to a close.

2 It took France fifty years to acknowledge the Vichy state's collaboration with the Third Reich.

3 The words of Max Ernst, as reported in 'Ecritures', *Nouvelle Revue Française*, Paris, 1970; quoted in Michèle C Cone, *Artists under Vichy: a case of prejudice and persecution*, Princeton University Press, New Jersey, 1992, p.118.

4 Benjamin was interned at Clos St Joseph near Nevers (Nièvre) and released in November 1939. A year later he was caught crossing illegally into Spain; fearing repatriation to a French internment camp, he killed himself with morphine tablets during the night of 26 September 1940.

5 For a fuller discussion of repressive policies during the Vichy Government and their effect on artists see Cone, op. cit.,1992; and Stephanie Barron, ed., *Exiles + Émigrés, The Flight of European Artists from Hitler*, Los Angeles County Museum of Art, 1997.

6 See Varian Fry, *Surrender on Demand*, Random House, New York, 1945, p.206.

7 See Anne Grynberg, *Les camps de la honte: les internés juifs des camps français (1939–1944)*, La Découverte, Paris, 1991.

8 Two other drawings by Hofstatter, *A View of the Camp at St Cyprien* and *The Kitchen in the Camp* (Yad Vashem, The Art Museum) are thematically and stylistically related to those discussed above. Other drawings, such as those by Vladimir Segal at Saint-Sulpice, Leo Breuer at Gurs and Louis Asscher in the *Sternlager* (Star camp) at Bergen-Belsen, foreground the barbed-wire fences and boundaries.

9 Arrested on the morning of 10 May 1940, Schwesig was deported to St Cyprien in a train convoy with German, Flemish and Austrian prisoners. He remained until the end of October when floods forced the camp's evacuation. Transferred to Gurs and later to the Noé camp, Schwesig produced a vast number of drawings of internment.

10 Schwesig was a regular contributor to the journal *Rote Hilfe* (Red Help). He made posters, photomontages and graphics for the Belgian organisation, *Secours aux Enfants Espagnols* (Help the Spanish Children), and painted anti-Fascist murals and hoardings.

11 The Schlegelkeller drawings were exhibited at the Palais Egmont, Brussels, during the 'European Amnesty Conference for Political Prisoners in Germany' (which Schwesig attended and at which he spoke on 5 July 1936) as well as Amsterdam and the Museum for Modern Western Art in Moscow in 1937. The series was last seen in the offices of the Comintern in 1939. An edition was planned, with an introduction by Heinrich Mann, but never materialised. Other images in the cycle allude to separate incidents during his internment: *Anyone could participate in the beatings; Released to two crime officers after hourly calls for his release; Police prison resembled a field hospital; Police officers were the nurses; In the bed lay a prisoner*, etc.

12 See, for instance, the works of Caspar David Friedrich (1774–1840) and Philipp Otto Runge (1777–1810) in which figures alone, or in pairs, are depicted in contemplation of the sublime.

13 In *Karl Schwesig (1898–1955) Paintings, Watercolours, Graphics, Documents*, Galerie Remmert und Barth, Düsseldorf, 9 September–7 November 1981.

14 Breuer's work of the 1950s reveals strong affinities with the geometric abstract works of Sophie Tauber-Arp, Victor Vasarely and Auguste Herbin.

15 It is carefully inscribed *Karl Schwesig, St Cyprien, Okt 11 1940, im meer baden Sonnenbaden*. Schwesig obtained a children's box of watercolours from the Joint Distribution Committee.

16 Nussbaum's registration form 'Notice Individuelle' confirms the date of his arrest at St Cyprien on 10 May (Archives de la préfecture des Pyrénées Atlantiques, Pau).

17 The provisions of a truce agreed with Germany on 22 July (an attempt by the French Government to divest itself of its Jewish refugee problem), allowed Nussbaum to apply to the camp's inspectorate for repatriation. Transferred to a transit point in Bordeaux, Nussbaum escaped with his childhood friend Georg Meyer, travelling by Red Cross transport through France to Paris and on to the Gare de Midi, in Brussels. Other Jews were deported to Auschwitz from similar collection points at Poitiers and Angers. See Martin Gilbert, *Atlas of the Holocaust*, Pergamon Press, Oxford, 1988, p.134.

18 Nussbaum's entry in the Jewish Register of the City of Brussels, B.E.171849 of 24 December 1940, confirms his presence in the city at this time. On the reverse of this painting is a *Still-life with books and a black glove*, c.1936–38; the *pentimenti* beneath this layer, however, reveals yet another composition, possibly a garden enclosure or harbour scene.

19 Books, writing paper and artists' materials were provided after this date by the Joint Distribution Committee, a Jewish welfare organisation.

20 The drawing is inscribed and dated *Entwurf zu einem Gemalde Felix Nussbaum, 1940* and dedicated to *Meiner lieben Familie Weichmann freundlichst gewidmet*. Nussbaum returned to the subject two years later, in *St Cyprien* (Unfinished), 18 June 1942, when considering the possibility of flight.

21 Hanging over the shed opening in *Prisoner*, 1940, is a small sign inscribed *J 12*, Nussbaum's barracks in the section of the camp known as *Ilot 2*. This detail is not apparent in the final state of *Self-portrait in the Camp*. The camp consisted of ten *Ilot* or islands isolated from each other by barbed-wire fences. Three sections were closed off as quarantine zones for prisoners suffering from typhoid and other illnesses. See Karl George Kaster, *Felix Nussbaum Art Defamed, Art in Exile, Art in Resistance, A Biography* (translated by Eileen Martin), The Overlook Press, Woodstock, New York, 1997, pp.330–31.

22 Inmates slept on loose straw scattered on the sand, and in the absence of clean water used straw to perform their ablutions.

23 Karl George Kaster offers a compelling, if unsupported, comparison between Nussbaum's *Self-Portrait at the Easel*, autumn, 1943 (Felix Nussbaum Collection, Osnabrück) and Otto Dix', *Self-Portrait at the Easel*, 1926 (Leopold Hoesch Museum, Düren), exhibited at Otto Meyer's Gallery (Nussbaum's patron and dealer) in Osnabrück in 1929. See Kaster, op. cit., 1997, pp. 403–5. It is tantalising to compare Nussbaum's *Self-portrait at the Easel*, 1943, with James Ensor's depiction of a respectably dressed skeleton, palette and brushes in hand, gazing attentively at the viewer in *Le Peintre Squelettisé dans l'atelier*, 1896 (Koonlijke Museum, Antwerp). Nussbaum was acquainted with Ensor's skeletons and would almost certainly have borne them in mind when working on *Death Triumphant*, 1944.

24 Painted in a palette of deep earth colours, suggesting also a lingering affinity with Rembrandt's *Self-Portrait*, 1660 (Louvre, Paris). Van Gogh's *Self-portrait* was based in turn on a portrait of the artist by his contemporary, resident in Paris, John Russell (1858–1931).

25 Boris Taslitzky, quoted in Laurent Gervereau, 'Un parcours avec Boris Taslitzky', *La Déportation, le système concentrationnaire Nazi*, Musée d'Histoire Contemporaine-BIDC, Paris, 1995, pp.262–65.

26 A term coined by Terence des Pres, *The Survivor, An Anatomy of Life in the Death Camps*, Oxford University Press, New York, 1976 (1980 edition), chapter III, pp. 51–71.

27 Alexander Donat, *The Holocaust Kingdom*, Holt, Reinhart & Winston, New York, 1965; quoted in Terence des Pres, ibid., 1976, p.64.

28 Primo Levi, *If this is a Man*, Abacus, London, 2000 (first published 1958), p.46.

29 Jorge Semprun, *Literature or Life*, Viking Books, New York, 1997, p.45.

30 2,000,000 French workers between the ages of 19 and 45, the so-called *travailleurs libre*, were resettled in Germany and forcibly employed in factories and farms. This policy, which was openly backed by Maréchal Pétain, stunned ordinary French citizens and secured the women's support for the Resistance from this moment on.

31 They were published in book form, together with Barosin's texts in Jacob Barosin, *A Remnant*, The Holocaust Library, New York (undated publication).

32 Laurent Gervereau, op. cit., 1995, p.262.

33 St Sulpice was established on 16 October 1940 as a camp for undesirables; communists, trade unionists and Jewish foreign nationals rounded up during the mass arrests of August 1942 swelled the camp's populations.

34 Quoted in Véronique Alemany-Dessaint, Danièle Baron, *Créer pour Survivre*, Musée des Beaux Arts de Reims, 1995, p.114.

35 The drawing has been convincingly attributed by Pnina Rosenberg to the German artist, Lili Rilik-Andrieux. See P. Rosenberg, *Salon des Refusés, L'Art dans les Camps d'Internement Français 1939–45*, Beit Lohamei Haghetaot, spring 2000. See also biographical entry at the end of this catalogue.

36 See Dawid Sierakowiak, *The Diary of Dawid Sierakowiak: Five Notebooks from the Lodz Ghetto*, Oxford University Press, New York 1996; see also Nechama Tec, 'Diaries and Oral History: Some Methodological Considerations', *Religion and the Arts*, Boston College, Boston, vol. 4, no.1, 2000.

37 I am indebted here to the discussion contained in Monica Bohm-Duchen's essay *Charlotte Salomon's Life or Theatre? An Introduction* (unpublished manuscript). For further reading, see also Charlotte Salomon, *Life or Theatre*, Royal Academy of Arts, London, 1998; Mary Lowenthal Felstiner, *To Paint her Life. Charlotte Salomon in the Nazi era*, Harper Collins, New York, 1994; Astrid Schmetterling, 'Tracing the Life (or Theatre?) of Charlotte Salomon', *Architecture, Art & Design*, 1997, pp.115–28.

38 Charlotte's father, Albert Salomon, was interned in the Sachsenhausen concentration camp for a period following the infamous Kristallnacht of November 1938.

39 Felstiner dates the work's inception to as late as mid-1941. Mary Lowenthal Felstiner, *To Paint her Life. Charlotte Salomon in the Nazi era*, Harper Collins, New York, 1994.

40 The wider family circle included an astonishing array of eminent figures: the architect Erich Mendelssohn, the scientist Albert Einstein, the theologian Albert Schweitzer, Rabbi Leo Baeck and the painter Max Liebermann.

41 Paula Lindberg (known in the cycle with the fictionalised name of Paulinka Bimbam) was active in the Jüdischer Kulturbund until its dissolution in 1941. Paula also took part in clandestine activities, procuring false papers for Jewish artists and intellectuals and providing a lifeline for their escape from Germany.

42 Wolfsohn's manuscript *Orpheus oder Der Weg zu einer Maske* (Orpheus, or the Way to a Mask) proved a crucial source of inspiration and is recalled in *Life or Theatre?*

43 Her parents, Albert and Paula Salomon, had fled from Berlin to Amsterdam in 1939 and survived the war by escaping from the Dutch transit camp of Westerbork and going underground with the help of the Resistance. They recovered Charlotte's *Life or Theatre?* in 1947, during a visit to Villefranche.

44 A reference to the fact that the entire work was created using only three colours, the primaries yellow, red and blue, plus white.

45 Katznelson's diary chronicles the fate of a transcient population at Drancy, echoing Feder. Yitzhak Katznelson, *Vittel Diary*, Tel Aviv, 1972, quoted in Martin Gilbert, *The Holocaust, The Jewish Tragedy* Fontana/Collins, Glasgow 1986, pp.385, 391–92.

46 I am indebted to Avi Hurvitz for his suggestion that Landau's young man may have returned in one of the empty trains from a Polish death camp.

47 Windows, too, are a recurring image in Charlotte Salomon's *Life or Theatre?*, described by Bohm-Duchen as 'a dramatic and sinister leitmotif' which echoes the unwitting suicide of several members of Charlotte's family, including her mother and grandmother.

48 In this year, Freundlich settled in Paris and produce his first abstract work.

49 Edda Maillet has commented on this apparent dichotomy in Otto Freundlich's work, possibly reflecting the life-threatening

circumstances in which he found himself. Conversation with the author, 3 February 1999. These works have only recently come to light and deserve greater attention.

50 Association Les Amis de Jeanne et Otto Freundlich, inv. no. D.198.88.e.

51 Association Les Amis de Jeanne et Otto Freundlich, inv. no. D.1986.65.

52 *Il parait que ces damner de réfugiés ne crèvent pas toujours de faim. Chaque fois que je me renseigne sur leur conduite morale je trouve cent balles dans la lettre.* The anecdote epitomises a climate in which theft, large and small, went unpunished. Association Les Amis de Jeanne et Otto Freundlich, inv. no. D.1986.49.

53 Otto Freundlich, Transcript. Association 'Les Amis de Jeanne et Otto Freundlich', Pontoise.

54 Freundlich had experimented earlier with a similar device, placed at the centre of the large *Composition Inachevée*, 1940 (Donation Freundlich, Musée du Pontoise), which likewise remained incomplete at the time of the artist's death in March, 1943.

55 Friedrich Nietzsche, *Der Wille zur Macht* (The Will to Power) and *Also Sprach Zarathustra* (Thus spoke Zarathustra), 1883–85. I am indebted to the essay by Ivo Frenzel, *Friedrich Nietzsche* contained in *German Art in the 20th Century, Painting and Sculpture 1905–1985*, Royal Academy of Arts, London 1985, pp.74–81.

56 Gilbert, op cit., London, 1987, p.94. Gilbert describes the deplorable conditions which Jews deported from Prague, Vienna and other West European cities encountered in the Lublin region, the lack of shelter or accommodation and the shortage of food and drinking water.

57 Another closely related drawing by Haas, dated 3 November 1939, shows a *minyan* or ten men at prayer, wearing *tallits*, their heads covered, inside the wooden huts. See Janet Blatter & Sybil Milton, *Art of the Holocaust*, Rutledge, New York, 1981, p.59.

Chapter 4

1 The presence of a Jewish community in the Czech lands of Bohemia and Moravia can be traced to the tenth century in the district of Malá Strana, below Prague Castle. Physically separated from the Old Town by high walls, it enjoyed a degree of political as well as legal autonomy. Its isolation provided some protection against hostility, such as the anti-Jewish riots (1096–98), or discriminatory measures such as the land-holding prohibitions of the Fourth Lateran Council (1215), which limited Jewish commercial activity to money lending (since Christians were prohibited by the Church from practising usury). These communities, which came to be known as ghettos were to be found across most of Europe. The Edict of Toleration (1781) affirmed the principle of religious toleration in the Austrian empire. Schools and universities opened their doors to Jewish enrolment. The guarantees of administrative, social and judicial autonomy that had prevailed in the ghetto were abolished in 1784. The German language would henceforth dominate all spheres of life,

replacing Yiddish as the language spoken among acculturated Jews.

2 In September 1941, Heinrich Heydrich announced a purge of Jews from the Protektorat and decreed that a centre for the assembly and deportation (*vorhübergehendes Sammellager*) of Jews from Central Europe as well as the Czech Lands of Bohemia and Moravia would be established at Theresienstadt. The mass deportation of Jews 'to the East' began on 14 October (with 5,000 evacuees) and on 16 October, the first convoy departed for Lodz.

3 This number would increase. Conditions were subhuman: only 457 Czech and 198 Viennese survived the camp. For a detailed discussion see Martin Gilbert, *The Holocaust, The Jewish Tragedy*, London, 1987.

4 An intensive Nazi presence converged in the area, at Litomerice, the site of a massive armaments and munitions factory lodged in underground tunnels and in the 'Small Fortress' of Terezín which served as a detention centre for 32,000 Czech, German, Russian, British political prisoners and Jewish detainees. The Small Fortress was the site of great physical hardship and summary executions. Even here, a number of prisoners, among them Alois Bučánek, Josef Kylies and Josef Klouček, produced works of enduring interest, with a direct bearing on their camp experiences and with emphasis on the inmate population, depicted in countless individual portrait drawings and caricatures.

5 In the opinion of Paul Rossel, the IRCC official, Eppstein, had extensive powers within the ghetto and administered these stringently. This view is not universally accepted, however, and has been forcefully contested by some survivor groups. Report to the IRCC; Archives, 23 June 1944; published in *Documents du Comité international de la Croix-Rouge concernant le ghetto de Theresienstadt* Geneva, 1990.

6 Hannah Arendt, 'Auschwitz et Jerusalem' in *Agora*, Deux-Temps, Paris, 1991, p.215.

7 Add to this, the vast amount of hand-written material – letters, postcards (e.g. from a young internee to his non-Jewish fiancée on the outside), diaries, poems, dedications and birthday wishes. SS Adolf Eichmann partially reinstated the postal service between the ghetto and the Protectorate, i.e., postcards, containing not more than thirty words and written in large capitals, could henceforth be submitted to the German censor.

8 Heilbrunn was a trained architect whose methodical and often incisive depiction of the geography contrasts with the allegorical, storytelling aspect of Fritta's works.

9 The book is bound in soft covers, hand-sewn and numbered, giving the impression that only a small number were published.

10 Transcript from Claude Lanzmann's 'A Visitor from the Living', from Frances Cline's 'A Holocaust Bloodhound Gently Tracks a Target', *New York Times*, 24 June 1999.

11 Tadeusz Borowski, *This Way to the Gas Ladies and Gentleman*, Penguin Books, London, 1976, p.30.

12 Our knowledge of the overcrowding and

living conditions is reliant on the drawings produced at the time. Mořitz Nágl's detailed drawings and watercolours served as the model for the recent reconstruction of a dormitory in the Magdeburg Barracks.

13 Letter dated 2 September 1943, quoted in Etty Hillesum, *An Interrupted Life: The Diaries and Letters 1941–43* (translated by Arnold J Pomerans), Persephone Books, London, 1999, p.425

14 Germaine Tillion, *Ravensbrück* (translated by Gerald Satterwhite), Anchor, New York, 1975; quoted in Tzvetan Todorov, *Facing the Extreme, Moral Life in the Concentration Camps*, Weidenfeld & Nicolson, London, 1999, p.77.

15 By January 1944, they comprised sixty per cent of its inhabitants with an average age of fifty.

16 An insufficient diet consisted of a black liquid (a coffee substitute), gruel and two or three boiled, often rotten, potatoes and the evening's bread ration. Basic rations were supplemented by potato peelings, stalks and leftovers from the vegetable gardens cultivated for the German command. For a more detailed discussion of a typical diet, see Ruth Bondy, 'Women in Theresienstadt and the Family Camp in Birkenau', in Dalia Ofer and Lenore J. Weitzman, eds., *Women in the Holocaust* Yale University Press, New Haven, 1998, p.317.

17 The health service provided treatment against contagious diseases—lowering dramatically the number of deaths caused by typhus—by encouraging preventative measures such as quarantine, vaccination and hygiene. Even so, 18,000 deaths were recorded from infectious diseases between 1942 and 1944. On top of these, 16,000 deaths were caused by endemic illnesses, pneumonia and common infections. A dental clinic, laboratory and basic radiology service opened later. Specialist treatment was dispensed in areas such as urology, gynaecology, dermatology, neurology, psychiatry.

18 Such inscriptions reveal the personalities, circumstances and events portrayed. We learnt from the inscriptions at the foot of this sheet, *Terezín dne 11/III.944 M. Müller Urologische Station 8. Kurt Weiner Zimmer no 312, Kaserne Langgasse, 11* that Dr Kurt Weiner presided over the camp infirmary's Urology Department. He arrived in Terezín on 30 July 1942 and was deported to Auschwitz on 28 September 1944.

19 Two hundred and thirty births were recorded in Terezín. But in July 1943, abortion was made compulsory and all babies born after that date were sent with their mothers on transports to the East and gassed. See Ruth Bondy, 'Women in Theresienstadt and the Family Camp in Birkenau' in Ofer, Weitzman, eds., op. cit., 1998, pp.311–26.

20 Fleischmann ran the psychiatric services at Terezín together with Victor Frankl.

21 Fleischmann worked on them from 3–30 June 1942. Other studies include: Felix Bloch's *Autopsy at Night*, 1942 (Jewish Museum in Prague) and Leo Haas' *Mortuary in Theresienstadt*, 1943 (Památník Terezín). Norbert Troller's *Performing Surgery in Terezín* 1943 (Památník Terezín) shows an opera-

tion in progress: a group of doctors and nurses in sterile garments attend the patient.

22 The remains of another 3,000 dead were disposed of in a mass grave.

23 Leo Haas, 'The Affair of the Painters of Terezín', Margaret S Strom, Arnošt Lustig, Arno Parik, eds., *Seeing Through Paradise, Artists and the Terezín Concentration Camp*, Massachusetts College of Art, Boston, 6 March–4 May 1991.

24 Grosz's influence can be traced specifically to the crowded scenes of Café Terezín by Fritta, Haas and Adolf Aussenberg (1914–44). Aussenberg's *Kaffeehaus*, 1944 (Yad Vashem, Art Museum) caricatures the prim waitresses in their starched pinnies, their pouting lips and exaggerated noses, with vigorous humour.

25 This is Haas' *Technická Kancelář* (Technical Office) Památník Terezín (PT 1886). Inscribed *11.II.1943*, it suggests a date for the completed drawing some time in February 1943.

26 The inscriptions read *Heren Ing. Grünberger von Leo Haas Theresienstadt 1943* and *Kreslírna vpravo ved. kan. Fríbl stojící dr. Leo Heilbrunn*. A third inscription, *papír nárěz*, above the drawing cabinet (far left).

27 Arno Parik suggests this could be Hilde Zadiková; in correspondence with the author 7 June 2000. This is a far from comprehensive record of the artists active in the ghetto. Among the women, Friedl Dicker-Brandeis, Hilda Zadiková and Amalia Seckbach have been the focus of studies elsewhere. Recently published material has brought to light the works of two hitherto lesser known draughtsmen, Arthur Goldschmidt and Petr Lowenstein. See 'Peindre et dessiner à Theresienstadt', Sabine Zeitoun, Dominique Foucher, eds., *La Masque de la Barbarie, Le ghetto Theresienstadt 1941–1945*, Centre d'Histoire de la Résistance et de la Déportation, Lyon, 1998, pp.91–149.

28 The inclusion of the artist's hands, drawing implements and sketch pad along the lower edge of Haas' *Life in the Ghetto*, Theresienstadt, 1943 (Yad Vashem, Art Museum), is a self-conscious reference to his role as witness.

29 This was Block 'M', opposite the Brunnenpark, the ghetto's 'picturesque' central square. In time, they obtained permission and the materials required to build a studio within the mansard roof, fashioning their own furniture, shelves and worktables. The walls were lined with reproductions of the Old Masters, among them Goya, Lippi and Rembrandt. From an unpublished transcript by Jan Burka 'Terezin…After 55 Years… Awoken Memories', Yad Vashem Art Museum, Jerusalem.

30 Burka, ibid., p.5.

31 This was the name given to the 30-ft wide road which ran between the railway tracks and the woods at Sobibor, where groups of new arrivals were led by the Nazis to their deaths. Burka's drawing is a remarkably precocious attempt to bring elements like these together, notwithstanding the uncertainties and drama they convey.

32 Author's emphasis, Leo Haas, op. cit., 1991.

33 Much of this detail is already present in the preparatory *Sheet of studies for 'Film and Reality*, 1943–44 (Collection Thomas Fritta Haas).

34 The film is often referred to incorrectly as *Der Führer schenkt den Juden eine Stadt* (The Führer Donates a Town to the Jews). See Karel Margry, '"Theresienstadt" (1944–45): The Nazi Propaganda Film Depicting the Concentration Camp as Paradise', *Historical Journal of Film, Radio and Television* vol. 12, no. 2, 1992.

35 An earlier effort in December 1943 to commission the Czech scriptwriter Jindrich Weil was soon abandoned. It was filmed by *Aktualita*, a Prague-based newsreel company. Gerron's synopsis, two versions of the script, notes toward a spoken commentary, a proposal for the film's editing and other documents survive.

36 An idea put forward by Karel Margry, who sites a number of sources, including historian H. G. Adler to substantiate the claim.

37 Gerron himself was deported to Auschwitz on 28 October 1944 along with the rest of the film's crew. Gerron was replaced by the Czech film-maker Karel Pečeny, who was not a prisoner. The film received a number of private screenings to chosen audiences but was never officially released.

Chapter 5

1 The term refers to communities set in the impoverished rural areas of eastern Europe, cut off from the mainstream culture, where traditionally Jewish religious observance thrived.

2 Of a total population of 33 million, ten per cent (or 3.3 million) were Jews. The cynical Nazi-Soviet non-aggression pact divided Poland between Germany and the USSR and placed two million Jews from the General Government under German control.

3 As Operation Barbarossa, Germany's invasion of the Soviet Union, proceeded at lightning pace, the *Einsatzgruppen*, following on the heels of the German Wehrmacht, carried out the first group of large-scale massacres of Jews, assisted by brutal Lithuanian, Ukrainian and Latvian auxiliaries.

4 Yosef Zelckowicz, 'In those Nightmarish Days', p.171; quoted in Michal Unger, ed., *The Last Ghetto, Life in the Lodz Ghetto 1940–1944*, Yad Vashem, The Holocaust Martyr's and Heroes' Remembrance Authority, Jerusalem, 1995, p.100.

5 '… The experience of the ghetto has forever broken us. I paint a little, I draw what you find here, [but] I have yet to overcome, as I write these words. I have not written anything until today, because I wanted to convey my thoughts on creativity and painting in the pictorial arts. Extract from Jacob Lifchitz's last letter from the Kovno ghetto, 6 July 1944 (United States Holocaust Memorial Museum, Washington). Germany invaded Lithuania on 22 June 1941; the final destruction of the Kovno ghetto took place on 13–15 July, 1944.

6 From the Diary of Rodashevsky, a Vilna schoolboy; quoted in *Ghetto*, National Theatre, London, 27 April 1989 (unnumbered pages).

7 Formed soon after the defeat of Poland by the Germans in the autumn 1939 and located in London after the fall of France, it was officially recognised by the other Allied governments. Karski's mission was to impress on Western leaders the need to take appropriate measures to forestall the destruction of European Jewry and to arm Jewish Resistance and self-defence groups. Karski's experiences are collected in Jan Karski's *Story of a Secret State*, Boston, 1944, p.321; quoted in Walter Lacquer, *The Terrible Secret*, Holt, New York, 1998, p.108.

8 Claude Lanzmann, *Shoah*, Da Cappo Press, New York, 1995, pp.154–61.

9 Lanzmann, ibid., pp.183–84.

10 The inscriptions found right and left of centre read in Hebrew letters

אֵין שׁ לָאדֹזשׁ

meaning: 'No God in Lodz'. The letter *shin* (the most sacred of Hebrew letters, being the first letter of the word for the deity), is positioned centrally on a white rectangle next to a doorway or gate, thus being a reference to the *mezuzah*, the small piece of parchment affixed to the doorposts and gates of Jewish homes containing the traditional Hebrew prayer *Shema Israel*, 'Hear Oh Israel, Hear our cry', etc.

11 Adam Czerniakow, leader of the Warsaw Ghetto until the mass deportations in July 1942, wrote in his diaries '[Rumkowski] is replete with self-praise, a conceited and witless man, and a dangerous man too, since he keeps telling the authorities that all is well in his preserve.' See Israel Gutman, 'The Distinctiveness of the Lodz Ghetto', Unger, op. cit., 1995, pp. 22–24.

12 This optimistic assessment was not shared by all. Emanuel Ringelblum was convinced that only Germany's military defeat would bring about an end to the murders and deportations.

13 'Officials from the city administration and the ghetto administration, from the Gestapo and the KRIPO, dressed like kings from the results of Jewish toil.' Gutman, op cit., 1995, p.26.

14 Intended perhaps as a certificate of apprenticeship or a dedication—like the *Ketubot* (marriage contracts) and other documents and gifts produced to mark a special occasion—Kowner worked to commission, thus meeting the almost constant demand for documents of this kind in the ghetto.

15 The general mortality rate in Lodz, in 1940, was 6,197 or 39.2 per thousand while in 1942 it was 18,134 or 159 per thousand; this compares with a pre-war rate of 9.6 per thousand.

16 The drawing's verso contains profuse annotations. However, the inscription *Ordinung Dienst/ Ulica Zawisza/ Transport chleba w Getcie Łódzkim/1942/ W Lipcu* refers misleadingly to the distribution of potatoes, not (as the drawing clearly shows) of the daily ration of bread.

17 'My favourite place was the forge, where I made many drawings of ploughs, wagons, wheels… The stables of the Landwirtschaft provided many inspiring moments…'. From an unpublished transcript by Jan Burka, 'Terezin…After 55 Years… Awoken

Memories', Yad Vashem, Art Museum, Jerusalem.

18 Ringelblum's diaries formed part of the *Oneg Shabbat* archives, a secret chronicle of the Warsaw ghetto produced during the Nazi oppression. See Emmanuel Ringelblum, *Last Writings*, Yad Vashem, Jerusalem, 1992, vol. 2, pp.51–52; quoted in Dalia Ofer & Lenore J. Weitzman, eds., *Women in the Holocaust*, Yale University Press, New Haven, 1998, p.151, fns.1, 32.

19 Fearful of arrest, men were confined to their accommodation or conscripted into forced labour. They also fled in large numbers to the forests, joining clandestine groups or searching for shelters or hide-outs for themselves and their families. See 'Gender in Ghetto Diaries and Testimonies', in Ofer, Weitzman, op. cit., 1998, pp.143–63.

20 This and the two drawings by Lurie discussed below were made during the artist's internment in the Leibitsch labour camp in the Czech Sudeten, though for the majority of the war the artist was interned in the Kovno ghetto, the subject of most of her wartime works.

21 Yosef Zelckowicz, 'In those Nightmarish Days', p.189; quoted in Unger, op. cit., 1995, p.99.

22 Primo Levi, *If this is a Man*, Abacus, London, 2000, pp.38–39. Levi was speaking of Auschwitz, though this too was the experience of the ghetto.

23 There is a remarkable similarity between this and the photograph of the young Zvi Nussbaum (now a medical doctor in New York), taken outside the Hotel Polski (from Jurgen Stroop, *The Stroop Report On The Destruction Of The Warsaw Ghetto*) during the Warsaw ghetto uprising; both images powerfully convey the sense of a tormented and largely captive population.

24 Born and educated in Paris, Norblin was responsible for encouraging a Polish School of painting in the years of the country's Independence in 1770–95. His etchings in particular evoke Rembrandt's.

25 Like Trębacz, Cracow-based artists Adolf Messer (1886–1931) and Artur Markowicz (1872–1934) portrayed the inward looking world of the Jewish *shtetl*.

26 Though it was not an extermination camp in the usual sense of the term, Daghani came to refer to Mikhailowka as such, by virtue of the fact that all those detained there, with the exception of the Daghanis themselves, who escaped, were brutally murdered by their Nazi and Ukrainian guards.

27 As the inscription suggests, the original was realised sometime in 1942 (whereabouts unknown). This work is reminiscent of the strongly coloured *Women's Quarter*, 1943 (Yad Vashem, Art Museum).

28 In a more muted version, *Typhus in the Camp, Transnistria*, 1943 (YIVO, New York) the ladder plays an equally defining role. See Janet Blatter & Sybil Milton's, *Art of the Holocaust*, Rutledge, New York, 1981, p.98. A signed pencil drawing of the subject that includes the tilting ladder is reproduced in Arnold Daghani, 'The Grave is in the Cherry Orchard', *Adam International Review*, ed., Miron Grindea, XXIX (1961), p.19.

29 Arnold Daghani, 'The Grave is in the Cherry

Orchard', *Adam International Review*, ed., Miron Grindea, XXIX (1961), p.18.

30 Two very similar images entitled *Interior with Candlelight I & II* depict the couple's hiding place in the Bershad ghetto (which they occupied during their escape to Bucharest in winter 1943–44). They are dated respectively 1943 and 1974 and are juxtaposed on a single page, epitomising the unconventional methods which Daghani employed. The earlier one is clearly made from observation, while the latter is a reworking of the same theme. Minor adjustments, i.e. in the treatment of light, or a foreshortened perspective, confirm the lucid reworkings of memory. Elsewhere in *What a Nice World*, 1970–77 (Centre for German-Jewish Studies, University of Sussex), Daghani had recorded the executions carried out in Czernowitz in July 1941 and the murder of Rabbi Dr Mark.

31 Arnold Daghani, *What a Nice World*, 1970–77 (unnumbered pages). In fact, a number of clandestine photographs were taken inside ghettos by Jews and gentiles. Mendel Grosman photographed Lodz, even though expressly forbidden to do so by the *Judenältester* Mordecai Rumkowski; and Walter Genewien, Director of the Finance Department, took colour slides of the ghetto.

32 Leon Thorne, *Out of the Ashes*, Rosebern, New York, 1963, p.13; quoted in Terrence Des Pres, op. cit., 1976, p.40.

33 Jozef Zelkowicz, 'Days of Nightmare', reprinted in Lawrence Langer, ed., *Art from the Ashes, A Holocaust Anthology*, Oxford University Press, New York, 1995, p.207.

34 Lodz was the longest-surviving ghetto; its final liquidation took place in June through August 1944.

35 Gita Sereny, *Into that Darkness*, Deutsch, London, 1995 (first published 1974), pp.230–31.

36 From a letter to the author, dated 14 April 1999.

37 Celnikier may have seen Rouault's works in reproduction in the studio of Emile Filla, with whom he studied on his return to Prague in 1946.

Chapter 6

1 Eugen Kogon, remarking on the use of forced labour at Buchenwald, says that 'Some of the work in camp was useful but some of it was utterly senseless, intended only as a form of torture, a diversion engaged in by the SS…The Jews especially had to build walls, only to tear them down the next day, rebuild them again and so on.' Eugen Kogon, *The Theory and Practice of Hell*, Medallion Books, New York, 1968, p.90; quoted in Daniel Goldhagen, *Hitler's Willing Executioners*,1997, pp.286, 570, fn.17.

2 Conditions at Buna were deplorable, as elsewhere; prisoners worked twelve hour shifts, beaten and harried by guards and dogs. 25,000 workers died of disease and starvation during construction of the complex.

3 Over two and a half years the SS received in the order of DM 20,000,000 from I. G. Farben for supplying labour for the Buna plant, later known as KL Auschwitz III Aussenlager.

4 This was how *SS Hauptsturmführer* Karl Fritzsch, first camp leader at Auschwitz, routinely welcomed new arrivals.

5 Otto Friedrich, *The Kingdom of Auschwitz*, Penguin Books, London, 1994, p.9.

6 Gawron reworked this theme in a painting produced in the United States in the 1960s and closely based on this drawing. For details pertaining to the artist's escape, see Lucy Milton, Janet Blatter, *Art of the Holocaust*, Rutledge, New York, 1981, p. 248.

7 The following have written extensively about those relationships and their value to survival: Terence Des Pres, *The Survivor, An Anatomy of Life in the Death Camps*, Oxford University Press, New York, 1976 (1980 edition); Primo Levi, *The Drowned and the Saved* (translated by R Rosenthal) Abacus, London, 1996 (first published 1986); Tzvetan Todorov, *Facing the Extreme, Moral Life in the Concentration Camps*, Weidenfeld & Nicolson, London, 1999

8 Alfred Kantor, *The Book of Alfred Kantor*, McGraw Hill, New York, 1971 (unpaginated).

9 The first transport of Polish prisoners arrived in Auschwitz from Tarnów on 14 June 1940, marking the camp's opening. Siwierski's *Soup* was probably completed soon after his arrest and deportation on 22 September.

10 The sculpture workshop at Auschwitz was active from 1941 onwards, producing a variety of decorative ornaments, including inlaid or carved boxes, knife handles, wooden spoons, chain links whittled out of a broomstick, mostly for Nazi consumption, but also used as tender in the barter and exchange of goods with other prisoners. Sculpture was made by Bruno Apitz (1900–80) at Buchenwald, Maria Albin Boniecki (active 1939–64) at Pawiak and Majdanek, and the Abbé Jean Daligaut (1899–1945) at Hinzert and Dachau.

11 Todorov, op. cit., 1999, p.160.

12 Ziva Amishai Maisels' assertion that, 'the thumbprints are those of Szajna himself' is not borne out by the evidence, i.e., the heterogeneous nature of the markings. See Ziva Amishai Maisels, *Depiction & Interpretation, The Influence of the Holocaust on the Visual Arts*, Pergamon Press, Oxford, 1993, p.248, fn. 37.

13 At Sachsenhausen, where the number of registered prisoners exceeded 200,000 (the real figure is thought to be higher), dead prisoners' numbers were assigned to new arrivals. Those not selected for work were sent directly to the gas chambers and crematoria. No records were kept of this transient population.

14 Olomucki added, 'I still recall the look in my mother's eyes at the Umschlagplatz, the ghetto railway station, where the trains bound for Treblinka stood. It is an expression of love and sorrow. And it contained a parting message… "Try to save your life. You have to remain alive for the sake of your drawings."' Miriam Novitch, Lucy Dawidowicz, Tom Freudenheim, eds., *Spiritual Resistance, Art from Concentration Camps, 1940–45*, Kibbutz Lohamei Haghetaot, Israel, 1981, p.17.

15 See also *Self-portrait After Four Selections* (Olomucki Collection, Israel) reproduced in Milton, Blatter 1981, p.202.

16   See Dalia Ofer & Lenore J. Weitzman, op. cit., eds., *Women in the Holocaust*, Yale University Press, New Haven, 1998.

17   In 1939, KL Rävensbruck (45 kilometres from Sachsenhausen) was established as the only camp specifically for women in the General Government. At its height, the population of the camp reached 132,000. Among these were women affiliated to political organisations hostile to the Nazis and Jews. The camp was liberated in April 1945.

18   An inadequate dietary intake and other factors interrupted women's normal menstrual rhythm, a fact greeted with relief.

19   In *Legacies of Silence*, my observations are based on first hand examination of the drawings (an imperative in any project of this kind). Regrettably, I was unable to extend the course of my research to include Ravensbrück camp and have therefore limited my remarks here, in the hope of one day being able to see the drawings in the camp's archives.

20   Hannah Krall and Marek Edelman, *Shielding the Flame* (translated by Joanna Stasinska and Lawrence Weschler), Henry Holt, New York, 1977, op. cit., p.7; quoted in Todorov, op. cit., 1999, p.97.

21   See Ziva Amishai Maisels, 'The Complexities of Witnessing', *Holocaust and Genocide Studies*, vol.2, no.1, 1987, pp.123–47. Reprinted in Monica Bohm-Duchen, ed., *After Auschwitz, Responses to the Holocaust in Contemporary Art*, Northern Centre for Contemporary Art, Sunderland and Lund Humphries, London, 1995; pp.25–48. See also Milton, Blatter, 1981, illus. p.195.

22   Maisels, ibid. This is one of the key essays on the visual and artistic responses to the Holocaust.

23   In addition to the drawing simply titled *Oswiecim*, Bromberg also showed two still-lifes, a *Church of the Holy Virgin in Lodz*, *A Jewish Street in Lodz* and *Deportation of Children*. Efraim Kaganowski, *Wystawa Zbiorowa* Centralne Żydowski Towarzystwo Kultury I Sztucki, Lodz 1948 (exhibition handlist).

24   Jozef Sandel, *Lexicon of Jewish Art* (unpublished typescript) 1946. Archives of Żydowski Instytut Historyczny w Polsce, Warsaw suggest a date of 1946 for the drawing.

25   Primo Levi, op. cit., 1996, p.6.

26   Dina Wardi, *Memorial Candles, Children of the Holocaust*, Tavistock Routledge, London, 1992, p.132.

27   The dated contributions begin in 1943 and continue into the post-war period (when the book was deposited with the Auschwitz Museum). Annotations are primarily in Polish, with some entries in Cyrillic.

28   Milton, Blatter, op. cit., 1981, p.142.

Chapter 7

1   Excerpt from a speech by Reichsfürer SS Heinrich Himmler, Chief of the German Police to senior SS officers, 4 October 1943; reproduced in *Documents on the Holocaust*, 1999, op. cit., pp.344–45.

2   This circular, signed by Martin Bormann but issued by Hitler's office states, 'where the Jewish Question is brought up in public there may be no discussion of a future overall solution (*Gesamtlosung*). It may however be mentioned that the Jews are taken in groups for appropriate labour purposes'. *Circular 33/43 g. Re: Treatment of the Jewish Question*, 11 July 1943; reproduced in *Documents on the Holocaust*, Yad Vashem, Jerusalem, 1999 (eighth edition), pp.342–43.

3   Sarah Bick Berkowitz, *Where are my brothers?*, Helios, New York, 1965, pp.42–43; quoted in Des Pres, op. cit., 1976, p.33.

4   The *Sonderkommando*'s task was to remove the corpses from the gas chambers, pull teeth, shave the women's hair, classify the victims' clothing, oversee the operation of the ovens, extract the burnt remains and dispose of the ashes.

5   Primo Levi, *The Drowned and the Saved* (trans. R Rosenthal), Abacus, London, 1996, pp.37–38.

6   It continues to present artists with difficulties. This question is explored in some detail in Maisels, op. cit., pp.50–98. See also Elisabeth Maxwell, Roman Halter, *Remembering for the Future, Drawings by Victims of the Holocaust from Concentration Camps and Ghettos, 1940–1945*, (private imprint), London, 1990.

7   Gitta Sereny, *Into that Darkness*, Deutsch, London, 1974, p.197.

8   The words of Jorge Semprun at Buchenwald recreate this atmosphere: 'For two years I'd seen a fraternal spirit gleaming in the hour of those around me... They passed by, shuffling like automatons, subdued, adjusting their stride... their eyes half closed, to protect themselves from the brutal radiance of the world, sheltering the tiny, vacillating flame of their vitality from icy drafts.' Jorge Semprun, *Literature or Life*, Viking Books, New York, 1997, p.17.

9   Primo Levi, op. cit., 1996, p.6.

10   The camp's population included the artists Abraham Berline, David Brainin, Jacques Gotko and Isis Khishka, as well a former and future French prime minister Leon Blum, a senior French cabinet minister Georges Mandel and the Spanish-born writer exiled in France, Jorge Semprun (later Minister of Culture in post-Franco Spain).

11   In her insightful thesis, *Léon Delarbre 1889–1974, Les Effets de la Guerre dans l'Oeuvre de Peintre Déporté*, Université Franche-Comté (unpublished Master's dissertation), Anne Drizard shows how Delarbre returned after the war to the concerns of his pre-war work *sur le motif*, though without the vitality of handling which characterized his earlier paintings.

12   '...the tree is all charred and burned inside, now it's nothing but an empty, rotting carcass, an American incendiary bomb liquidated Goethe's beech tree [sic], the day they bombarded the camp kitchens...' Jorge Semprun, *The Long Voyage*, Penguin Books, London, 1964, pp.119–20.

13   Semprun, op. cit., 1997, pp.93–94.

14   Tadeusz Borowski, *This Way to the Gas Ladies and Gentleman* (translated by Barbara Vedder, with an introduction by Jan Kott), Penguin Books, London, 1976, p.29.

15   Victor Frankl. *From Death-Camp to Existentialism* (translated by Ilse Lasche), Beacon Press, Boston, 1959, p.13; quoted in Des Pres, op. cit., 1976, p. 182.

16   *Dead Christ* (J Paul Getty Museum, Los Angeles) is a study for the *predella* of the *Pietá* (National Gallery of Ireland, Dublin) originally painted for the base of Pontormo's altarpiece in the Church of San Michele Visdomini, Florence with its specific religious connotations.

17   Belsen was liberated by British troops of the 8th Armoured Division on 15 April. Scenes of the atrocities they found there sent shock-waves around the world.

18   Konzentrationslager Dachau was the first of the 'model camps'. Established by Himmler (Head of the SS and chief architect of the concentration camp system) in March 1933, the number of prisoners passing through exceeded 200,000. A typhus epidemic claimed huge casualties in the closing months of the war (in all some 76,000 prisoners perished in the camp). The SS began the partial evacuation of the camp on 26 April 1945, which was liberated by the American 7th Division on 29 April. Himmler was captured by the British in May and committed suicide.

19   Zoran Music, quoted in Michael Peppiatt, *Zoran Music*, Sainsbury Centre for Visual Arts, University of East Anglia, Norwich February–April 2000; Estorick Collection of Modern Italian Art, London, June–September 2000, p.22. I am grateful to Michael Peppiatt for allowing me to quote extensively from his interviews with the artist.

20   Earlier precedents include Leonardo, *Baroncelli pendu* (Bayonne, Musée Bonnat); Jose Ribera, *Pendu à un pieu* (San Francisco Museum of Art); Jacques Callot, *An Execution*, c.1633.

21   This is a study for *Twenty-nine Russians are hung at roll-call in the presence of their comrades, officers, petty officers and German soldiers who have come as spectators*, Dora, 21 March, 1945.

22   Zoran Music, quoted in Peppiatt, op. cit., 2000, pp.21–24.

23   Semprun, op. cit., 1997, pp.42–43.

24   Zyklon or HCN, a highly poisonous and extremely active compound (made up of hydrocyanic or prussic acid), was produced by *Deutsche Gesellschaft für Schädlingsbekämpfung*, a part of I G Farben Industrie According to the records, in 1942–43 the Firm of Tesch und Stabenow (Testa) supplied 19,652 kilograms of the compound to Auschwitz. These documents show that the net profit derived from the sale of the compound by both firms totalled DM 173,720. The gassing would have taken approximately 20 minutes to complete. The chamber was then opened, the bodies removed and the floor cleaned of bodily *excreta*, in preparation for the next group of victims.

25   Likening this work not to Ingres but to Delacroix's *Death of Sardanapulus*, Ziva Amishai Maisels has suggested that Siminski has relied on exemplars in order to depict a scene he had not actually witnessed. One way or another the drawing suggests Siminski's complicity, actual or imagined. Not enough is known about the circumstances that led to its making. We do know that it was commissioned by a Dr E Lolling, at Sachsenhausen (but his identity is not clear). Maisels quite rightly derides Siminski

for his betrayal of the subject, remarking that he 'succumbed to the danger of wringing pleasure, aesthetic and sensuous, from the depiction of an atrocity.' Maisels, op. cit., 1993, p.45.

26 From the Diaries of Rudolf Höss, Władysław Bartoszewski, Mieczysław Kieta, ed., *KL Auschwitz Seen by the SS*, Auschwitz Birkenau State Museum, Oswiecim 1997, pp.78–79. Höss was not alone in witnessing these events. Other high-ranking officials also witnessed the exterminations at Auschwitz: the Chief Inspector of Camps, Richard Glücks, *SS Reichspürer* Himmler, Adolf Eichmann and Robert von Grawits, SS Senior Surgeon and Chairman of the Red Cross.

27 See discussion in Gitta Sereny, *Into that Darkness*, Deutsch, London, 1974.

28 Sereny, ibid., p.202.

29 Primo Levi, *If this is a Man*, Abacus, London, 2000, p.32.

30 Mauthausen was the last camp in the former Reich territory to be liberated by Allied troops on 5 and 6 May 1945.

31 This is one of a series of 111 drawings produced at Buchenwald and published soon after the war. See Boris Taslitzky, *Cent onze dessins faits à Buchenwald*, Association Française Buchenwald-Dora, Editions Hautefeuille, Paris, 1945, reprinted 1978, no. 24. Other drawings describe in detail the prisoner's clothing. For instance, in *Hongrois sortant des douches*, 1945, a diminutive figure, wrapped in a hooded cover, emerges from the showers at Buchenwald. The inscription at the foot of the drawing reads '*couverte vermillon fatigué et pantalon vert bouteille*.

32 Between January and April 1945, no less than 15,400 deaths were registered in Buchenwald. In some blocks, the living and the dead were thrown together.

33 *Le Petite Camp de Buchenwald* was exhibited in *Art et Résistance* at the Musée National d'Art Moderne in February 1946 and purchased by the museum.

34 Jacques Gaucheron, 'Entretien avec Boris Taslitzky' *Arts de France*, 1950, Paris, nos. 29–30, pp.36–73.

35 Ziva Maisels, 'Art Confronts the Holocaust'; quoted in Bohm Duchen, M. ed., *After Auschwitz, Responses to the Holocaust in Contemporary Art* Northern Centre for Contemporary Art, Sunderland and Lund Humphries, London, 1995. Elsewhere, Maisels compares these with the devices employed by the Italian-American artist Rico Le Brun, which share with Picasso, a common origin in Cubism. The conflating of forms in a Cubist-type space serves to distance the subject, thus 'turning documents into art'.

36 Leon Delarbre's *Croquis Clandestins: Auschwitz, Buchenwald, Dora, Bergen-Belsen* were first published in November 1945 and Taslitzky's *Cent onze dessins faits à Buchenwald* were also collected and published immediately after the war by Louis Aragon.

37 Photographs of atrocity, the victims of death by gas and other means had been reproduced in the New Masses on 22 December 1942 and 3 August 1943.

38 Maisels has shown conclusively how Cagli appropriated this figure from a photograph taken of the subject by the US Signal Corps

at Nordhausen after liberation, but removes it from its original setting. See Maisels, op. cit., 1993, figs. 160, 161.

39 Edward R Murrow's radio broadcast from Buchenwald, 16 April, 1945.

40 *Il transforme en beauté l'horreur humaine actuelle*. Seghers, Paris 1946; quoted in *Paris-Paris, Creation en France 1937–1957*, Centre Georges Pompidou, Paris, 1981; pp.97–115, 120–121.

41 Francis Ponge, 'Réflexions sur les statuettes, figures et peintures d'Alberto Giacometti', *Cahiers d'Art*, Paris, 1951; reprinted in Germaine Viatte, ed., *Aftermath: France 1945–54, New Images of Man*, Barbican Art Gallery, London, 3 March–13 June 1982.

Chapter 8

1 H O Bluhm, 'How did they survive? Mechanisms of defence in Nazi Concentration Camps', *American Journal of Psychotherapy*, 211, 3–32, 1948, p.25.

2 Anton Gill, *The Journey Back From Hell, Conversations with Concentration Camp Survivors*, Grafton Books, London, 1988, pp.442–59.

3 Jorge Semprun, *The Long Voyage*, Penguin Books, London, 1964, p.24.

4 Gita Sereny, *Into that Darkness*, Pimlico, London, 1995 (first published 1974), pp.230–31.

5 H H Price, *Thinking and Experience*, 1969; quoted in Richard I Cohen, *Jewish Icons, Art and Society in Modern Europe*, University of California Press, Berkeley and Los Angeles, 1998.

6 In this opening discussion I am indebted to the 'Memory, Representation and Education' colloquium at 'Remembering for the Future 2000', Oxford 16–23 July, 2000 (forthcoming publication), as well as to representations made by David Cesarani, Jonathan Webber and others.

7 Jorge Semprun, *Literature or Life*, Viking Books, New York, 1997, p.126.

8 The literary works by the survivors, Robert Antelme, Primo Levi, Tadeusz Borowski, Aharon Appelfeld, Paul Celan, Dan Pagis attest to this fact. Yosef Hayim Yerushalmi, *Zohar, Jewish History and Jewish Memory*, University of Washington Press, 1982, p.98.

9 The catalogue of the artist's 1995 retrospective exhibition lists thirty-four works. Some, however, have estimated this at a higher number.

10 One in particular shows four figures laid out in a receding order. See Jean Clair, ed., *Zoran Music*, Réunion des Musées Nationaux, Grand Palais, Paris, April–July, 1995.

11 Music attributes this ability to organise the flat surface of his painting to his encounter with the Byzantine mosaics of the Slovene countryside.

12 The suite would occupy the artist over the following 17 years. Music explains how the title came about. While contemplating a four-metre pile of corpses in front of the crematoria a friend at Dachau remarked, 'a thing like this will never happen again.' Music phrased his response some time later, 'when I could no longer hold things in, when the

memories of the camp surged up inside me, then I realised it was not true. We are not the last.'

13 '*Le Carso est la matrice de toute ma peinture. Une paysage dépouillé, presque désertique. Pétrifie, dirait-on.*', quoted in *Zoran Music*, Paris, 1995, p.231.

14 Music was first drawn to the strange shapes of the landscape and mountains around Sienna during a visit to Tuscany in 1948. See *Zoran Music*, 1995, pp.235, 238.

15 Michael Peppiatt, *Zoran Music*, Sainsbury Centre for Visual Arts, University of East Anglia, Norwich, February–April 2000; Estorick Collection of Modern Italian Art, London, June–September 2000, p.33.

16 Peppiatt, ibid., pp.21–24.

17 A progressive diminution of Music's eyesight in the mid-eighties and early nineties is accompanied by a corresponding richness in the tactility of the surface. The loss of one sense sharpens another. He was always responsive to the distinct weave of linen, working on the unprimed surface of the canvas (a practice also preferred by Francis Bacon, whom Music greatly admired).

18 Peppiatt, op. cit., pp.22.

19 This is one of the themes developed in Tom Segev's *The Seventh Million: The Israelis and the Holocaust*, Hill & Wang, New York, 1994.

20 This rupture characterised the battles between 'modernists' and traditionalists in Israel. Dalia Manor detects a *malaise* or climate of indifference toward Holocaust themes in Israeli Art; see Dalia Manor 'From Rejection to Recognition: Israeli Art and the Holocaust', *Israel Affairs*, vol. 4, nos.3 & 4, spring/summer 1998.

21 Their arrival was followed soon after by two outstanding graphic artists, Hermann Strück and Jakob Steinhardt. Their presence encouraged a diversity of expressive languages in Israel, unusual in so young a country.

22 Other exponents of this tradition include: Aviva Uri, Moshe Gershuni, Liliane Klapisch and Moshe Kupfermann.

23 Goya's references included Quevedo's *Dreams*, the satirical plays of Antonio de Zamora, the vogue for witchcraft and Moratín's accounts of the gruesome witches' trials in his *Auto de Fe*. See Juliet Wilson-Bareau, *Goya's Prints*, British Museum Press, London, 1981, pp.23–41.

24 Osias Hofstatter's iconography is informed by, among others, Breughel, the Medieval 'passions', the satirical *image d'epinal*, elements from the guts-and-gore of the *Grand Guignol* theatre, the hilarity of *Punchinello*, Balzac's *Comédie Humaine*.

25 Hofstatter's later reputation is based on the graphic works produced after his arrival in Israel in 1957 and in particular those produced after 1967 and shown in *Michael Gross, Osias Hofstatter, Mordechai Moreh*, XI São Paolo Biennale, September–November 1971.

26 It may be worth recalling in this context the crucial role played by Hofstatter's companion, Anna Schebestova, in the artist's development (see biographical entry, p.107).

27 The earliest of Yehuda Bacon's diaries was begun in July, 1945, in the Stirjin rehabilitation home, near Prague.

28 Bacon frequently refers to the trial, confirming its importance for him.

29 At the time of my last visit to Bacon's studio in December 1998, I counted 191 workbooks bound in near identical covers measuring 11 x 17 in (28.5 x 43.5cm) when open.

30 Bacon recalls the impression made on him by Otto Benesch's study of Rembrandt's drawings.

31 We might reflect here on the special place assigned in Picasso's art to his female companions as muse or *anima*.

32 The Cairo *genizah* yielded a repository of valuable texts, some more than a thousand years old, discovered by the Cambridge scholar and theologian, Solomon Shechter (1847–1915).

33 In Bacon's *Escape with the Torah*, Prague, 1946, a young man flees a continent engulfed in flames, the *Torah* scrolls (the first five books of the Bible or Pentateuch) held securely as a proud symbol epitomizing the hopes for spiritual and communal renewal after the war. The late Biblical narrative of the Megillat Esther (scroll of Esther), read on Purim, which commemorates Jewish deliverance from genocide in the Persian Empire, has echoes not just for Bacon but for other Israeli artists, like Moshe Kupferman and Raffi Lavie.

34 *Memorbücher* are discussed in Yosef Hayim Yerushalmi, op. cit., 1982, p.46.

35 Books are important in other ways to the Bacon household. His wife and companion of many years Dr Leah Bacon is a distinguished writer and, until recently, lectured in English and American literature at the Hebrew University.

36 Hans Günther Adler, *Theresienstadt 1941–45. Das Antlitz einer Zwangsgemeinschaft. Geschichte, Soziologie, Psychologie*, J.C.B.Mohr, Tübingen, 1955.

37 Compare for instance, Klee's *Angelus Novus* with the more sinister *Angel Applicant* (Engel Anwärter) 1939 (Metropolitan Museum of Art, New York) and *The Angel of Death* (Der Todesengel) 1940 (Felix Klee Collection, Berne).

38 The year 1920 marked a high point in Klee's career with an exhibition at the Hans Goltz Galerie *Neue Kunst* in Munich, the publication of two monographs and an invitation to join the staff at the Bauhaus.

87 **Bedřich Fritta**
Men's Dormitory, Sudentenkasserne,
Terezin, 1943–44
pen and ink on paper
378 x 285mm
Thomas Fritta Haas
Cat. 53

Catalogue

All works on paper unless otherwise stated

LEGACIES

Käthe Kollwitz
1. *Lamentation, In Memory of Ernst Barlach*
Klage
1938–39
bronze, edition of 10
265 x 260 x 60mm
Tel Aviv Museum of Art, Israel
Gift of Helen and Eric Cohn,
New York, 1970

Paul Klee
2. *Mephisto as Pallas*
Mephisto Als Pallas
1939
watercolour, tempera on black Ingres
paper on board,
480 x 309mm
Ulmer Museum, Ulm

Jankel Adler
3. *Orphans*
Waisen
1942
oil and gesso on paper
lined on to panel
570 x 780mm
Private Collection

Isaac Celnikier
4. *Uprising*
Révolte
1981–84
oil on canvas
1970 x 2235mm
Collection the artist

PRECURSORS

Emile Nolde
5. *Prophet*
1912
woodcut
323 x 220mm (image)
British Museum, London

Ludwig Meidner
6. *Self-portrait as Prophet*
Selbstporträt als Prophet
1918
pen and ink, pencil
649 x 550mm
Marvin and Janet Fishman Collection,
Milwaukee

Jacob Steinhardt
7. *Praying Jew*
Illustration to Arno Nadel's *In Tiefer Nacht*
c.1912
etching
210 x 152mm
Tel Aviv Museum of Art, Israel

Lovis Corinth
8. *Death and the artist*
from the suite *Totentanz*
1922
etching
234 x 178mm
British Museum, London

Otto Dix
9. *Gassed*
from the suite *Der Krieg*
Gastote, Templeux-la-Fosse, August 1916
1923
etching and aquatint
194 x 287mm
British Museum, London

Marc Chagall
10. *Praying Jew*
De betende Jude
1922–23
woodcut, edition 20
280 x 203mm (image)
478 x 330mm (sheet)
Private Collection

Marc Chagall
11. Study for *The Falling Angel*
Etude pour 'La Chute de l'Ange'
1934
oil, Indian ink, crayon and pencil
on cardboard
495 x 630mm
Private Collection

Jacob Steinhardt
12. *The Ten Plagues*
frontispiece from *Haggadah shel Pesach*
1923
woodcut
239 x 177mm
The Israel Museum, Jerusalem

Jacob Steinhardt
13. *Haggadah shel Pesach*
1923
woodcut illustrations, with lettering
designed by Franzisca Baruch
265 x 385mm (open)
Private Collection

Jacob Steinhardt
14. *The Book of Yehoshua Eliezer ben Sirah*
Illustrations to verses from the Apocrypha
with a foreword by Arnold Zweig
1929
woodcut and letter press
195 x 280mm
The Israel Museum, Jerusalem

Jacob Pins
15. *Dance of Death*
1945
woodcut and wood engraving
483 x 383mm
British Museum, London

Felix Nussbaum
16. *Skeleton playing the clarinet*
Study for *Death Triumphant*
c.1944
pencil and gouache on buff paper
306 x 223mm
Felix-Nussbaum-Haus, Osnabrück mit der
Sammlung der Niedersächsischen
Sparkassenstiftung

Ludwig Meidner
17. *Suburban Street in Berlin*
1913
drypoint
170 x 139mm
British Museum, London

Jacob Steinhardt
18. *Pogrom*
1913
drypoint
133 x 195mm
The Israel Museum, Jerusalem

Max Beckmann
19. Transfer drawing for *The Street*
from the suite, *Die Hölle*
1919
pencil, black chalk
673 x 535mm
British Museum, London

Bruno Schulz
20. *Self-portrait*
c.1933
pencil
115 x 98mm
Muzeum Literatury im Adama
Mickiewicza, Warsaw

Bruno Schulz
21. *Scenes at a table – Josef wearing a hat*
seated between two women
Scena przy stole – Józef (autoportret)
w kapeluszu miedzy dwiema kobietami
pencil
145 x 190mm
Muzeum Literatury im Adama
Mickiewicza, Warsaw

Bruno Schulz
22. *Vehicle – Astronomical Refractor*
Illustration for *Sanatorium Under the Sign of*
the Hourglass
Pojazd – refraktor astronomiczny
c.1936
pen and ink on tracing paper
145 x 185mm
Muzeum Literatury im Adama
Mickiewicza, Warsaw

Otto Pankok
23. *The Synagogue*
1940
charcoal and black chalk
970 x 1290mm
Otto Pankok Museum
Haus Esselt, Germany

Felix Nussbaum
24. *Bombardment I*
Fassung I
1941
pen and ink wash
510 x 650mm
Jüdisches Museum der
Stadt Frankfurt-am-Main

IN TRANSIT, FRANCE

Osias Hofstatter
25. *View of St Cyprien*
1940
pen and ink
150 x 101mm
Art collection
Beit Lohamei Haghetaot, Israel
Ghetto Fighters' House Museum

Osias Hofstatter
26. *The Beach*
St Cyprien, 1940
pen and ink
90 x 205mm
Art collection
Beit Lohamei Haghetaot, Israel
Ghetto Fighters' House Museum

Karl Schwesig

27. *Naked figure asleep on the Beach*
St Cyprien, 1940
pen and ink
205 x 268mm
Art collection
Beit Lohamei Haghetaot, Israel
Ghetto Fighters' House Museum

Karl Schwesig

28. *The Flood*
St Cyprien, 1940
pen and ink
167 x 220mm
Art collection
Beit Lohamei Haghetaot, Israel
Ghetto Fighters' House Museum

Karl Schwesig

29. *Immigrants by the Sea, Night*
Emigranten am Meer
St Cyprien, 1940
pen and ink wash
210 x 261mm
Art collection
Beit Lohamei Haghetaot, Israel
Ghetto Fighters' House Museum

Karl Schwesig

30. *Canigou Mountains under Snow*
St Cyprien, 1940
watercolour on tracing paper
230 x 300mm
Art collection
Beit Lohamei Haghetaot, Israel
Ghetto Fighters' House Museum

Felix Nussbaum

31. *Huddled Prisoner*
1940
charcoal, chalk, pen, ink and
gouache on buff paper
515 x 425mm
Felix-Nussbaum-Haus Osnabrück mit der
Sammlung der Niedersächsischen
Sparkassenstiftung

Felix Nussbaum

32. *Self-portrait with key*
1941
oil on board
472 x 551mm
Tel Aviv Museum of Art
Gift of Mr Philippe Aisinber & Mr Maurice
Tzwern, Brussels, in memory of Uniyl
Tzern (Czenstochova 1904–1943Brussels)
and all the victims of Fascism

Jacob Barosin

33. *Latrines*
Gurs, 1943
graphite
250 x 180mm
Yad Vashem Art Museum, Jerusalem

Jacob Barosin

34. *Deportees*
Gurs, 1943
graphite
180 x 250mm
Yad Vashem Art Museum, Jerusalem

Boris Taslitzky

35. *During a lecture in the camp*
Durant une conférence au camp
St Sulpice-la-Pointe,
1944
pen and ink
208 x 310mm
Musée de la Résistance Nationale,
Champigny

Boris Taslitzky

36. *Prisoners reading*
Prisonniers lisants
St Sulpice-la-Pointe, 1944
pen and ink
210 x 310mm
Musée de la Résistance Nationale,
Champigny

Adolphe Feder

37. *The Reader (Jew with Yellow Star)*
Drancy, 1943
charcoal and pastel
490 x 376mm
Art collection
Beit Lohamei Haghetaot, Israel
Ghetto Fighters' House Museum

Leon Landau

38. *Portrait of a Young Man*
Malines, 1943
pencil
355 x 265mm
Art collection
Beit Lohamei Haghetaot, Israel
Ghetto Fighters' House Museum

Otto Freundlich

39. *L'Indélicat*
The Offending Postman
Saint-Paul-de-Fenouillet, c.1941
pencil
283 x 231mm
Association 'Les Amis de Jeanne et Otto
Freundlich', Pontoise

Lili Rilik-Andrieux

40. *Three women leaning over a stove*
Gurs, 1940
pen and ink
150 x 160mm
Art collection
Beit Lohamei Haghetaot, Israel
Ghetto Fighters' House Museum

Leo Haas

41. *Laundry Room*
Wäscherei
Nisko, 1939
pencil
222 x 281mm
Památník Terezín

Irene Awret

42. *Open Window with Still-life,*
Vase and Shells (summer)
Malines, c.1944
pencil
250 x 182mm
Art collection
Beit Lohamei Haghetaot, Israel
Ghetto Fighters' House Museum

Irene Awret

43. *Open Window (winter)*
Malines, 1944
pencil
245 x 182mm
Art collection
Beit Lohamei Haghetaot, Israel
Ghetto Fighters' House Museum

Irene Awret

44. *Clouds*
Malines, 1944
pencil
244 x 182mm
Art collection
Beit Lohamei Haghetaot, Israel
Ghetto Fighters' House Museum

Otto Freundlich

45. Study for *My Sky is Red*
Etude pour 'Mon Ciel est Rouge'
1933
pencil
270 x 210mm
Association 'Les Amis de Jeanne et Otto
Freundlich', Pontoise

Otto Freundlich

46. *Unfinished composition*
Composition (inachevée)
1943
gouache on board
650 x 500mm
Donation Freundlich, Musée de Pontoise

TEREZÍN

Bedřich Fritta

47. *View of Theresienstadt*
Terezín, 1943–44
pen and ink
593 x 440mm
Thomas Fritta Haas

Joseph Spier

48. *Picture of Theresienstadt*
Bilder Aus Theresienstadt
Terezín, 1944
album containing 18 hand-coloured
lithographs
170 x 440mm (open)
Yad Vashem Art Museum, Jerusalem
Gift of Ze'ev Shek, Israel

Leo Haas

49. *Members of the Lagerkommandantur*
on the beat
Terezín, 1943–44
pencil
175 x 125mm
Památník Terezín

Otto Ungar

50. *Street Scene with Crowds*
Terezín, c.1943
pen, ink and gouache
440 x 600mm
The Jewish Museum in Prague

Leo Haas

51. *Arrivals*
Terezín, c.1943
gouache, pen and ink wash
363 x 462mm
Yad Vashem Art Museum, Jerusalem
Gift of Ze'ev Shek, Israel

Otto Ungar
52. *After the arrival of the Transport*
Po Příjezdu transportu
Terezín, c.1943
gouache, pen and ink wash
440 x 600mm
Památník Terezín

Bedřich Fritta
53. *Men's Dormitory, Sudeten Barracks*
Mužské ubikace v Sudetských kasárnách
Terezín, 1943–44
pen and ink
378 x 285mm
Thomas Fritta Haas

Karel Fleischmann
54. *Living Quarters, Sudeten Barracks*
Terezín, 1943
pen and ink wash
225 x 330mm
Yad Vashem Art Museum, Jerusalem

Mořitz Nágl
55. *Small Dormitory*
Ubikace ve světnici
Terezín, c.1942
oil on linen mounted on board
295 x 398mm
The Jewish Museum in Prague

Charlotte Burešová
56. *Dormitory*
Terezín, undated
pen and ink wash, graphite
and chinese white
313 x 233mm
Yad Vashem Art Museum, Jerusalem

Bedřich Fritta
57. *Fortune Teller*
Kartářka
Terezín, 1943–44
pen, brush and ink wash
587 x 422mm
Thomas Fritta Haas

Otto Ungar
58. *Old Man with Soup Bowl*
Starý muž s jídelní miskou
Terezín, 1942–44
pen and ink wash on
watercolour paper
533 x 356mm
Památník Terezín

Karel Fleischmann
59. *Old Man with a Cup*
Terezín, 1943
graphite
440 x 300mm
The Jewish Museum in Prague

Bedřich Fritta
60. *Going to Work*
Nástup do Práce
Terezín, c.1942–44
pen and ink wash
256 x 327mm
Thomas Fritta Haas

Bedřich Fritta
61. *The Morgue*
Terezín, 1943–44
pen, brush and ink wash
474 x 360mm
Thomas Fritta Haas

Karel Fleischmann
62. *Invalid veterans' prostheses*
Protézy válečných invalidů
Terezín, 1943
pen and ink wash
330 x 440mm
The Jewish Museum in Prague

Leo Haas
63. *Technical Drawing Studio*
Kreslírna II
Terezín, 1943
graphite and black chalk
363 x 529mm
Památník Terezín

Jan Burka
64. *Nude*
Terezín, 1944
pen and sepia wash
300 x 162mm
Yad Vashem Art Museum, Jerusalem

Jan Burka
65. *Study of Irises*
Reclining Nude, verso
Terezín, c.1942
pen and ink, watercolour and
sanguine on buff paper
257 x 232mm
Yad Vashem Art Museum, Jerusalem

Bedřich Fritta
66. *Deluge*
Terezín, 1943–44
black chalk, pen and ink wash on heavily
abraded paper
420 x 583mm
Thomas Fritta Haas

Bedřich Fritta
67. *Film and Reality*
Terezín, 1943–44
pen and ink
320 x 570mm
Thomas Fritta Haas

Bedřich Fritta
68. *Sheet of studies for 'Film and Reality'*
Terezín, 1943–44
pencil and mixed media
sheet from a sketchbook
(dimensions unknown)
Thomas Fritta Haas

Leo Haas
69. *Funeral Hearses*
Terezín, c.1943
pen and ink wash
373 x 500mm
Yad Vashem Art Museum, Jerusalem

Bedřich Fritta
70. *Transport of the Elderly*
Terezín, 1942–44
pen and ink wash
417 x 596mm
Thomas Fritta Haas

Felix Bloch
71. *The Hearse, Transport*
Terezín, 1943
black chalk
298 x 432mm
Yad Vashem Art Museum, Jerusalem

Karel Fleischmann
72. *Collecting corpses*
Svážení mrtvol
Terezín, 1943
pen and ink wash
224 x 330mm
The Jewish Museum in Prague

Otto Ungar
73. *Funeral*
Pohřeb
Terezín, 1942
black chalk and gouache
220 x 298mm
Památník Terezín

GHETTO
Jankel Adler
74. *What a World: The Destruction of Lodz*
1923–24
oil on board
635 x 425mm
The Israel Museum, Jerusalem
Gift of Dr and Mrs Isaac Friedman,
Plantation, Florida to American Friends
of the Israel Museum

Jacob Lifchitz
75. *Crowd Gathering*
Kovno Ghetto, c.1944
pen and ink
98 x 205mm
Yad Vashem Art Museum, Jerusalem

Jacob Lifchitz
76. *Internee*
Kovno Ghetto, c.1944
pen and ink
345 x 250mm
Yad Vashem Art Museum, Jerusalem

Esther Lurie
77. *Women Prisoner*
Leibitsch, 1944
pencil on a cotton spool
paper wrapper
110 x 62mm
Yad Vashem Art Museum, Jerusalem

Esther Lurie
78. *Women Prisoner*
Leibitsch, 1944
pencil, pen and ink
108 x 75mm
Art collection
Beit Lohamei Haghetaot, Israel
Ghetto Fighters' House Museum

Esther Lurie
79. *Women Prisoner, back view*
Leibitsch, 1944
pen and ink
103 x 75mm
Art collection
Beit Lohamei Haghetaot, Israel
Ghetto Fighters' House Museum

Esther Lurie
80. *Woman Prisoner*
Strutthof, 1944
pencil
105 x 73mm
Art collection
Beit Lohamei Haghetaot, Israel
Ghetto Fighters' House Museum

Josef Kowner

81. *Self-portrait*
    Lodz Ghetto, 1941
    watercolour
    495 x 385mm
    Yad Vashem Art Museum, Jerusalem
    Gift of Leon Kowner, Israel

Josef Kowner

82. *Untitled sheet with decorated borders showing ghetto tradesmen: a cobbler, tailors, metal-worker and carpenter*
    Lodz Ghetto, 1943
    pen and ink
    270 x 370mm
    Żydowski Instytut Historyczny w Polsce, Poland

Roman Kramstyck

83. *Jewish Family in the Ghetto*
    Rodzina Żydowska w getcie
    Warsaw, c.1942
    red sanguine chalk
    536 x 378mm
    Żydowski Instytut Historyczny w Polsce, Poland

Anonymous

84. *Sewage Collection*
    Wywóz Fekalii w getcie Łódzkim
    Lodz Ghetto, 1943
    oil on composite board
    332 x 453mm
    Żydowski Instytut Historyczny w Polsce, Poland

Israel Lejzerowicz

85. *Sewage Carts*
    Lodz Ghetto, 1941–42
    soft pastel
    430 x 672mm
    Yad Vashem Art Museum, Jerusalem
    Gift of Nachman Zonabend, Sweden

Arnold Daghani

86. *Evensong*
    1954
    gouache
    274 x 262mm
    Arnold Daghani Archive
    Centre for German-Jewish Studies, University of Sussex

AUSCHWITZ

Mieczysław Kościelniak

87. *A Friendly Favour*
    Koleżeńska przysługa
    Oświęcim, c.1944
    black chalk
    210 x 295mm
    Państwowe Muzeum, Oświęcim

Mieczysław Kościelniak

88. *Prisoners of Oświęcim*
    Więźniowie Oświęcimscy
    Oświęcim, 1944
    pen and ink
    300 x 210mm
    Państwowe Muzeum, Oświęcim

Włodzimierz Siwierski

89. *Soup*
    Zupa
    Oświęcim, 1940
    pencil
    100 x 162mm
    Państwowe Muzeum, Oświęcim

Włodzimierz Siwierski

90. *Sculptor*
    Rzeźbiarz
    Oświęcim, 1941
    pencil
    157 x 112mm
    Państwowe Muzeum, Oświęcim

Halina Olomucki

91. *Women in Birkenau*
    1945
    pencil on tracing paper
    320 x 215mm
    Art collection
    Beit Lohamei Haghetaot, Israel
    Ghetto Fighters' House Museum

Józef Szajna

92. *Penal company, Sonderkommando and tyfus*
    Karna kompanie, Sonderkommando i tyfus
    Buchenwald, 1944–45
    pencil, brush and tusche
    340 x 298mm
    Państwowe Muzeum, Oświęcim

Franciszek Jaźwiecki

93. *Portrait of Stefan Antoniak*
    Portret Stefana Antoniaka
    Buchenwald, 1944
    pencil
    200 x 140mm
    Państwowe Muzeum, Oświęcim

Franciszek Jaźwiecki

94. *Portrait of the Russian Prisoner Ivan Zwigincew*
    Portret Iwana Zwigincewa R70271
    Buchenwald, 1944
    pencil and colour crayon
    200 x 140mm
    Państwowe Muzeum, Oświęcim

Franciszek Jaźwiecki

95. *Portrait of the French Prisoner Ros Pedra*
    Portret Ros Pedra F34922
    Buchenwald, 1944
    pencil and colour crayon
    200 x 140mm
    Państwowe Muzeum, Oświęcim

Franciszek Jaźwiecki

96. *Portrait of Yugoslav Prisoner Milana Savica*
    Portret Milana Savica J35103
    Buchenwald, 1944
    pencil
    200 x 140mm
    Państwowe Muzeum, Oświęcim

Franciszek Jaźwiecki

97. *Portrait of the Polish Prisoner Julian Rudzkiego*
    Portret Juliana Rudzkiego P63671
    Sachsenhausen, 1943–44
    pencil and colour crayon
    200 x 140mm
    Państwowe Muzeum, Oświęcim

Franciszek Jaźwiecki

98. *Self-portrait*
    Autoportret Franciszka Jaźwieckiego P75057
    Buchenwald, 1944
    pencil and colour crayon
    200 x 140mm
    Państwowe Muzeum, Oświęcim

Maurycy Bromberg

99. *Five Jews Harnessed to a Roller*
    Pięciu więźniów zaprzężonych do walca, Oświęcim
    c.1945–48
    wax crayon and solvent spirit
    279 x 381mm
    Żydowski Instytut Historyczny w Polsce, Poland

David Olère

100. *My Private War*
     Paris, 1945
     pencil, pen and ink wash
     280 x 380mm
     Art collection
     Beit Lohamei Haghetaot, Israel
     Ghetto Fighters' House Museum

Władysław Siwek

101. *Devil!*
     Kaduk!
     Oświęcim, c.1950
     pencil, watercolour
     690 x 490mm
     Państwowe Muzeum, Oświęcim

Mieczysław Koúcielniak

102. *Wheelbarrows*
     Taczki
     Warsaw, c.1947
     pencil and tempera
     610 x 860mm
     Państwowe Muzeum, Oświęcim

WITNESS TO ATROCITY

Léon Delarbre

103. *Goethe's oak*
     Le Chêne de Goethe
     Buchenwald, 1944
     pencil on joined sheets
     142 x 250mm
     Centre George Pompidou, Paris
     Musée nationale d'art moderne
     on loan to Musée de la Résistance et de la Déportation de Besançon

Léon Delarbre

104. *The crematorium the morning after the bombardment*
     Le crématoire le lendemain du bombardement
     Buchenwald, 1944
     graphite
     135 x 170mm
     Centre George Pompidou, Paris
     Musée nationale d'art moderne
     on loan to Musée de la Résistance et de la Déportation de Besançon

Léon Delarbre

105. *In the Small Camp, dysentery: while his trousers dry-off*
     Au petit camp, dysenterie: pendant que sèche le pantalon
     Buchenwald, 1944
     pencil on newsprint
     170 x 135mm
     Centre George Pompidou, Paris
     Musée nationale d'art moderne
     on loan to Musée de la Résistance et de la Déportation de Besançon

Léon Delarbre
106. *The morning after Liberation: too late!*
Le lendemain de la Libération: trop tarde!
Bergen-Belsen, 1945
pencil and black chalk
260 x 280mm
Centre George Pompidou, Paris
Musée nationale d'art moderne
on loan to Musée de la Résistance et de
la Déportation de Besançon

Léon Delarbre
107. *On the roadside: a fellow prisoner dead on*
route from the station to the camp
Sur le bord de la route: un camarade mort
pendant le trajet de la gare au camp
Bergen Belsen, 1945
105 x 150mm
Centre George Pompidou, Paris
Musée nationale d'art moderne
on loan to Musée de la Résistance et de
la Déportation de Besançon

Zoran Music
108. *Hanged man*
Pendu
Dachau, 1945
ink
299 x 212mm
Centre George Pompidou, Paris
Musée nationale d'art moderne

Zoran Music
109. *Corpses in coffins*
Corps en cercueils
Dachau, 1945
ink
211 x 278mm
Centre George Pompidou, Paris
Musée nationale d'art moderne

Zoran Music
110. *Corpse carried by two men*
Corps emporté par deux hommes
Dachau, 1945
brown chalk
210 x 297mm
Centre George Pompidou, Paris
Musée nationale d'art moderne

Zoran Music
111. *Oven in the Old Crematorium*
Die Öfen im Alten Krematorium
Dachau, 1945
brown chalk
212 x 299mm
Centre George Pompidou, Paris
Musée nationale d'art moderne

Aldo Carpi
112. *The Courtyard of the Railway Station,*
Corpses in front of Block 31
Gusen, 1945
pencil
260 x 186mm
Art collection
Beit Lohamei Haghetaot, Israel
Ghetto Fighters' House Museum

Paul Goyard
113. *Carnage*
Charnier
Buchenwald, 1945
pencil
215 x 290mm
Musée d'Histoire Contemporaine, Paris

Corrado Cagli
114. *Lying Corpses*
Buchenwald, 1945
pen and ink
200 x 330mm
Archivio Cagli, Rome

Corrado Cagli
115. *Boy in the Camp*
Ragazzo nel Lager
Buchenwald, 1945
pen and ink
254 x 330mm
Archivio Cagli, Rome

Aldo Carpi
116. *The Little Jew*
Il Piccolo Ebreo
Gusen, 1945
pencil
260 x 205mm
Art collection
Beit Lohamei Haghetaot, Israel
Ghetto Fighters' House Museum

Aldo Carpi
117. *The Famished*
Mauthausen 1944
pen and ink wash
260 x 186mm
Art collection
Beit Lohamei Haghetaot, Israel
Ghetto Fighters' House Museum

Boris Taslitzky
118. *Hungarian leaving the showers*
Hongrois sortant des douches
Buchenwald, 1945
pencil
122 x 105mm
Musée de la Résistance Nationale,
Champigny

Boris Taslitzky
119. *Along the barbed fence*
Le long des barbelés
Buchenwald, 1944
pencil
127 x 100mm
Musée de la Résistance Nationale,
Champigny

Boris Taslitzky
120. Study for *Le Petit Camp á Buchenwald*
Buchenwald, 1945
watercolour, pen and ink
212 x 311mm
Musée de la Résistance Nationale,
Champigny

SURVIVORS
Zoran Music
121. *We are not the last*
Nous ne sommes pas les derniers
1973
acrylic on canvas
970 x 1460mm
Collection the artist

Zoran Music
122. *We are not the last*
Nous ne sommes pas les derniers
1978
brown chalk
500 x 350 mm
Collection the artist

Zoran Music
123. *We are not the last*
Nous ne sommes pas les derniers
1975
charcoal
210 x 295mm
Robert and Lisa Sainsbury Collection, UEA

Zoran Music
124. *We are not the last*
Nous ne sommes pas les derniers
1975
from a box set of seven etchings
332 x 259mm
Robert and Lisa Sainsbury Collection, UEA

Zoran Music
125. *We are not the last*
Nous ne sommes pas les derniers
1975
from a box set of seven etchings
332 x 259mm
Robert and Lisa Sainsbury Collection, UEA

Zoran Music
126. *We are not the last*
Nous ne sommes pas les derniers
1975
from a box set of seven etchings
332 x 259mm
Robert and Lisa Sainsbury Collection, UEA

Osias Hofstatter
127. *Diagonal*
1968
pen and ink wash on newsprint, layered
onto board and heavily abraded
430 x 320mm
Collection of Herzliya Museum of Art

Osias Hofstatter
128. *Three Profiles*
1968
pen and ink wash on newsprint, layered
onto board and heavily abraded
350 x 278mm
Collection of Herzliya Museum of Art

Osias Hofstatter
129. *Untitled (Mother and Child)*
undated
pen and ink wash
434 x 330mm
Collection of Herzliya Museum of Art

Osias Hofstatter
130. *Untitled (Woman-Bird-Man-Beast)*
undated
pen and ink wash
500 x 350mm
Collection of Herzliya Museum of Art

Osias Hofstatter
131. *Untitled (Man-Beast-Child)*
undated
gouache, ink, graphite
615 x 405mm
Collection of Herzliya Museum of Art

Osias Hofstatter
132. *Untitled (Hand and Heads)*
undated
pen and ink wash
730 x 550mm
Collection of Herzliya Museum of Art

Yehuda Bacon

133. *Forty workbooks*
1973–99
pencil, black chalk, pen and ink wash,
watercolour and mixed media
bound in black covers
285 x 435mm (open)
Collection the artist

Yehuda Bacon

134. *Diary*
1945
Collection the artist

Yehuda Bacon

135. *Diary*
1994
Collection the artist

Arnold Daghani

136. *What a Nice World*
1942–77
album containing 200 sheets
mixed media, bound
540 x 770 x 70mm (open)
Arnold Daghani Archive
Centre for German-Jewish Studies,
University of Sussex

Arnold Daghani

137. *The building in which we had a narrow
escape*
1977/78
album containing 81 sheets
mixed media, bound
320 x 490mm (open)
Arnold Daghani Archive
Centre for German-Jewish Studies,
University of Sussex

Arnold Daghani

138. Commentary on an original text by
Pierre Jean Jouve, *Le Monde Désert et le
Monde Bizarre peuplé par le locataire dans ce
livre*
1965
mixed media, bound
214 x 135mm
Arnold Daghani Archive
Centre for German-Jewish Studies,
University of Sussex

List of Lenders
(numbers refer to list of exhibits)

Czech Republic
The Jewish Museum in Prague 50, 55, 59, 62, 72
Památník Terezín 41, 49, 52, 58, 63, 73
Thomas Fritta Haas 47, 53, 57, 60, 61, 66, 67, 68, 70

France
Association 'Les Amis de Jeanne et Otto Freundlich', Pontoise 39, 45
Centre George Pompidou, Paris, Musée national d'art moderne 103, 104, 105, 106, 107, 108, 109, 110, 111
Donation Freundlich, Musées des Pontoise 46
Isaac Celnikier 4
Musée d'Histoire Contemporaine, Paris 113
Musée de la Résistance Nationale, Champigny: 35, 36, 118, 119, 120
Private Collection 10, 11
Zoran Music 121, 122

Germany
Felix-Nussbaum-Haus Osnabrück mit der Sammlung der Niedersächsischen Sparkassenstiftung 16, 31
Jüdisches Museum der Stadt Frankfurt-am-Main 24
Otto Pankok Museum, Haus Esselt 23
Ulmer Museum, Ulm 2

Israel
Beit Lohamei Haghetaot (Ghetto Fighters' House Museum) 25, 26, 27, 28, 29, 30, 37, 38, 40, 42, 43, 44, 78, 79, 80, 91, 100, 112, 116, 117
Herzliya Museum of Art 127, 128, 129, 130, 131, 132
The Israel Museum, Jerusalem 12, 14, 18, 74
Tel Aviv Museum of Art 1, 7, 32
Yad Vashem Art Museum, Jerusalem 33, 34, 48, 51, 54, 56, 64, 65, 69, 71, 75, 76, 77, 81, 85
Yehuda Bacon 133, 134, 135

Italy
Archivio Cagli, Roma 114, 115

Poland
Muzeum Literatury im Adama Mickiewicza, Warsaw 20, 21, 22

Państwowe Muzeum, Oświęcim 87, 88, 89, 90, 92, 93, 94, 95, 96, 97, 98, 101, 102
Żydowski Instytut Historyczny w Polsce 82, 83, 84, 99

United Kingdom
Arnold Daghani Archive, Centre for German Jewish Studies, University of Sussex 86, 136, 137, 138
British Museum, London 5, 8, 9, 15, 17, 19
Private Collections 3, 13
Robert and Lisa Sainsbury Collection, University of East Anglia 123, 124, 125, 126

USA
Marvin and Janet Fishman Collection, Milwaukee 6

Photographic Credits
(numbers refer to illustrations)

Frontispiece, 3, 10. © Tel Aviv Museum of Art
Frontispiece, 3 both © DACS 2001
1, 4. Paul-Klee-Stiftung, Kunstmuseum Berne. © DACS 2001
2, 15, 18, 49, 86. © The Israel Museum, Jerusalem
2, 49, 86. David Harris © DACS 2001
15, 18. Avshalom Avital
5, 74, 80, 81. Imperial War Museum, London
5 © ADAGP, Paris and © DACS 2001, London 2001
80, 81 © DACS 2001
6. © The artist
7. © Tate, London 2001. © DACS 2001
8, 12, 17. British Museum, London & © Nolde-Stiftung Seebüll 12 © DACS 2001
9. The owner. © Ludwig Meidner-Archiv, Jüdisches Museum, Frankfurt-am-Main
11. © Leicester City Museum Services. © DACS 2001
13. The owner. © ADAGP, Paris and © DACS 2001, London 2001
14, 69, 73. Réunion des Musées Nationaux. CNAC/MNAN/DIST RMN. © ADAGP, Paris and © DACS 2001, London 2001
16. Felix-Nussbaum-Haus Osnabrück mit der Sammlung der Niedersächsischen Sparkassenstiftung. © VG Bild-Kunst Bonn

2001, Christian Grovermann. © DACS 2001
19. Scottish National Gallery of Modern Art. © DACS 2001
20. Muzeum Literatury im Adama Mickiewicza, Warsaw
21. Otto Pankok Museum, Haus Esselt,Germany
22, 52. Jüdisches Museum Frankfurt am Main
23. Staatziche Museen Kassel
24. Courtesy Neue Gallerie New York and Sothebys, London. © DACS 2001
25, 30, 31, 53, 65, 78. © Art collection - Beit Lohamei Haghetaot, Israel (Ghetto Fighters' House Museum)
30, 31, 53, 78 Glenn Sujo
26. Galerie Remnant und Barth
27, 75. Glenn Sujo. © ADAGP, Paris and © DACS 2001, London 2001
29. Jewish Historical Museum, Amsterdam. © Charlotte Salomon Foundation
32. Association 'Les Amis de Jeanne et Otto Freundlich', Pontoise
33. Musées de Pontoises
34. AKG, London
35, 38, 45. Památník Terezín
36, 42, 47, 48, 87. Le Centre d'Histoire de la Résistance et de la Déportation á Lyon. © Artist's estate
37,40, 43. The Jewish Museum in Prague
39, 41, 44, 46, 51. Yad Vashem Art Museum, Jerusalem
39. Glenn Sujo
41, 44, 46, 51 Zev Radovan.
50, 54, 66. Żydowski Instytut Historyczny w Polsce, Poland
55, 56. University of Sussex. © Arnold Daghani Trust
57, 58, 59, 61, 62, 63, 64, 67, 68. Państwowe Muzeum, Oświęcim. © Artists' estate. 63 © Państwowe Muzeum, Oświęcim
70. The J Paul Getty Museum, Los Angeles
71, 72. Musée de la Résistance et de la Déportation de Besançon, France. Cliché JP Tupin.
76, 77. © Archivio Cagli, Roma
79, 82. Herzliya Museum of Art, Israel
83. The Warburg Institute, London
84, 85. Douglas Guthrie. © The artist.